The Ripper's Vi
in Print

The Ripper's Victims in Print

The Rhetoric of Portrayals Since 1929

REBECCA FROST

McFarland & Company, Inc., Publishers

Jefferson, North Carolina

LIBRARY OF CONGRESS CATALOGUING-IN-PUBLICATION DATA

Names: Frost, Rebecca, 1985– author.
Title: The Ripper's victims in print : the rhetoric of portrayals since
1929 / Rebecca Frost.
Description: Jefferson, North Carolina : McFarland & Company, Inc.,
Publishers, 2018 | Includes bibliographical references and index.
Identifiers: LCCN 2017057156 | ISBN 9781476669892 (softcover : acid
free paper) ∞
Subjects: LCSH: Jack, the Ripper. | Murder victims—England—
London—Case studies. | Serial murderers—England—London—
Case studies. | Poor women—England—London—Social
conditions—19th century.
Classification: LCC HV6535.G6 L6365 2018 | DDC 364.152/3209421—dc23
LC record available at https://lccn.loc.gov/2017057156

BRITISH LIBRARY CATALOGUING DATA ARE AVAILABLE

ISBN (print) 1-4766-6989-2
ISBN (ebook) 978-1-4766-3143-1

Front cover image © 2018 samposnick/iStock

Printed in the United States of America

*McFarland & Company, Inc., Publishers
Box 611, Jefferson, North Carolina 28640
www.mcfarlandpub.com*

To the memory of Brittany Nicholas,
who looked for—
and brought out—
the best in everyone

Acknowledgments

First and foremost I would like to thank Dr. Kette Thomas, who agreed to guide me through an independent study on Jack the Ripper's victims at our very first meeting. Her support and encouragement meant that I could then pursue the dissertation I had imagined. Dr. Diane Shoos, Dr. Marilyn Cooper, and Dr. Adam Feltz also agreed to be on my dissertation committee, and each provided specific, faceted insights into my research. Thank you for your perspectives.

Thanks also go to the circle of colleagues and friends who have impacted my research and my work, listed in alphabetical order because I would never be able to form a hierarchy: Dr. Kirsti Arko; Angela Badke; Natasha Fetzer; Colleen Hix; Rae Hix; Dr. Karla Kitalong; Katie Trotter; and members of the UP-Write group. Your support has been perhaps a bit unorthodox at times, but always present and very much appreciated.

And last but not least, I must express gratitude toward my family: my parents, who have read nearly every word I have ever written (poor Xander); and my husband Eric, who has heard more about Jack the Ripper than he ever wanted to in his life.

Table of Contents

Introduction

In the summer of 2007 I entered a bookshop in London and asked, quite naively, if it had any titles about Jack the Ripper. I was directed toward the proper section and confronted with a shelf and a half of choices and no idea where to start. In the end I arbitrarily chose between the two thickest books and ended up with Philip Sugden's *Complete History of Jack the Ripper*. Whenever anyone asks where my interest in true crime began, I name Sugden.

Three years later I had read what I thought was a vast number of books on the Ripper and I went to my first meeting with Dr. Kette Thomas ready to propose an independent study course—but not on the Ripper. I sat down with Kette and outlined my realization: every time an author writes about a serial killer, there are more victims than killers in the narrative. This held true whether the killer in question was the Ripper, John Wayne Gacy, Ted Bundy, Gary Ridgway.... Any serial killer had more than one victim, no matter which definition of "serial killer" happened to be current. The true crime books I had read, however, overwhelmingly devoted space on the page to the killer.

It was, as I explained to Kette, quite a revelation for me when I realized that, as I was delving into an historical mystery full of clues and evidence, I was participating in the representation of the victims as objects. (I did not word it so cleverly then, but this same sense of injustice drove my dissertation years later, in which I was able to express these ideas more eloquently.) What I wanted to do with my independent study was breathe life back into the victims of Jack the Ripper to recreate the women they might have been.

I was able to take my independent study paper and turn it into my very first conference presentation based solely on my belief that this cultural trend of bringing the serial killer to the spotlight and leaving the victims in the shadows—unless, of course, their bodies held some crucial clue—

1

was in need of discussion and consideration, and certainly not on any prior experience with conferences. Until then I had focused mainly on American crime narratives for my dissertation, with a foray into Stephen King's serial killers as both a conference presentation and a book chapter, but my collection of works about Jack the Ripper grew steadily. Unlike my first encounters, I stopped reading them to learn the answer to the mystery of the killer's identity and started reading them for what they had to say about the victims.

I consulted the Casebook: Jack the Ripper website[1] for its list of nonfiction titles about the Ripper, not minding when it advised that certain ones were outdated or had since been proven wrong because I was not looking for facts. I was hoping to track down books across a wide range of years to trace the rhetoric surrounding the Ripper's victims. This book is the result of that search.

I examine representations of the five canonical victims from Leonard Matters' 1929 *The Mystery of Jack the Ripper*, considered the first nonfiction book on the subject, up through titles published as recently as 2017. In many I am only interested in a few pages since my focus is not on these women as victims or corpses, and certainly not as clues that point to the Ripper's identity, but in these women as women. I am further not concerned with whether the descriptions of and information about them is accurate, but rather in what information is presented, and in what language. My focus is the rhetoric of victimhood as presented throughout the decades in the specific case of the victims of Jack the Ripper.

I chose to focus on the canonical five victims—Mary Ann "Polly" Nichols, Annie Chapman, Elizabeth "Liz" Stride, Catherine "Kate" Eddowes, and Mary Jane or Marie Jeanette Kelly—not because Jack the Ripper killed these five women and only these five women, but because they are the most likely to appear in any given text about him. It is a matter of having access to evidence and not a statement of personal belief on the number or identity of Ripper victims. Each will be discussed in connection with individual texts the way their names are written in that text.

The sheer number of English-language narratives concerning Jack the Ripper that were produced around the century mark of the killings, during the following decade of the 1990s, and even since the beginning of the twenty-first century means that, in some chapters, the books discussed are representative samples. My working bibliography is by no means exhaustive—although I hope to continue to make progress toward that goal—but does include works by the more well-known Ripperologists as well as the more popular ones of recent decades.

The organization of this book is chronological based on the original publication date of the material being examined. Many of the original documents have been reproduced in later publications so as to be more accessible—and, indeed, more legible—for the average amateur Ripperologist, and that information is treated as contemporary to the crimes.

Chapter One, "Enter the Victims: The Ripper Crimes of 1888," surveys what was known at the start of it all, covering newspaper and inquest information. Although many more recent works refer to any number of primary documents, the most common are coroners' reports, which give few—if any—details about the victim herself and instead concentrate on what her injuries have to say about the killer.

Chapter Two, "Fifty Years Later: The Earliest Ripper Books," addresses the early works of the 1920s and 1930s, beginning with Leonard Matters' *The Mystery of Jack the Ripper* from 1929. These titles have been published when sources and readers might remember the crimes, and thus their connection to the events is the most immediate for book-length narratives.

Chapter Three, "'Ladies of the pavement': Ripper Narratives of the 1950s and 1960s," explores the next Ripper narratives for information about the canonical victims. There were no books published in the 1940s, and thus authors and audiences find themselves situated in the post-war world, which may have effects on the narratives produced then.

Chapter Four, "Royals, Freemasons and Schemes: Presenting Victims in the Conspiracy Theories of the 1970s," focuses on the decade in which Queen Victoria, her personal physician, and her grandson all came under suspicion as having played a role in the Ripper crimes. To explain the motives behind the killings, many theories relate the victims to each other in new ways and explore their identities and personalities to make these accusations of guilt seem plausible.

Chapter Five, "One Hundred Years Later: Writing for the Anniversary of the Crimes," concentrates on the 1980s, an interesting decade in Ripperology for multiple reasons: it holds the hundred-year anniversary of the murders; saw the American true crime boom; marked the FBI beginning to state itself as an authority on serial killers and serial killing, terms that had only recently been coined; and saw, in 1989, the execution of Ted Bundy, who had become a modern foil for the Ripper. This change in attention to and authority concerning serial killing allows for new language to be used in the chronicling of the Ripper crimes and in the description of his victims.

Chapter Six, "More Than a Century Later: Discussing Murder in the 1990s," draws upon a selection of books from the 1990s, a decade in which the first female author is heard and books seek to offer new and exciting information on a case more than one hundred years old. Past inconsistencies are highlighted and past rumors dismissed, but the discussion of the victims remains open for new approaches and close readings in order to determine whether, after all these decades of varying narratives, these women are receiving a different kind of attention.

Chapter Seven, "More of the Same? An Introduction to the 21st Century Books," tackles a selection of representations from the twenty-first century that seem to follow along in the historically-established vein. These books are indeed "more of the same" in both their theories and victim descriptions, creating an argument for how much—or how little—cultural approaches to victimhood have changed.

Chapter Eight, "Enter DNA: Victim Descriptions in Light of 21st Century Uses of Technology in Ripper Theories," focuses on texts that have advertised themselves as using modern technology to form their approaches to the crimes and those involved. This chapter includes the popular 2003 book by Patricia Cornwell, *Portrait of a Killer*, as well as the more recent—and controversial—2014 *Naming the Ripper* by Russell Edwards, both of which rely heavily on DNA evidence gathered through the personal work of the authors and the great personal expense of hiring experts. Although the technology and terminology surrounding the case have advanced, has the approach to the victims changed?

Chapter Nine, "Crimes for a New Age: Variations and Changes in Victim Representation of the 21st Century," makes a short survey of the more recent Ripper texts that have gone beyond the usual and oft-repeated narrative. Some do not concern themselves with the victims at all, and the way in which they do so may be just as enlightening as the way the victims have been represented, or ignored, in prior decades.

Finally, the Conclusion considers more than a century of information on Jack the Ripper to ask the larger questions: what has changed? What influenced those changes? And what is still in need of change?

Frequent readers of true crime or Ripper texts may notice a common element is missing here. I have chosen not to include photographs of the victims, since the majority of uncontested photographs come from the morgue. Much has been written and theorized about the victims as corpses, but the focus of this book is the representation of the victims as living women.

• ONE •

Enter the Victims
The Ripper Crimes of 1888

This is not a book about Jack the Ripper. That would be an understandable misconception—his name is, after all, in the title, and multiple books claiming to be about the victims or other surrounding topics do indeed end up focusing on the Ripper himself. The Ripper's identity is one of the great historical mysteries and the focus of more than one hundred books. This is not one of them.

Although many pages have been devoted to concluding exactly how many women were killed by Jack the Ripper, the most commonly agreed-upon victims make up the so-called canonical five: Mary Ann "Polly" Nichols, Annie Chapman, Elizabeth "Liz" Stride, Catherine "Kate" Eddowes, and Mary Jane (or Marie Jeanette) Kelly. These women were found murdered in the latter half of 1888 in the poor East End area of London and have been resurrected in nearly every Jack the Ripper narrative published since. Although none of these women lived to be fifty, their names are still spoken more than one hundred twenty-five years after their deaths.

Because of the repetition of the Jack the Ripper narrative and the fact that these five women are commonly agreed to have been his victims, we are thus able to trace their narratives and the rhetoric surrounding their victimhood across the decades. This investigation is not interested in descriptions of the wounds inflicted to their bodies, or in their corpses—instead, this study focuses on the descriptions of the women themselves, in life. How were they presented? What terms and phrases are used to describe these women? Are they lumped together as five variations on a singular theme of victim, or are they allowed individual traits? And do these descriptions serve to flesh out these specific lives of women in London's East End, or do they function solely to point to the identity of their killer?

Whitechapel, 1888

For those living through the terror of 1888, little explanation of the time and place was needed. Although those in the West End may have learned a bit about the lives being lived by the poorer citizens of the East End, they still occupied the same time period and shared many of the same world views. This cannot be said for readers situated in the twenty-first century, who may require more of a background so that they may clearly picture the time and place in which these women lived. These descriptions, some pulled from contemporary documents, are more common in recent books about Jack the Ripper, reflecting both the distance from the events and the acknowledgment that situation plays into these murders—or at least into identifying the murderer.

The East End, including Whitechapel, was largely home to newly arrived immigrants. In the late nineteenth century, many of these immigrants were Jewish, seeking refuge from pogroms and general persecution in Eastern Europe. Due to religious practices and daily customs, many of these immigrants tended to keep to themselves and settle among fellow Jews instead of mixing with others in the area. To further the divide between poor Londoners and these immigrants, Victorian England did not provide social services for the poor, while the Jewish community did. Since the Jewish community looked out for their own, instead of leaving the unfortunate to fend for themselves, this led to increasing anti-Semitism among the English—or at least among contemporary seekers of Jack the Ripper, who were all too eager to accuse him of being foreign, Jewish, or otherwise "other."

Life in the East End was difficult enough without seeing others—and foreigners to boot—having a slightly easier time of it. Those who ended up in the East End had not done so by choice, only occupying the filthy streets and dilapidated buildings because the poor and unwanted had been pushed further and further east as the city proper expanded. In the East End alone there were nearly one hundred thousand paupers, and the vast majority of them did not have a fixed address. Many East Enders spent their days gathering pennies to spend the night in a doss house or lodging house, paying for their beds one night at a time. If they had no money and could bring themselves to accept the harsh conditions, they might have lined up for a place at a work house. Homelessness was rampant in the East End and led to people being on the street at all hours, not being allowed to linger in the kitchens of lodging houses or in the public houses without being able to pay.

While Victorian London may be portrayed as uptight and prudish, the East End seemed to be a different world entirely. Some young men of the higher class of Londoners may have engaged in the practice of slumming as a means of passing the time, experiencing the life of the lower classes for a limited period of time, but otherwise the upper classes avoided such rough areas. In more than one report surrounding the Ripper case, cries of "Murder!" were ignored because of their frequency. It was not the sort of area many people would have entered into willingly.

One escape from the rough life of the East End would be the numerous public houses, frequented by the victims themselves. These pubs opened around five in the morning and closed around midnight, if indeed they ever closed at all. At the time, alcoholism was not considered a disease but was thought to be a sign of a weak mind or lesser constitution. This was not helped along by the fact that many women of the East End were not only given to excessive drinking but were also prostitutes, combining sins. Clearly, drinking was for the lower classes, and the higher classes had little to no business being in the East End in the first place. They would likely have been able to ignore the poverty of the East End altogether if not for the Jack the Ripper murders.

Those who made their homes in the East End generally struggled to find lodging for the night, once their daily business had been concluded and they no longer wished to—or could afford to—stay in a pub. Even with the large number of doss houses, there were not enough beds for every homeless member of the East End to have one, a fact that was highlighted during the Ripper murders. Single beds cost four pence a night and were generally available in doss houses that accepted a single gender, while double beds were eight pence in houses that allowed men and women to sleep together. Prostitutes would thus charge clients four pence per encounter or allow a man to spend the night with them if he paid for the double bed—a more certain arrangement, since any money earned during the day could easily be spent on food or, more likely, drink. If a single bed was too expensive or a lodger only had two pence to spend, she could pay to sleep on a "line." This was merely a rope or webbing of ropes arranged to keep the sleeper off of the floor and was hardly conducive to a good night's sleep, although it at least provided the lodger with a place to pass the night.

Doss houses were owned by people of means who may never have set food inside and thus may have not known the truth of their conditions. Linens were supposedly washed once a week, which was more than could be said for the various bodies that slept on them, although the job itself might be done by potential dossers in exchange for a bed for the night. There were kitchens that served as little more than common rooms with fires since they did not serve food. Lodgers who had their own food could warm it and themselves by the fires—keeping an eye on the food so it would not be stolen—and socialize with others in the given space. Even those without food or money for a bed might attempt to get comfortable in the space before inevitably being kicked out into the street. Lodging houses did not deal in credit.

As bad as the doss houses sound, the workhouses were worse. Although the poor hated them, there were always long lines that formed early, since space was limited. Each petitioner would be searched and rejected if a single penny was found—absolute poverty was necessary to enter the workhouse. Tobacco, knives, and matches were not allowed in the workhouses, either, and it was unlikely that petitioners would have risked having their meager possessions taken from them at the gate. Anyone who passed this initial inspection and allowed inside would be washed in a common tub, dried with workhouse towels, and sent off to sleep in a communal ward. The cots did not have mattresses but were instead strung with rope, like hammocks. Breakfast was served at six and consisted of oatmeal or moldy meat before inmates were sent to pound stones, pick oakum, or work in the infirmary or mortuary. Dinner at eight consisted of leftovers from the infirmary. If the lodgers were willing and able to put in this long day of work, they were given a second night. Those who refused to work were kicked out and denied even the scanty meals and protection of the common ward at night. This work, it may be added, was tantamount to that performed by prisoners. Any East Ender who willingly sought out the work house was clearly desperate.

Aside from toiling for a day in a workhouse, women might earn their doss money through prostitution. The number of prostitutes living and working in Whitechapel is debatable between various contemporary reports that either underestimated or perhaps inflated the population, but it was clearly in the thousands. It was not as straightforward a proposition as simply finding a man and exchanging the deed for money, and not as safe as a single random encounter with a stranger. Gangs would roam the streets and wait for prostitutes to finish their transactions so that they might rob them. If these gangs happened upon a prostitute without money, or if a client decided to seek revenge on a woman for inflicting him with disease, she might face anything from a beating to the loss of her life. These women lacked even the dubious protection a pimp may have provided and instead led wandering, dangerous lives in which their absences—and indeed their deaths—may not have been noticed immediately. It was the violence accompanying the Ripper murders that led them to gain so much attention.

The police force was relatively new in the 1880s and policemen were largely untrusted by the common citizen. Officers were required to wear their uniforms off duty as well as on, to prevent any underhanded spying, and in the case of the Ripper murders the suggestion of plain-clothed policemen was met with strong resistance. Some officers were assigned to stand at fixed points during their shifts, while others walked very specific beats at a carefully measured pace. This meant that their routes could be timed and anticipated and in the East End, with its labyrinth of streets, it was very easy to get out of sight of someone even if they could still be heard. In an attempt to throw off the casual criminal, policemen intermittently spent their shifts walking their beat in the reverse order, although presumably they passed the same locations at the same intervals as before.

Along with the newness of the police force, Londoners in 1888 were also faced with the newness of readily available mass media. The Central News Agency, which was to play a role of its own in the Ripper murders, had been founded in 1870 and news could now be relayed via telegraph and spread faster than before. Especially of interest in the case of the Ripper, death inquests were open to the public, and reporters made sure to attend. In this era of "new journalism," death and crime certainly sold papers. Granted, it was illegal for those papers to publish certain key details of those death inquests, but nothing would get in the way of the good story. Even the truth was often sacrificed in order to neaten up a narrative around the edges, providing background information, scandal, or other juicy details to the reading public.

In spite of the usual danger of the East End, which was after all so crime-ridden that cries of "Murder!" were ignored by the populace and the deaths themselves ignored by greater London, the murders attributed to Jack the Ripper made headlines the world over. Mutilation of corpses was a previously unknown phenomenon that baffled the Victorian mind, and the crimes themselves were without any apparent motive. The discovery— and condition—of the bodies of Mary Ann, Annie, Liz, Kate, and Marie Jeanette, as well as all information available from their death inquests and any other witnesses reporters could track down, were all considered newsworthy and fit for the average citizen to read, discuss, and share with anyone who had not yet heard it.

Mary Ann Nichols

Mary Ann Nichols, commonly labeled Jack the Ripper's first victim, was discovered dead early on the morning of August 31, 1888, in Buck's Row. The men who first came upon her initially suspected she was passed out drunk, which would have been common for women of the area who happened to be out alone in the wee hours of the morning. Newspapers of the day recorded not only personal interviews but details of the inquest, so there were multiple voices present to describe who Mary Ann was. This initial impression of Mary Ann is multifaceted, although likely tempered by the violence of her death and the publicity of the statements. Cultural resistance to speaking ill of the dead might indeed be a factor.

Mary Ann had been separated from her husband for nine years at the time of her death, and it is revealed that this separation came because she was so often drunk. William Nichols is therefore presented as having left his wife—and, perhaps, abandoned her to her brutal fate—because of her own personal failings. It comes as a further black mark that the couple had five children and that the youngest was only about two years old when she left. Mary Ann therefore failed not only as a proper sober woman, but also as a wife and mother, and had no choice but to seek her own way in the world because she could not fit the roles presented to her.

Initially William Nichols allowed his wife a weekly allowance that would be enough to see to her room and board, but all manner of supported ended in 1882, "it having come to his knowledge that she was living the life of a prostitute."[1] From then until her death, Nichols neither saw nor heard from his wife, and presumably did not take it upon himself to seek her out. Now truly forced to fend for herself, Mary Ann turned to the workhouses, which gave the outward appearance of taking in the destitute for honest work in exchange for room and board. This "honest work" consisted of backbreaking labor, while the room and board were minimally clean and nutritious. Mary Ann was identified because of her petticoats, which were labeled as property of the Lambeth Workhouse, one of the workhouses in which she had stayed.

At some point in her history Mary Ann had attempted both honest labor, working as a maid, and living with her father. Her employment did not last long because she stole some clothes and ran away, and it was explained that she left her father because they had fought the previous evening. It is strongly hinted that, in both cases, it was Mary Ann's love of drinking that ended the possibility of a better life. The theme of drink destroying good women—or at least women who had once possessed the potential to fit their expected roles—is common throughout these narratives.

Despite this negative tendency, reports held that Mary Ann was not necessarily a bad or unpleasant person. Because of the manner of her death, police looked for any reason anyone would have wanted to harm her, and they came up short. Both her current companions at her series of lodging houses and her father agreed on this point. Even allowing for the improvement of character after a death and evidence given in such a public forum, a solid answer of a threat could have led to the identification of the Ripper himself. Since the Ripper was never identified, despite multiple murders and presumably the best efforts of the London police force, the suggestion that she was relatively inoffensive outside of her drinking might well hold true. If anyone had witnessed Mary Ann aggravating another, reporting it would have garnered a witness instant fame. Along the same lines, anyone who held an opposing opinion might also have likewise held his tongue rather than take on the position of being a suspect.

Aside from having been labeled as living the life of a prostitute, it was also reported that Mary Ann "evidently formed irregular connexions"[2] even during the time she was living with her father. It was suggested at the inquiry that she had wanted to remove herself from paternal oversight when she left her father so that such encounters could continue without judgment. Yes, the newspapers admitted, perhaps it was because they had fought, but it still could have been a fight over Mary Ann's behavior, a proposal that is clearly the more scandalous. The newspapers and inquiry reports thus make it clear how they suspected Mary Ann had been making a living, even when a fellow lodger chose to disagree. This same lodger, although she would not admit that Mary Ann had been a prostitute, did acknowledge that she had been known to drink to excess, which was not a trait associated with proper women. The fact that she claimed ignorance of Mary Ann's means of making a living and then immediately admitted to her drinking habits might be seen, then, to be a hint or admission in its own right.

Despite these points against Mary Ann, the inquisition did reveal one tidbit that might be in Mary Ann's favor: there was the claim that she had left William, and not the other way around, because he had gone to live with the woman who had nursed her after the birth of her youngest child. Despite initial newspaper reports that William Nichols had left his wife because of her drinking or the factual statement that Mary Ann had left her children when they were still so young, this counter proposal presents Mary Ann as the sympathetic party. If William had indeed cheated on his wife when she was in her final confinement, this colors the reports of her drinking. Instead of being a weak-willed woman unable to refrain from alcohol, Mary Ann might be mourning the choice of an unfaithful husband. This suggestion is, however, mentioned only once and not overly emphasized. The overall impression of Mary Ann is that she was a nice enough woman, but prone to drink, and ended up living the life of a prostitute because she could not—or would not—do otherwise.

Annie Chapman

Annie Chapman, the second of the Ripper's canonical victims, was found dead on the morning of September 8, 1888, in the backyard of a house on Hanbury Street. Because of the timing of Annie's death and the length of the inquest into Mary Ann's death, the murders were already connected during Mary Ann's death inquest. Even though there was no evidence that Annie and Mary Ann may have crossed paths in life, they were connected in death almost immediately.

Like Mary Ann, Annie was also separated from her husband, who had been giving her a larger weekly sum until the time of own death about eighteen months before her murder. Unlike Mary Ann, Annie was solidly connected to another man, a laborer named Edward Stanley. According to some reports, "with that exception she was not known to be acquainted with any particular man."[3] Although Annie was indeed known to associate with a man who was not her husband, it may have been only with this single man, and then there is also the possibility that this only occurred after she was widowed. At a time when women were incredibly dependent on men for their wellbeing, it might have been understandable, even to the general population of London, if Annie had indeed been associated with a man, especially since the death of her husband meant she had lost the security of her weekly allowance.

Annie was also reported to have worn two brass rings, the single instance of these women to have worn jewelry. Being brass, they were not expensive and thus unlikely to be hawked. However, sentiment might be tied to the wearing of a wedding ring, as one of them was labeled, especially with her husband having been deceased. No evidence is given about the state of their marriage or why they parted. If, on the other hand, Annie wore the rings as testament to her laborer instead, it is still a sign of devotion to one man and therefore more respectable than Mary Ann's label of prostitution.

This image of Annie as a one-man woman, however rosy, does not last through the inquiry documents. The night watchmen of the lodging house where she routinely stayed backed up the impression that she was routinely seen with just the one man, but another witness mentioned how Annie routinely spent Saturday nights with a pensioner—not a laborer—and that she also "brought other men to the lodging-house."[4] Even if Edward Stanley was identifiable as both a laborer and a pensioner, that mention of the "other men" cements the idea of Annie's means of earning a living. Lest anyone assume that these men went no further than the lodging house kitchen, the one Annie frequented allowed men and women to share beds.

Annie seems to be more complicated not only because of reports she was indeed loyal to a single man, but because she is presented as having made a living by selling trinkets like flowers and crocheted items. Add to this the fact that her friend Amelia Farmer chose to describe her as having both industry and cleverness, neither of which would seem to be necessary for prostitution. Annie, it seems, had the mind, the skills, and the materials to turn to other paths to make a living. Adding to this positive picture of Annie were reports that she was friendly to others in the lodging house, and the only enemy that surfaced turned out to be a woman and therefore not likely to have been the murderer.

Her drinking seems to have been limited to Saturdays, perhaps solely with the aforementioned pensioner, with the assumption that Annie would have made her money Saturdays by selling the things she had crafted during the week. This sunny, almost respectable picture of a woman down her luck is further tempered when Amelia Farmer adds that she knew her friend was often out late at night and, despite the talent and supplies, was apparently not entirely discriminatory about how she made her coins. Women who sell flowers or crochet things generally do not need to be out late at night. It is possible that all of Annie's attempts to avoid prostitution failed her, simply because she ended up in the East End and without a regular income. Although she may have made every attempt to avoid prostitution, Annie still ended up in a yard with the Ripper.

Elizabeth Stride

Elizabeth Stride was the first of two women to have been discovered murdered in the early morning hours of September 30, 1888, and is the only Ripper victim who was thought to have been Swedish. Her body was discovered in Dutfield's Yard. Both the deputy of the lodging house she frequented and a longtime friend agreed that she had been born in Sweden and had at one time been married, but had lost her husband and at least some of her children during the sinking of the pleasure ship the *Princess Alice* in 1878. Liz herself was meant to have been only one of a handful of passengers who had survived the sinking. There was no explanation of why or when she had come to England and little information about her past, outside of the *Princess Alice* story, until the last three years of her life.

Michal Kidney was able to provide this information since he had been living with Liz "nearly all that time."[5] That "nearly" meant Liz would leave Kidney apparently whenever she felt like, but he volunteered that this departure was due to her drinking habits and not because of any apathy she may have felt toward him. Kidney took pride in being the man Liz preferred. Like Mary Ann and Annie before her, Liz was afflicted with the compulsion to drink. Unlike the others, however, Liz had a steady man in her life who reported that he took her back every time she returned. Kidney further protested that Liz had not left him on the night of her death because she had taken off with anyone else, rejecting any suggestion that she might have made her living as a prostitute. Although it is not clear at this time what Liz did for a living, Kidney's presence in both her life and at the inquest suggest that she might have been cared for well enough without having had to resort to prostitution.

Again, though, these statements are augmented by other witnesses at the inquest. The deputy at the lodging house where she usually stayed reported the positive fact that she knew Liz to be clean and sober, but also the more troubling information that she used to stay out late at night. Proper women in Victorian England had no reason to stay out late at night. Further, even Kidney did not hide the fact that Liz drank, even if only occasionally. Whenever she drank, though, she left him for days at a time, once again linking her life and tendencies to those of Mary Ann and Annie. Outside of this little information, however, Liz remains mysterious.

Catherine Eddowes

Catherine Eddowes was the second victim of the early morning of September 30, 1888, discovered not far from Liz in Mitre Square. Like Liz, Kate had been living with a long-term companion named John Kelly who, at the inquest, referred to Kate as his wife. Kate still had family living in the area, so her biography is more complete than that of Liz.

Similarly to Mary Ann or Annie, Kate had previously been with another man for about twenty years, long enough to have had three children with Tomas Conway. The couple did not marry. In a familiar, tale, it is reported that Conway was the one to have left Kate because of her drinking habits, although again, this was not the only version of events. Kate's sister, Eliza Gold, testified, "I cannot tell whether they parted on good or bad terms,"[6] and the couple's daughter, Annie Philips, reported that her father had simply left without saying why, and that was the last she saw of him. Annie Philips had not been on good terms with her father, so it is possible that Kate had reason to feel the same way. Since Conway himself is not present to testify, neither member of the couple could shed light on the true circumstances of their separation.

Despite her lack of contact with her father, Annie Philips had indeed seen her mother since her parents parted. The fact that her daughter did indeed see her mother is not necessarily a positive assessment of Kate's character, since Annie Philips reveals that she had to hide her brothers' addresses from Kate to prevent discussions of lending money, although it is unclear which party would be the beggar. Were Kate's sons so ill-off that they would have asked their mother for money, or did the reports of the inquest mean to say that mother would have been the one begging, if she had known where to find them? Annie Philips certainly reports that Kate frequently asked her for money, so it makes little sense for her to imply her brothers would have been the ones asking their mother for some coins.

As often as she may have gone to Annie Philips for spare coins, Kate was also known to have found work when she could. Her sister, her common-law husband John Kelly, and her lodging-house deputy Fredrick William Wilkinson all agreed that Kate would hawk wares on the street, while Wilkinson added that she also did some cleaning when she could. Further, Wilkinson added, "I have never heard of her being intimate with any one but Kelly,"[7] a strong endorsement especially in comparison with the narratives surrounding Liz's relationship with Michael Kidney and Annie's with her laborer or pensioner.

While Kate's sister described her as being sober, Kelly himself was the one who admitted that Kate would at times get drunk. In fact, much of the possibly negative information about Kate comes from Kelly, whether he states it outright or words it in such a way as to indicate what possible truth he is arguing against. There was the positive report that, in all the time he and Kate had been together, he had been a moralizing influence on her and would not let her engage in prostitution. This indicates that she did indeed need a moralizing presence—or perhaps simply a source of income—in order to take such a high road. Kelly further argues that Kate never brought him money she had earned the previous night, although it is a statement of such exactitude that it leaves open the possibility that Kate may have indeed earned such money without giving it to him. Even with such a steady man in her life, Kate still drank and was of the class expected to have resorted to prostitution, and thus it cannot be entirely eliminated from the narrative of her past.

One final point of interest in this initial description of Kate is the fact that her list of belongings extends over three pages. Although Mary Ann, Annie, and Liz were like Kate in that they did not have their own rooms to which to return every night, Kate carried the most numerous possessions with her, meager as they were. These included such items as a packet of tea and sugar, various colors of thread, and pawn tickets, including those for Kelly's boots. The pair had pawned them during her last day, presumably leaving Kelly barefoot, in order to have enough money for food. She was also wearing the most layers of clothing of any of the victims, all of which paints a picture of an itinerant woman struggling to make a living in Victorian England.

Marie Jeanette Kelly

Marine Jeanette Kelly, referred to by this French version of Mary Jane in these earliest reports, is often considered to be the Ripper's final victim. She is regularly set apart from the previous women, in part due to the fact that she rented a room of her own instead of staying at doss houses or workhouses, and in part because of the severity of her injuries. Marie Jeanette's body was discovered in her rented room in Miller's Court on the morning of November 9, 1888.

Like Elizabeth Stride, Marie Jeanette did not have any family nearby, and thus her life is likewise narrated by the man she most recently lived with. Joseph Barnett had been staying with Marie Jeanette for a total of about eighteen months, although he had moved out of her rented room shortly before her murder. The reason for his departure changes depending upon the report. First, he is recorded to have said that it was "in consequence of not earning sufficient money to give her and her resorting to prostitution."[8] This is only the second time that the word prostitution is stated outright in connection with these women—Mary Ann's husband refused to continue paying her an allowance when he learned she was living the life of a prostitute, but the other women stayed out late, were not particularly in how they earned a living, never brought their men money, and so on. This blunt admission after her death is supported when a friend of Marie Jeanette, who also admitted to being a prostitute, observed that Marie Jeanette herself did not lie about what she did to earn a living and thus was never heard to call herself a charwoman or other such euphemism. If she refused to adopt such terms in life, then it would seem strange to use them after her death.

Later reports from Barnett, however, seem to attempt to restore him to the level of John Kelly: a man who supported the woman in his life and, perhaps, felt his manhood was questioned when earlier publications made much of the fact that he had lost his income. At the inquest his story has changed to the fact that he left Marie Jeanette not because he had lost his job and she had once again taken up prostitution, but because she had brought a fellow prostitute to stay with them in her tiny rented room. All the same, this correction does not necessarily place Barnett in the best of light. It is only because he left Marie Jeanette that she took to prostitution once more, and it was this return to walking the streets that placed her in harm's way. Clearly the East End would have been alert to the dangers facing women who did not have a bed for the night, so Marie Jeanette's invitation to her friend was one of kindness and good will.

Although Barnett was still presumably earning money up until the point when he had left the now-overcrowded room, Marie Jeanette's death was discovered when her landlord sent someone to seek out the back rent that she owed. While it would be unlikely that a prostitute who could not afford a bed at a doss house would have been able to help Marie Jeanette with the rent, it would seem that Barnett had not been offering assistance, either. In fact, considering the length of time it had been since the rent was paid, he may have been living off Marie Jeanette's generosity himself. It is possible that he felt her kindness to her friend meant less for him, thinking more along the lines of money than actual physical space.

Other than the fact that she rented a room while they frequented doss and lodging houses, Marie Jeanette is separated from the other women by dint of being the youngest victim and through the stories of her past. Those who knew her commented on her appearance as being unusually presentable as well as striking, and she was supposedly educated far beyond the other women of the East End. In general the story of Marie Jeanette is of a woman whose descent was swift and dire. Lacking friends and family who had known her longer, Barnett could only report what she had told him about her life prior to their first meeting. According to this tale, Marie had once been a prostitute in the West End and had even gone with a gentleman to France for a time. Apparently France was not to her liking, since she left both the country and her gentleman to return to London, although this time to the East End. Why anyone would give up the life of a kept woman in France in exchange for Whitechapel is neither questioned nor explained.

Like the other women, Marie Jeanette was also "much given to drink, and had rapidly gone from bad to worse"[9] after her return to London. Even though she was younger than the other women, likely in her twenties instead of in her forties, and in spite the fact that she was able to rent a room of her own instead of seeking out a doss house bed each night, Marie Jeanette was still poor, still a prostitute, and still a drunk. Despite her youth and rumored beauty, Marie Jeanette was still a woman of London's East End, and she met the same fate as the other victims of the Ripper's knife.

A Flash in the Pan

Despite the worldwide interest in the crimes of Jack the Ripper, and the possible further murders attributed to the killer over the next few years, the written narratives were confined to newspapers for decades. The inquest into Marie Jeanette's murder was halted after a single day and those news-paper articles ceased almost as suddenly. While the police insisted that the Ripper was no longer a threat due to suicide, imprisonment on another charge, or because he was now in an insane asylum, editors were strongly encouraged to keep the Ripper from the headlines in order to refrain from inciting public panic. Granted, if the police had honestly identified Jack the Ripper, it is highly unlikely that they would have kept his name a secret and not allowed it to appear in print.

Part of what had allowed the Ripper to command so much space in the newspapers was the fact that someone, or multiple someones, proceeded to write numerous letters posing at the killer. The first of these was sent to the Central News Agency instead of to the police, and was initially regarded as a joke. Once the letter writer's predictions seemed to come true after the night of the "double event" of the murders of Elizabeth and Catherine, the letter was published—and many more were soon to follow. It was one of these letters that introduced the epithet "Jack the Ripper" and the reason why we know the killer as such today, instead of calling him "the knife" or "the Whitechapel fiend."

The publication of these letters continued to fuel the news stories that permeated all of London and kept the Ripper murders on the front page. Although current thought tends to dismiss most, if not all, of the letters as hoaxes, at the time some were reproduced in the hope that readers would recognize the handwriting. One letter even accompanied a piece of kidney, ostensibly part of the one that had been removed from Catherine's body, and lamented the fact that it had to be written in red ink instead of blood. The debate over whether or not the piece was indeed a kidney, human, and had come from the Mitre Square victim allowed journalists even more fodder for their articles.

With arguments over kidneys, letters, victims, methods, and the identity of the killer, the Ripper crimes saturated the newspapers of the day. Where murders in Whitechapel had previously been too common to create such conversation and to interest those outside of the district, much less those around the world, this series of murders was a continually updated narrative meant to interest audiences beyond those in the immediate area. The number of papers printed and distributed each day created a demand for the most current knowledge, as well as for angles and tidbits that other headlines had not already touched. The conversation was continual.

And yet, after the protracted inquest into the murder of Marie Jeanette, silence fell. Between the sudden lack of new murders and the pressure from the police, the story dried up. The Ripper may have left the headlines but he did not leave public consciousness. Marie Belloc-Lowndess published the first fictional novel based on the Ripper in 1913, and her book, *The Lodger*, went on to inspire filmmakers like Alfred Hitchcock himself. Then, in 1929, forty years after the events, the first nonfiction account of the Jack the Ripper murders was published.

Two

Fifty Years Later
The Earliest Ripper Books

Despite the immense amount of interest in the Ripper crimes leading up to Marie Jeanette's death, an interest that spiked with individual brutal murderers in the following few years, little was written about them outside of the contemporary newspaper reports. There are anecdotal reports of reporters being silenced from further discussion, and published papers by those who were involved in the investigation of the crime hint strongly that the Ripper's identity was known. Further publication, then, was stifled in order to keep the panic from rising: the Ripper was not identified in print, but neither could it be suggested that he was still a threat.

Unlike today, book-length accounts of true crime events were not common. In fact, the first book about the Ripper crimes may be the first book-length true crime narrative to have been published. Even then it came forty years after the crimes themselves, when the killer—whoever he may have been—was likely dead or incarcerated, since no further crimes had been committed. The emotional distance from the crimes may have further been increased by the fact that the audience for this book had lived through the First World War, which was a very different attack on the Homefront. The story of a lone man with a knife—who, after all, only killed a handful of women—may have been almost a relief in the wake of a war.

The Victims of Dr. Stanley

The first book to be published on the subject of Jack the Ripper came forty years after the events themselves, at a time when there were still people who could remember the crimes, but also at a time removed from the specific culture that had surrounded the crimes. Blanket statements about the victims or indeed all women of the East End are common, perhaps in an attempt to properly set the scene by explaining there was nothing special about these women in particular. Leonard Matters, in his 1929 book *The Mystery of Jack the Ripper*, prefaces his discussion of the crimes by flatly declaring that in "each case the story of human failure and descent was the same."[1] There is little need—or perhaps little cause—to approach the women of the East End, much less the five canonical victims of Jack the Ripper, as individuals.

Matters prefers to present his victims in a seagoing theme, as wrecks who have somehow managed to wash up or drift into the East End. They are thus perhaps like ships, borne along by the whim of the wind and tide, not in control of their movements or final resting places. To an extent this could be argued to be an apt comparison, since a Victorian woman without a husband had very few options open to her and indeed little to say about the direction of her life. It remains to be questioned whether Matters thought that the Ripper's victims were destined distinctly for their gruesome deaths.

When the body of Mary Ann Nicholls is discovered, Matters sets the scene by informing readers that the man who found her is familiar with the area and predicted that he was seeing one of the many prostitutes of the area, simply so drunk that she could not remove herself from the gutter. Readers are thus made aware that women of the area, if not Mary Ann herself, tended to drink themselves into stupors and then generally be ignored by men on their early walks to work. The idea of drinking to excess is thus already planted in the reader's mind, specifically as a common reaction of women of the district.

Mary Ann is identified as being separated from her husband and "of dissolute habits,"[2] confirming excess drinking in this specific case. Later on the very same page her father is seen arguing that Mary Ann was in fact continually sober, but his voice is the sole dissension. Mary Ann's estranged husband offers up a tale more likely to sell—and therefore more likely to be printed in—newspapers. According to William Nicholls, Mary Ann had left him years before, not simply on her own but in favor of another man. The married couple must have remained in contact in some way even after her departure, because William clarifies after her death that it had been months since he had seen her or heard anything from her. William Nicholls might not be a grieving widower, but this is not shown to be a black mark on his name. His wife left him, presumably after cuckolding him, and thus their separation is placed entirely at her feet while giving him a reason to be less than charitable in his descriptions of her.

Mary Ann is also likely responsible for her own presence on the street the night of her death, since Matters tells us she was not allowed to stay in her lodging house because she did not have money for the night. Beds had to be paid for each night in advance, and credit was not accepted. Any charitable assumption of where Mary Ann's money had gone—or question of whether she had been in possession of any in the first place—is answered when the last person to have seen Mary Ann alive reported that she had been too drunk to stand and was leaning against a wall. Mary Ann had thus either been in possession of money and spent it on drink, or found someone to buy her a drink, likely in exchange for favors.

Matters does not say bluntly that Mary Ann was a prostitute, but he includes coroner Wynne Baxter's comment that "[i]t was an extraordinary thing … that nobody had seen her in the company with any man"[3]—and besides, how else would she have been able to make money in the middle of the night? There is no outright discussion that indicates she was involved with prostitution, but no other suggestion of occupation, either, or how she was usually able to afford her bed in the lodging house. There is, in fact, very little discussion of Mary Ann herself. Readers learn that she was married, that her husband was still alive, and that the pair had been separated, but little else seems necessary prior to her movements on the final night of her life. The rest is just filler information about the woman whose name is only known because she crossed paths with Jack the Ripper.

Annie Chapman is also described as being overly fond of drink, although in her case this is balanced by the fact that she was also "quiet and inoffensive."[4] Matters takes an interesting approach to Annie, often tempering any negative comments with these and similar positive ones, and introducing her as the least of the least. Out of all the victims, the future looks bleakest for Annie. Exactly why Matters chooses to present her in such a way is not clear, but he alternately robs her of humanity by describing her as a poor creature before restoring again and making her a singularly unhappy woman. Annie is reduced far beyond Mary Anne in these descriptions, although the language surrounding her also offers her more emotion and more sympathy, despite the similarities in their brief biographies.

Matters informs readers that Chapman was a widow—thus without a husband to spread tales of how she had been in life and during their marriage—but again, like Mary Anne, she had not been living with him for some time before his death. Annie had also been inhabiting various boarding houses in the slums in and around Whitechapel, but again Matters' description of the situation uses more evocative and sympathetic language than when he explained Mary Anne's plight. He does continue to play with Annie's identity, alternating between animal descriptions and the use of human language. Whatever Annie is, Matters paints her as a pitiful figure, pointing out that, on her last night and in search of her doss money, she likely walked quite a distance and over a long period of time in search of a man willing to so much as look at her. While the figure of the East End prostitute has sunk low, apparently Annie Chapman has managed to end up lower than most—and somehow, by being the most pitiful of the pitiful, inspired Matters to sympathy instead of disgust.

With as little information as Matters gives about Mary Ann and Annie, Elizabeth Stride has even less. He relates her tale of the sinking of the *Princess Alice*, once again drifting toward empathy when he writes that she watched her two children drown, and it was this tragedy that resulted in her drinking habit—and her life on the street to support it. Instead of drink driving a separation and propelling the woman in question into the East End, Matters suggests that this tragedy struck Elizabeth first and thus she had a cause for drinking. Matters is unable to discover what had become of the children's father, but after the sinking Elizabeth is left entirely alone, with no one to drive her away because of her sudden decision to drink and no one to provide for her.

Aside from this tragic tale, Matters notes that she was forty-five years old and living among the various other homeless populations in the East End. He does provide an interesting bit of commentary, though, when he adds that Elizabeth was a woman of such stature that she "could have been expected, if given the chance, to fight tenaciously for her life."[5] There are many things he might be implying with this statement: first, that she was not given the opportunity to fight for her life and was surprised by the Ripper; second, that she did indeed fight, but the Ripper was physically superior and managed to overpower her; or third, he might wish to question whether such a life was worth fighting for at all, or if Elizabeth might have submitted to her fate as a way of committing suicide. It is an intriguing statement since it is simply offered without being followed up by any such suppositions, perhaps to indicate that none of the other women could have been expected to physically resist in any way.

Catherine Eddowes is described in familiar terms, being of the same general age and appearance of Mary Anne and Annie—and indeed perhaps the majority of women who found themselves in the East End. On the night of her death Catherine had been locked up for being publicly drunk and was released only a handful of hours later, still not entirely recovered. Matters seeks to clarify the relationship between Catherine and drink when he adds that, "though usually sodden with gin, she was not originally a subject for the police."[6] Catherine may not generally practice sobriety, but neither is she a generally disruptive drunk, so her final night seems to have been out of character.

Outside of this, the only information Matters seems to find important is that Catherine very much belonged in the group that held Mary Ann, Annie, and Elizabeth. He does not outright state that she is a prostitute, instead referring to class instead of occupation, but women of this lowest class, left on their own, were likely simply assumed to have taken themselves to the streets. Catherine has also left her husband and has no other means of support, by this time a familiar tale. Perhaps by this point Matters believes he had proven his point, and that these details were indeed very much the same and his readers might find themselves bored with further information on Catherine's biography, since her story seems to be very similar to the previous women's.

This lack of attention disappears, however, when Matters comes to Marie Jeanette Kelly. She is not only the focus as the Ripper's final victim, but also in the narrative that Matters later presents to Jack the Ripper's motives and why the killings indeed stopped after her death. From the start Matters separates her from the others, listing her in contrast: she was younger than the others, only in her twenties, who still retained her good looks despite the fact that, like the others, she was indeed a prostitute. In fact, Matters seems to struggle to reconcile a beautiful woman to someone of her occupation, nothing that "[s]he was given to drink and was immoral, but being so young she had not fallen to same depths as the other, older victims."[7]

Marie Jeanette is further separated from the other women because she, unlike them, was not forced to walk the streets so often, or in such desperation. She rented her own room and did not have to come up with pennies every night for a bed. Somehow she was able to secure a steady enough income in order to be able to afford this, but Matters must present her as a prostitute instead of assigning her some other occupation in order for his theory to play out. Marie Jeanette stands apart from the others all the same—where Annie Chapman inspired pity, Marie Jeanette inspires awe.

Marie Jeanette was a widow like Annie, having lost her husband in a mining accident while she was still quite young. Matters does not trace her path from widowhood to the East End, but he does report that she was friendly with the prostitutes of the area and, like the others, was fond of drink. Joe Barnett, who had been living with Marie Jeanette in her small room until shortly before her murder, defends this behavior by saying that "she was otherwise a respectable person."[8] Respectability is not a term often associated with women in the East End, and not one that Matters has allowed to be attached to any of the previous women. Even though Marie Jeanette drank just like they did, and even though she spent her time in behavior that sounds suspiciously like prostitution, Matters allows her to be respectable, if only by comparison.

Her identity as a prostitute, as well as this respectability, both play a role in Matters' narrative of his Ripper suspect. He proposes that the Ripper was a doctor, and gives him the pseudonym of Dr. Stanley so as to protect the man who made a deathbed confession. Dr. Stanley wishes to kill Marie Jeanette because she afflicted his son with a sexually transmitted disease that led to the young man's death. During her encounters with the younger Stanley, Marie Jeanette "was just one of those light-hearted creatures who seemed to have been destined for the night-life into which she fitted so naturally."[9] She is not only young and beautiful, but cunning as well, having had her "apprenticeship" at a brothel in the West End. This attractive Marie Jeanette knows her appeal to young gentlemen of the upper classes and has trained herself to use this to her advantage, entering into prostitution quite willingly and making full use of her charms. Instead of being forced into the streets, prostitution is her personal choice.

This Marie Jeanette not only uses the young Stanley but also many other men, being ostensibly irresistible to the men of her own class, as well. The young Stanley is perhaps a bit naïve when he does not realize her profession, but men of the lower classes wish to support Marie Jeanette because she seems to be above them in some way. She uses what men she can find, one after another, for as much as she can get from them. This explains why she was able to afford her own room instead of staying at lodging houses, although it makes Barnett just the latest in a string of men to be duped by her charms. Instead of engaging in casual acts of prostitution recognized as such by both parties, she fools men into supporting her in a semblance of a long-term relationship while in actuality simply using them.

Matters is convinced that this scheme will not last, since although Marie Jeanette is young and beautiful, her penchant for drink will soon force her the way of the others. Whatever Matters thinks of Mary Ann, Annie, Elizabeth, and Catherine, Marie Jeanette is far worse because her beautiful exterior hides a twisted and devious character. Devious, it seems, only toward men who gravitate toward her, since she was popular with the women in the area, especially when she could do them a favor. It is a sign of insecurity that Matters reports Marie Jeanette did not like to be alone, but preferred to go about with at least one other woman in her company. Somehow both sides of her existed at the same time, and her metaphorical claws only came out when she found herself with a likely man she could use. Since she was meant to have infected a doctor's son, who was an up-and-coming doctor himself, her preference for men—or perhaps her appeal to the same—was not limited to a single class.

Marie Jeanette, although given by far the most narrative attention, therefore comes across as something of a complicated contradiction. This is a young woman who was willing to buy drinks for her friends—perhaps so she simply would not be drinking alone—but was also something of a danger to any man who foolishly crossed her path. She was intelligent enough to keep herself from being used while at the same time knowing how best to present herself to make a living off of men. By spending more time in his description of Marie Jeanette, Matters presents her as a complicated human being with many of the failings of the other women, but with a few unique characteristics, as well.

Even discounting the extended treatment of Marie Jeanette, Matters disproves his own thesis that each woman's story was much like the last. Readers need only to refer to his sentimental treatment of Annie Chapman. Despite his attempts to present each woman as made from the same cloth, especially considering the factual similarities within their biographies, Matters still, perhaps unintentionally, differentiates his subjects. He barely touches on Elizabeth and Catherine, likely with the assumption that readers can fill in the blanks along the lines of the previous women's stories. However, the information he gives, along with the style in which he gives it and his choice of emotional vocabulary, already serve to separate Annie from Mary Ann and show that perhaps not every East End woman can be made to fit the same backstory, after all.

The Authority of a Detective

Edwin T. Woodhall's 1937 book *Jack the Ripper or When London Walked in Terror* does perhaps a better job of making Matter's argument for the mysterious Dr. Stanley even though he offers fewer details about the victims. Woodhall believes that his interpretation stands out, both because he was first a detective before turning to writing, and second because his authoritative statement is also affordable, being advertised as "cheap" even on the cover. His focus is, of course, on finding the identity of Jack the Ripper, and since he includes a retelling of the Dr. Stanley story, Marie Kelly once again receives more attention than the other women, some by a rather large margin.

Due to the small amount of space devoted to the crimes, each woman is typically only given a few descriptors. Together they are "defenseless women,"[10] "women of a certain type,"[11] and—more poetically, when describing victim Martha Tabram—"a Magdalene of the East End streets."[12] Even though Woodhall employs these and other euphemisms, it is clear that he intends his readers to take the next logical step and label them as prostitutes, plain and simple. Although he does not come out and specifically use this possibly offensive language fifty years after the deaths of his subjects, the hints are anything but subtle. For Woodhall, these women are not simply down on their luck, making a living in the East End by any means possible. They are, each and every one, clearly earning a living through sex.

Mary Ann Nichols is presented as wearing "a loud black and white check costume,"[13] immediately recognized by the constable who first came upon her body due to this unlikely and garish outfit. Perhaps his readers are far enough removed from the reality of life in the East End of London in the 1880s, since there is no doubt that her outfit is indeed a "costume" that presumably matches and was not acquired piecemeal. Further, the white checks are still white, despite the notorious air pollution of industrial London and the living conditions of the East End. Woodhall knows that Mary Ann was living on her own, with no relatives to help her, and that she spend her nights in lodging houses of the East End with no access to proper laundry services—or perhaps even an alternate outfit to wear while washing this one. He still dresses her in this ensemble that sounds rather ridiculous, adding insult when he, like Matters, calls Mary Ann a "derelict" and, later, "the poor 'creature of the streets' of East End London."[14] A derelict, in the language of shipwrecks, is cargo that has sunk to the bottom and cannot be recovered. Even though it once may have had a use, it must now be dismissed and left where it lies. Woodhall removes Mary Ann's humanity while she is still living, and thus she ceases to be a woman before she becomes a corpse.

Ann Chapman fares little better, being identified first by her name and age and then her looks. She is "pretty in a rather flashy way,"[15] although it seems little would be flashier than a black a white checked costume. She is at least, and remains, a woman instead of already an object, although the mention of her looks is still troubling. Mary Ann is neither pretty nor ugly, perhaps because her checked outfit detracted from her face. Ann, on the other hand, is pretty, a woman objectified if not an object. Woodhall offers a small gesture of sympathy, although the fact that he calls her poor and unfortunate might simply be statements of facts. He has already clarified that the Victorians used the word "unfortunate" to describe prostitutes, much in the way hat he himself is dancing around the term. The terse way he describes Ann the woman, as opposed to Ann the corpse, makes it difficult to tell which meaning he intends.

Woodhall's entire description of Elizabeth Stride is confined to a single sentence that explains he will not give any more information about her "for the reason that there were no fresh aspects, beyond the fact of the crime belonging to the same class of female mass-killings."[16] There were no fresh aspects as far as clues pointing to the killer, and—in an argument that supports Matters—no fresh aspects in the figure of Elizabeth herself. She is simply part of the same class, and therefore the same occupation, that has already been under discussion, and thus there is no use expounding on her presumably unremarkable life. Had there been more clues to be found on her corpse, perhaps her life—or at least the very end of it, in which she had encountered the killer—would have been worthy of discussion. As it stands, this is Woodhall's shortest discussion of any of these women, and it seems readers should count themselves lucky enough to know Elizabeth's name.

There is only a little more information about the life of Catherine Eddowes. She is solely more interesting to Woodhall because of the timeline of events. Catherine was murdered the same night as Elizabeth, with her body being discovered while police were still organizing the questioning of witnesses where Elizabeth was found. The police officer whose steady beat brought him through Mitre Square helped to narrow down the window of opportunity even further, which meant that the Ripper murdered and mutilated Catherine in a surprisingly short amount of time. And finally, Catherine is the only victim who, according to Woodhall, was seen in the company of the Ripper before her death. All of this is, however, focused on identifying the Ripper instead of on the person of Catherine herself.

He does reveal that Catherine had been arrested the previous afternoon, as was common practice when women were found drunk on the street. There is no indication as to whether Catherine was either frequently arrested or frequently drunk, leaving readers to come to their own conclusions based on this single instance. There is no discussion of her clothing or her looks, which can apparently be assumed to have both been plain and not worth mentioning.

In contrast, "Marie Kelly was a little different. She was younger, more refined, better dressed, and far nicer looking than any of them had been"[17]—and apparently she avoided wearing checks. Within the text describing the crimes, the space in which Woodhall discusses the other women and before he ventures into various theories, this is all we know of Marie prior to her death. The extent of her injuries quickly turns her from a human being into an object, although Woodhall does not dwell on those injuries. At least Marie is allowed to maintain her humanity until her encounter with Jack the Ripper.

She is even discussed again when Woodhall introduces the final theory he has chosen to discuss, that of Dr. Stanley. In his version of the tale, Marie becomes a "female 'night life butterfly'"[18] who, in all her glory, is capable of seducing the younger Stanley. As a butterfly of any kind she has already risen above the level of caterpillar, although Woodhall does not describe what that might have entailed for young Marie. Perhaps an innocent child, Marie entered into her chrysalis and emerged scheming and dangerous, as well as overwhelmingly attractive to men. Woodhall indicates that her choice of the young Stanley was a form of dubious compliment, since she had met such a large number of nice young men in her life—of his class as well as her own—and had for some reason battened on to him. She is no innocent young beauty but is rather fully aware and fully in control of her actions, as well as her men. This Marie also uses them for her own devices, and has clearly been blessed with the good looks and cunning in order to do so.

From wherever it was she had met the young Stanley, Marie disappeared into the vast populous of the greater city. Somehow, even though Woodhall insisted that she was able to stand out, she also apparently managed to disappear completely. After the death of his son, Dr. Stanley has a difficult time trying to track her down. Despite the fact that she stood out in the East End due to her looks and her age, he must search for months before he can track her down, murdering some of her "fellow-sisters"[19] along the way. This is a more subtle indication that, beauty or not, Marie was just like the other women and should be thought of as no better. She might even perhaps be worse, since she set out not to earn the simple price of a bed for the night, but to seduce and therefore ruin the life of a young, upcoming doctor.

It is the final line of Woodhall's book—a statement of Dr. Stanley's logic—that sums up the Ripper's approach to the women he killed: "What did a few lives of this type matter … so long as the one 'sacrificial victim' in the long run led him to the ONE woman he sought?"[20] His victims mattered to Dr. Stanley as little as Elizabeth Stride does to Woodhall, although Mary Ann, Ann, and Catherine could not be said to have mattered much more. They are sacrificed to the glory of his personal revenge for the death of his son. Their role in this story, as within this investigation, is to be discovered dead and to be subjected to a thorough post-mortem so that authors and readers might be convinced of the identity of the Ripper.

Murdered by One of Their Own

William Stewart's 1939 book *Jack the Ripper: A New Theory* does not pursue the Dr. Stanley theory, but rather proposes that Jack the Ripper was not a man after all, but a midwife. Instead of making up a pseudonym for this woman, he simply states her occupation and argues how a midwife would have been perfectly situated to perform the murders. She would have had knowledge of anatomy, as well as a reason to be out and about on the streets at all hours. Stewart further adds that the voluminous women's clothing of the day would have allowed her to hide any bloodstains she procured during the murders. For motive, he sticks with the popular idea of revenge, although his midwife is seeking it against the class of women who reported her to the police and had her arrested, instead of justice for a dead child.

Stewart is not only a former detective, but he is also an artist, and along with presenting information he says he has rediscovered, he includes his own personal sketches of the victims. These are presented alongside photographs of the locations in which their bodies were discovered. The photographs help to show the lengths to which he went in preparing for this book, although the sketches—around the size of a postage stamp—lead to Stewart revealing a lot more.

Although he furthers his authority by explaining various experiments he and his friends performed at the murder sites, mainly to determine how well sound would travel, it is his discussion of the victims' appearances that leads to closer scrutiny of his sketches. Stewart places the victims as the poorest in London, adding that "the older members had sunk so low that they looked like bad drawings of human beings."[21] Does this mean that his own sketches, if they appear to be poorly done, are in fact meant to look exactly as they do in order to be accurate representations? Is it possible to make a good sketch of a bad face? The size of his sketches means that the level of detail is sacrificed in favor of the larger photographs of the locations, but presumably the drawings are not themselves "bad." They simply represent women who had lived hard lives prior to their gruesome deaths, although it is difficult to see how such small images could inspire either attention or empathy.

Stewart's sympathy, or perhaps his romanticism, comes when he declares stoutly that "there is abundant proof that Annie Chapman and Mary Kelly are 'one-man' women."[22] To be a "one-man" woman presumably means to live under his care and protection, although that protection failed each of them. Annie was of course out late at night, having been turned away from her usual doss house because she lacked the money for a bed, and Mary, although in her own room, was alone on the night of her murder since Joe Barnett had moved out. Stewart shows resistance to classifying all five women as being of the same occupation, despite the other similarities in their stories. Ostensibly Annie and Mary are indeed "one-man" women out of devotion and care, and not through schemes to keep themselves fed and sheltered.

Mary Ann Nicholls, on the other hand, was indeed a prostitute, living a life in which women were expected to be "continually knocked about. Such assaults seemed one of the normal conditions of the profession,"[23] which Stewart presents as part of the thought process on the morning when her body was discovered. She might have been too drunk to move, yes, but she might also have been beaten. Mary's body was identified by her estranged husband, which leads to further questions: if she had been married, and if life on the street was so dangerous, why would she have left him? Stewart does not offer an explanation for their parting, or even indicate which spouse made the decision to leave the other, or if it was a mutual decision. It is difficult to see why a woman would willingly leave the relative security of a marriage in favor of fending for herself on the street, which suggests that her husband must have had a reason to call for the separation. Readers are left to speculate on that reason for themselves.

Stewart traces her path through various workhouses and her single attempt to work as a servant that ended when she stole money from her employer. This led to Mary being on the street, once again drifting from workhouse to lodging house. The only hint as to what she might have done with her stolen money, as well as why she might not have been able to afford a bed on her final night, is that, when she was last seen, she was drunk enough to be unable to walk straight. There is no attempt to argue whether this drunkenness was a common or uncommon state and thus whether it might have been the cause of other misfortune in Mary's life.

Stewart ends each chapter with numbered points about the "evidence" in each "case" and only here reveals Mary's age and the fact that she had five children. While this information is important enough to include in this summing up—and indeed will play into Stewart's proposed theory that he introduces later—it was not worthy of earlier mention. Although Mary's husband is included in that he identified her body, her children appear to have no role in either her death or her identification, and presumably her role of mother was minimal in the years since their separation.

The chapter on Annie Chapman opens with a lengthy first-person account of a journalist who rushes to the scene soon after her body as discovered, and only then moves toward the inquest descriptions that refer to Annie in her life. Although Annie had been married, her husband himself died a year and a half before her murder, leaving her a widow without the weekly payments he had faithfully provided. Although the fact that she received a weekly payment seems to indicate that they had not been living together, Stewart does not present Annie as ever actually having left her husband. Instead, she is simply a "one-man" woman and a widow, not at fault for her status of being without a husband.

Stewart continues his almost compassionate description of Annie when he reports that she was, in all likelihood, not "a regular street-walker."[24] Witnesses reported that Annie had sold flowers and crochet work instead of her body. Rather than show skepticism at these reports and question whether Annie's friends may have been presenting a dead women in the best light possible, Stewart includes this information in his summing up of reliable facts. Again, her age and number of children make their first appearance in this numbered list at the end of the chapter, indicating their importance for Stewart's forthcoming theory despite what little they add to the murder narrative.

The power of the "canonical five" victims is revealed when Stewart comes to Elizabeth Stride. He opens this chapter with the declaration that "[w]hile there is not a shred of evidence to support the belief that Elizabeth Stride was murdered by the Ripper this murder is included for ... no account of the East End murders would be complete without it."[25] That the Ripper murdered a minimum of five women was a theory already established within the first fifty years after the murders, linking these five women together in death even when an author wishes to argue against that linking. The entirety of information about her life comes from Michael Kidney, who had lived with her for a handful of months prior to her death. He relates the *Princess Alice* story, though in this version Stride herself worked aboard as a stewardess. Unlike in the case of Annie Chapman, Stewart does not accept this secondhand retelling of Elizabeth's life story as completely accurate, since his summing up of the chapter includes that point that, despite the *Princess Alice* tale that included the death of her husband and two children, all nine of her children were alive at the time of her death. Also in spite of the lack of such testimony, Stewart declared that Elizabeth was living estranged from her husband and does not allow her to rise to the position of a "one-man" woman despite Kidney's testimony.

Instead, Stewart argues for a kind of serial monogamy when his summing up states that Elizabeth spent her life going from man to man, and Kidney just happened to be the one she was living with at the time of her death. Somehow the "one-man" woman distinction is reserved for women who have in fact had two men in their lives—their husbands and one other—and not simply for women who are living with a man while avoiding prostitution. Kidney is thus not elevated to the level of Annie's nameless man, who receives a single mention as some kind of pensioner. Instead suspicion is thrown upon him when Stewart feels the need to clarify that it is impossible to prove that Kidney ever sent her onto the streets. Although no such evidence exists, the suspicion certainly does—and is worth mentioning in such an oblique way—and casts Kidney in a negative light. Presumably the only reason an East End woman would devote herself to a man would be for the protection he could provide, and a man who sent his woman out with the goal of prostitution was a poor provider and perhaps not much of a man, even for the East End. After all, Kidney believed the tales that Elizabeth had told him, when Stewart can flatly declare them to be untrue. Kidney might be under her spell, care so little for her that he would have accepted any tall tale that she told him, or perhaps be fully aware that it was a lie but repeat it out of respect for Elizabeth. Stewart does not present enough information for readers to guess.

One further point is a mention of Elizabeth that has nothing to do with her lack of beauty or her history: "She was an exceedingly powerful woman."[26] Stewart makes this observation after his statement of her age and before giving the number of children Elizabeth had borne, a puzzling place. Was she exceedingly powerful for a woman of forty-five, or is the fact that she had delivered nine children proof of how powerful she was? And further, if she were indeed powerful, what sort of man—or, as Stewart will argue, woman—could have murdered her? Stewart's theory suggests a means by which Elizabeth would have let her guard down, but this is a curious statement lacking in the description of any of the other women, including the younger and less alcohol-ravaged Mary Kelly.

Catherine Eddowes falls under the same almost contradictory umbrella as Elizabeth in that, although John Kelly testified that he had been living with her for quite some time, she is also not a "one-man" woman.

This identification is followed by the parenthetical notation that "[t]he face of the victim had been badly disfigured,"[27] meaning that Kelly must have identified her despite these injuries and others to her body. Is this meant to indicate that Kelly knew her well if he were up to the task, or that his knowledge of her was indecent because they were not married and yet he was able to recognize her naked body? Kelly himself is dismissed after two sentences, having served his purpose of identifying the victim. Although he is identified by name, unlike Annie's nameless pensioner, he is apparently lacking that certain something that would allow Stewart to identify him as Elizabeth's "one man."

Catherine is known to have been drinking the night before her murder because Stewart informs readers that she was not entirely sober when she was released from police custody hours later. Whether or not this was unusual for her is a subject not even considered—aside from her final movements, Stewart reports his standard statistic of age and number of children, then adds that Catherine was in and out of lodging- and workhouses. This, then, is the whole of what Stewart feels important enough about Catherine's life to impart to his readers.

Mary Kelly, as has now become common practice, is carefully separated from the other women. Stewart reports her landlord, John McCarthy, thinking of her as "a decent little woman ... different to others of her type."[28] Whether this difference rests solely in her decency or is for another reason, Stewart does not say. At the very least Mary was able to charm her landlord to a certain extent, since she was behind in her rent and he still thought of her so fondly. This is especially notable after so many of the previous women were thrown out of their lodging houses for lacking the mere pennies necessary for a single night's stay.

Mary's "one man" was named Joseph Barnett and had been living with her for a few months at the time of her death, although not in the days immediately prior to it. Despite his presence and support, presumably monetarily as well as emotionally, Mary was friends with the local prostitutes even if she did not herself engage in prostitution, and she often spent money on drink. Barnett left her because she had invited a prostitute to share their small room with its single bed. This fact could be used to shine a favorable light on Mary and an unfavorable one on Barnett. Although there had not been any further murders in the weeks since the night of the double event, newspapers were keeping the story of the murders alive, and Mary would have taken in her friend in order to protect her from becoming a possible victim. After all, it only took a single night on the streets to lead to a gruesome death. True, their room was small, but Barnett's absence made her more vulnerable despite the possession of a room to herself, especially since he left her to make up the missing weeks of rent.

Unlike Kidney's reporting of Elizabeth's history on the *Princess Alice*, Stewart presents Barnett's retelling of Mary's past as fact. According to Barnett and undisputed by Stewart, Mary had lived both in the West End and for a time in France, although she had left France of her own free will. Whatever had happened there was perhaps not as terrible as what waited for Mary next, since she ended up in the poorer East End. At least she had Barnett and her little room for a while, until he left her and she had to find a way to start paying for that room. A woman alone in the East End had few choices, and it was Barnett's absence that forced her onto the streets. Presumably Barnett had been honorable enough, unlike Kidney, to have kept her away from prostitution while they were living together—although the fact that they owed so much rent did not speak well for his earning power.

Just as Stewart presents Annie as sympathetic, he does the same for his second "one-man" woman. Much later in the text, after his chapter about Mary has been concluded, Stewart addresses the questionable tale of her time in France and subsequent quick decent by pointing out that she is a "born romantic" and, as such, would "find some measure of conso-lation by fabricating stories of some high estate" from which she was meant to have fallen.[29] He does not believe her story, after all, although he does not dismiss Mary's tales as suddenly and firmly as he did Elizabeth's in her biography. In this case he even seems to understand why such a young woman, in need of a man, might prefer to tell such a lie. This sympathy was not extended to Elizabeth.

There is one further statement Stewart makes specifically in reference to Mary Kelly that applies not only to the other women, but to many dis-cussions of victims of violent crime, past and present. He writes it bluntly: "Mary Kelly, like the previous victims, was an accessory to her own death, for she had lived a life which, while contributing to the Ripper's success, by that very reason helped to make the unsuccess of the police a certainty."[30] While other authors dance around the subject, suggesting that the Ripper selected his victims because they were used to going with strangers into dark corners, Stewart states it outright. He accuses Mary and all the others of putting themselves in this danger—as though they had a choice of voca-tion, or as though they should have fought back or otherwise protected themselves. This is not an argument that Jack the Ripper should not have killed women, but that these women should not have made themselves such easy prey.

The bluntness of this statement—"accessory to her own death"—reveals these underlying thoughts about murder victims, especially those who, in life, had been prostitutes. It also perhaps explains Stewart's limited details of these women's lives, since the salient fact is that each was a prostitute, and thus had a hand in arranging her own death. The Ripper specifically chooses prostitutes of the East End as his victims, selecting a class, gender, and profession that could be—and has been—so easily dismissed. Stewart, then, is not saying anything new when he accuses these women of being accessories to their own deaths. He has simply taken what Matters and Woodhall have merely hinted at and stated it plainly.

No Ripper texts were written in the 1940s, and certainly few authors ever spoke so plainly as Stewart. The next appearance of the Ripper narrative in books came in the 1950s and 1960s, after the Second World War in a world where tragedy could indeed have struck at home, but where few readers, if any, would remember the Whitechapel of 1888. Perhaps, after a war in which the enemy attacked with bombs that could strike anyone, reading about a single man with a knife who chose very specific victims was an escape.

THREE

"Ladies of the pavement"

Ripper Narratives
of the 1950s and 1960s

The first full-length book on Jack the Ripper was published forty years after the event itself and could not have been said to have opened the floodgates. Only two more were published in the following decade, and then twenty years passed before the next book. In those twenty years, the world experienced a number of changes.

Sixty years after the Ripper murders, audiences were even further removed from the culture in which they took place. Newspapers were no longer the sole source for timely information. Telephones, radios, and televisions had become common. While the East End may have remained a less prosperous region than the West End, all of London had felt the effects of the bombings during World War II. Men, women, and children alike had been threatened by the axis powers, and the level of fear may well have been comparable to the days when newspaper boys shouted details of the latest gruesome murder. Women had entered the workforce and then refused to be displaced when the soldiers returned home. The focus of attention was shifting.

The Ripper reappears in books more than a decade after the end of the war, assuming three new alias over a half-dozen years. None of these identities is enough to rival Hitler—a Russian surgeon, a failed barrister, and a Jewish slaughterman all fall short—but they represent a specific, localized threat that is now far in the past and likely no longer remembered firsthand. Readers and authors are far enough removed from these murders, as well as far enough removed from the most recent event of violent bloodshed, that the Ripper may once more be examined.

There is a notable change between the Jack the Ripper books of the

1920s and 1930s and those of the 1950s and 1960s. Although these pairs of decades boast a mere three books each, those of the earlier decades include very little information about the five women found dead. The amount of space devoted to them—to their biographies and years of life instead of to their corpses and coroners' reports—greatly expands in the fifties and sixties. It is possible that the experience of an entire country having been on edge and in fear of the next attacks, while at the same time coping and living through the danger in part by bringing women out of the home, allowed for the perspective of the Ripper's victims to be more fully considered as both important and valid.

Naming the Ripper with Another Alias

In his 1959 book *The Identity of Jack the Ripper*, Donald McCormick offers up a confusing solution in the form of a man alternately named Alexander Pedachenko and Vassily Konovalov. Multiple contemporary theories speculated that the Ripper had to be a foreigner, since no one could conceive of a proper Englishman committing such a crime. Further, there was great debate over whether or not the Ripper showed any medical skill during his mutilations of his victims, with the prevailing theory leaning toward the affirmative. A third question was whether or not the Ripper happened to be sane, since presumably an insane butcher of women would be more notable and should have been more easily caught. McCormick satisfies all of these concerns with his proposal of a mad Russian doctor, although Pedachenko may not have ever actually existed.

It is only in his final chapter that McCormick names his Ripper, and even then only after dismissing multiple other theories. He opens with the murders themselves, with Chapter 2 entitled "'Polly' of Thrawl Street" and Chapter 3 "Dark Annie." Their deaths are important enough not only for an entire chapter to be devoted to them, but to be named for them, as well. Liz and Kate must share a chapter given the broad title of "An Autumn of Terror," and even though Mary Kelly exists in her own chapter, it is named "Grand Guignol in Miller's Court" and named after the location of her death instead of using her own name. This is an interesting division— Polly, being the first victim, may be accorded the "honor" of a chapter title simply by dint of being first, but Mary, usually held separate from the others because of the brutality of her mutilation and the fact that she is usually considered to be the final murder, has a chapter that proclaims her address instead of her identity.

Within her chapter that at least holds her name and might be excused for giving her address as a form of identifying her against the other Pollys of the East End, Polly is a contradiction. McCormick declares that she "was generally liked, even by her own sex and by those who competed against her"[1] as fellow prostitutes, but when he expounds upon her biography, he finds little to like. McCormick breezes through her childhood and past her marriage to the point where she finally parted from her husband and her five children. The language is neutral enough that it is unclear whether Polly left her husband or he left her, but nothing is said about him apart from his occupation whereas Polly is shown to be too fond of drinking and careless in many aspects of her life. This carelessness is not subject to much scrutiny, but since drinking put Polly on the outs with her father, as well, perhaps nothing more needs to be said. Readers are able to connect her fondness for the bottle with her inability to remain in a household with a male figure well enough.

It is a pattern that repeats, since Polly is next seen running through a string of men who manage to put up with her for perhaps a month before they, too, react in the same way as her estranged husband. As likable as McCormick claims Polly to be, perhaps it is only to those who must endure her in small doses and not those who attempt to cohabitation for an extended period of time. Polly runs through various men and plenty of alcohol until she ends up even lower than many of the women around her.

And yet, whether or not she has been medicating herself with alcohol, Polly is still likable. McCormick argues that, when drunk, she was perhaps a bit loud, but always cheerful, hardly the worst reaction to an overindulgence. It is difficult to imagine incessant cheerfulness as a reason for so many men to abandon her in turn, but McCormick does not go into further details and indeed only names Polly's husband and father. The other men are perhaps in and out of her life too quickly to have left such a mark, or—it must be considered—have been constructed through hearsay and rumor in which the reality of the situation was blown all out of proportion. If Polly experienced any money troubles with these men, they were subsumed under the repetition of her alcoholism.

Even on her final night McCormick's Polly is not turned into the street for a lack of money but because she happened to show up drunk. This makes her declaration that it will not be long before she has money for her bed a rather confusing non sequitur, since McCormick made no indication that she lacked coins in the first place. Then again, a drunken Polly may well have given such a response, either as her way of denying her condition or because she had not fully understood in the first place.

Either way, a drunk Polly ends up wandering the streets, admitting to a friend that she was thrown out because she did not have any money and not because she was turned away at the door for drunkenness—after all, what doss house would have clients if men and women were turned away for drink? Just as it is difficult to reconcile a likable Polly with the biography McCormick presents, it is confusing to attempt to determine which explanation honestly led to her presence on the street that night.

Polly is likable but unable to hold a man's favor for long. She drinks, but this does not turn her mean or maudlin. She did not have money for a bed, but she was turned away at the door of the lodging house because of her drinking. It is possible that she had drunk enough to hope that she might have her bed on credit and it is not unbelievable that she would have told different tales to different people in her life. Two of these people—the men who had parted from her but had not been able to escape being known in her biography: her husband and father—even chose to insist that she had not been a prostitute in life, and McCormick does not offer any evidence to refute this. It would have been entirely possible for them to lay such blame at Polly's feet, since she could have easily been presented as abandoning her husband, children, and father in turn, but it seems she turned to serial monogamy instead of prostitution and was thus saved from such a label. In the end much of Polly's life remains a mystery, and despite this confusion, McCormick does not interpret the given information as in as poor a light as he could have.

Annie, who receives a chapter title that is solely her nickname, stands out for McCormick against all of the others. First and foremost he admits to her occupation as prostitute, although this places her far below the middle-class of her birth and marriage. This endears her to neither her fellow women of the streets nor to McCormick and garners no sympathy, although he does mention that the end of her marriage may have been the fault of her husband. Annie, like Polly, parted from both husband and children and had a drinking habit. Although McCormick makes no hesitation in dispelling any romantic notions of Annie as a "one man" woman, she did not turn to prostitution until after her husband's death, when her weekly allowance ceased. For McCormick, Annie's attempts to make money through crocheting and selling flowers were the supplement to her main income and not her first choice of vocation. He presents an Annie who, despite looking older due to her drinking and poor health, "frequently took men back to the common lodging house"[2] where she stayed.

Annie's movements during the final days of her life, important because they might reveal where and when she had crossed paths with the killer, are confusing. McCormick mentions she had been in the infirmary off and on all month due to illness, and then relates her fight with another woman during which she was badly injured. McCormick reports that she spent the night before her death with her sister, but he does not show Annie being kicked out of a lodging house or even attempting to enter one on the last night of her life. There is no firm explanation for what she might have been doing out so late—or so early—although the previous evening she had acknowledged to a friend that she needed money for lodging. Between this statement around five the previous afternoon and the murder around five in the morning, McCormick gives no indication of her actions.

In spite of the fact that she had been ill and the beating she had taken for pointing out another woman's attempted scam of a mutual friend, McCormick offers no sympathy to Annie. He specifically states that anyone offering such sympathy has been misled. He denies Annie both Polly's supposed serial monogamy and her universal likability, and there is no mention of how Annie acted when she was drunk. It is as though McCormick is personally offended by prior sympathetic representations of Annie Chapman and has set out, in this chapter titled with her nickname, to dispel them all and offer her up to a harsher light.

The facts presented of Annie's life, like those of Polly's, could have been interpreted more or less favorably as McCormick chose. The language he uses to discuss Polly, even in her negative aspects, is buffered and buoyed by this continual insistence on and his belief in her likability. Annie suffers from his determination to invert previous representations that he finds to be fraudulent. It is perhaps possible to find sympathy for a victim of Jack the Ripper, but McCormick has none for Annie.

In their shared chapter, McCormick bounces back and forth between information on Elizabeth and Catherine. Elizabeth, like Annie, is most definitely a prostitute, although other details are not as certain. It is uncontested that she was a Swede, but, Stride not being her maiden name, there is some confusion as to whether she is, or ever was, married. Despite being registered in the Swedish church as unmarried and known there as childless, McCormick reports Elizabeth's rescue from the sinking of the *Princess Alice* and the death of her husband and two children.

Even after admitting that there is no evidence to back up this claim, McCormick relates the fact that Elizabeth marked this moment as "the beginning of her downfall."[3] The story of the *Princess Alice* not only explains why Elizabeth was alone on the streets, as neither wife nor mother, but also provides a reason for her drinking. In this telling, the grief made Elizabeth crave hard liquor, and thus she worked as a prostitute in order to satisfy her craving and dull the pain. Unlike Polly or Annie, Elizabeth did not leave her husband or be driven out by him. If their parting was a result of his death then her situation would have indeed been desperate, especially if she needed to pay for drink as well as shelter and food.

She may have found help in this, since McCormick brings up the figure of Michael Kidney. Theirs does not seem to have been an entirely stable relationship, since they intermittently parted during the three years they lived together. McCormick does not mention whether Elizabeth and Kidney were in the on again or off again part of their relationship on the night of her death. In fact, Kidney is apparently of such little importance to Elizabeth that his name only appears the once.

Catherine's long-term relationship, John Kelly, fares little better, with his name appearing twice despite the fact that they had been together for seven years. Readers are once again faced with a strange contradiction when McCormick informs them that Kelly knew her the wife of a man named Thomas Conway before adding that, as far as evidence could be found, she had never actually married Conway. Barnett seems to have been under the impression that she was indeed Conway's wife, although presumably she had followed this up with the information that she was widowed or that they had separated. Certainly she was not receiving an allowance, the way Annie had until her husband's death. All the same, if Catherine had met Barnett after her relationship with Conway had ended, it brings up the question of why she would have introduced herself to him as Conway's wife without additional clarification of the current arrangement.

Questions of whether one half of the couple might have been using the other for money, Kelly depending on Catherine's prostitution when he was unable to find work as a laborer, or Catherine being supported by Kelly so she would not have to walk the streets, are not raised. Nor is the question of why the couple may have stayed together at all if they so often ended up penniless as they did in Catherine's final days. As with Elizabeth and Kidney, there is no investigation of this relationship or what it might have meant for either party. Kelly allows Catherine to pawn his boots less than twenty-four hours before her death so that they might eat, standing barefoot on the dirty cobbles in September. If the female victims are largely ignored within Ripper narratives, the character of their companions receives even less scrutiny.

Catherine's prostitution was not her only means of obtaining money, although McCormick stresses it as her most common. This Catherine, as McCormick relates through Catherine's daughter Ann Phillips, was an irritation because she would beg her daughter for any spare coins. Despite Kelly's identification of Catherine as Conway's wife, Ann Philips seems uncertain as to her paternity. What she does know is that "Conway left her mother because Catherine Eddowes drank so heavily."[4] Conway was in fact still living, although he had been living under an assumed name so that Catherine could not find him and hound him for money as she hounded her daughter.

Once again readers are faced with a woman who has separated from the man who, if not her husband, was the father of her child, and was therefore also separated from her children. She drinks to excess—if there were any hope that Catherine may have found sobriety in the wake of her relationship with Conway, this is quashed with the recollection that she spent her final evening in jail for public drunkenness. She, like Elizabeth, is in a long-term relationship with a man, although this does not prevent her from being on the street alone after dark.

The only woman who did not meet her end on the street after dark had recently lost the man who had worked to keep her off of them. McCormick clarifies that the Ripper's final victim went by various forms of her name, sometimes Mary Ann, sometimes Mary Jane, "and, occasionally, more pretentiously as Marie Jeanette Kelly."[5] Perhaps it is Mary Jane's youth and vivacity, so unlike many women in the East End, that has allowed her to feel so pretentious. Those who lived nearby knew who she was without having ever been introduced. At her death inquest, one woman noted that "you couldn't miss her. She was different from these other girls"[6]— and Miller's Court, where Mary Jane lived, was home to many young women. Mary Jane's difference must have been visibly clear.

Mary Jane may have been an object of jealousy for more than her age and her looks, since she lived there with the man she had introduced as her husband. She had met Joseph Barnett only the day before they had decided to live together, and, according to testimony at her inquest, the relationship seemed to be a good one. True, there were fights, and one in particular led to a broken window, but it was agreed that these only happened when Mary Jane drank. Overall Mary Jane was a lucky girl to have her looks, her youth, and her Joe Barnett.

Her Joe Barnett who, for whatever reason, was rapidly cooling toward her. McCormick guesses that Barnett "discovered his mistress had been secretly whoring again,"[7] a supposition that carries many levels of meaning. First, although Mary Jane can refer to Barnett as her common-law husband, she is instead his mistress instead of a common-law wife. Granted, a mistress is simply a woman involved in a long-term relationship who is not married, but the most frequent use of the word implies that the man in question is married and his mistress is the other woman.

Barnett is perhaps lucky that Mary Jane is his mistress and not his wife, although separation without divorce clearly happened in the Victorian era. Thus, when he discovers that Mary Jane has been prostituting herself without his knowledge, he is able to simply leave her. But why would Mary Jane walk the streets in the first place? If she had a room, a bed, and a man to provide for her, then she would hardly need to put herself in such a position. After all, the Ripper had already murdered four women before her, and the newspapers were hardly silent on the matter. McCormick does not mention it, but the Ripper murders could not have escaped her attention.

Did she need money for drink that she felt Barnett could not give her? Was he therefore insulted that life with him was not so grand that she felt no need to drink? Or was it instead an insult to his manhood because he could not provide for the two of them on his own? McCormick maintains that Barnett was under no illusions about Mary Jane's life before they had met, which included a rapid fall from a bordello in the West End and a series of men who left her because of how she acted when she was drunk. Her modus operandi was so repetitive that McCormick decides her sole purpose in prowling the streets was not for single encounters with men, but to find the next one to provide for her room and board. Was Barnett simply seduced by a pro and could not cope when he learned he was unable to change her?

Mary Jane may have been a mystery to many of those around her, but even her friend George Hutchinson is shown to have had a shrewd idea of the kind of woman she was. McCormick confides that Hutchinson "had always liked the girl"[8]—girl, not woman—and had often thought of coming to an agreement that would benefit both of them. Although Mary Jane would have apparently been up to the task, Hutchinson admits that he would not have been able to keep up with her, and that he had little to contribute, presumably in the face of all that made her such a phenomenon in the East End. Hutchinson, like so many others—and in contradiction to McCormick—clearly thought there was something about Mary Jane that elevated her above the other women in Whitechapel.

Elevated or not, Mary Jane found herself in a familiar situation. She was not turned away from or out of a lodging house, but she owed a large sum of rent going back many weeks. Barnett had left her and stuck her with paying it all on her own, but the fact that it had not been paid for weeks suggests that he had not been paying it, and, if Mary Jane had gone around "whoring" behind his back, it had not earned her enough to make up the difference, either. All the same, the need for money drove Mary

Jane onto the street during the last night of her life, at which time she asked Hutchinson for sixpence. McCormick has the penniless Hutchinson thinking of the fact that, for six pennies, he might have been able to spend the night in Mary Jane's room, in her bed, and likely with her. As much as Hutchinson admired Mary Jane, this shows all too clearly that he knew her morals and her price.

Behind in rent or not, those who saw Mary Jane that night agreed that she had been drinking, again mirroring so many of the women before her. McCormick neither speculates how Mary Jane might have obtained drink, or why she might have wanted it—after all, a woman who preferred to find long-term partners instead of engaging in casual prostitution may indeed have wanted a pint or two fortify herself for the task at hand.

But McCormick's Mary Jane, like many of his other victims, is a hardened drinker not thrust into prostitution, but accepting the position willingly. After Barnett leaves, Mary Jane has nothing left but to turn to the streets. At an earlier time in her life she had attempted to open a shop in London, but she was now penniless as well has having "no business sense and no education"[9]—no matter what some of her contemporaries believed about her—and there was nothing left but the streets. Mary Jane may have died in her room instead of on the pavement, but she still let the Ripper in.

It may be argued that the contradictions in McCormick's narratives of these women's lives comes from a simple lack of information compounded by hearsay, the rumor mill, and a desire not to speak ill of the dead. Perhaps he felt it would have detracted from his narrative to explore the discrepancies in his own biographies of these women to a depth that would have fleshed out the messiness of human life unable to be turned into a simple single-line narrative. At the very least he might have acknowledged these small disagreements, such as a Polly who was apparently universally well-liked but could not maintain a lasting and stable relationship with a man. It is this deeper investigation that would attempt to raise the victims from flat stand-ins who matter only as corpses to women existing in a complex world of gender and class expectations that is not familiar to readers of the day.

"Dregs of wretched humanity"

Like other authors before him, Tom Cullen seems to have a penchant for seafaring metaphors in his 1965 *Autumn of Terror* (also published as *When London Walked in Terror* and *The Crimes and Times of Jack the Ripper*).

Perhaps there is something about calling the East End "the abyss" that encourages ideas of descent to be watery instead of full of the dirt and smog that would have been more closely aligned with the truth. For Cullen, prostitutes of the East End find themselves on "the last rungs of the ladder descending into the abyss."[10] Presumably they might still have a step or two to go, since that ladder must be resting on some sort of surface, and thus there must be something lower, but Cullen does not name what that might be. It is this position on the ladder that made these women cross paths with Jack the Ripper—in this case, a young lawyer named Montague John Druitt.

Being in so low a position does not necessarily lend itself to humility, as the fragment of mirror found on Polly Nichols' body is a "concession to vanity,"[11] since even one such as she likes to check her reflection from time to time. There is no other suggestion of use given other than that of peering at herself, even though Polly has been both on the streets and in the bottle long enough that Cullen dismisses any allure she may once have had. Polly is not a woman who gives regular care to her looks, and any looks that she has left are long past caring for. Presumably there were no mirrors in the lodging houses where Polly stayed, since she had to carry her own, since there were so many concerns for the poor other than appearance. Yet here her mirror is, helping prove her identity by marking her as a dosser and giving an indication of where to look for her friends.

Neither Polly's marriage nor her apparently sole attempt at a respectable job can redeem her. Although she was a mother, Cullen reports that she generally abandoned her family in favor of saloons with their dual appeal of strange men and drink. She is little suited to being either wife or mother, and her attempt at being a maid is likewise doomed. There is almost a hint of sympathy as Cullen describes her standing at attention as the master of the house—a dry house—reads from the daily lesson, and at least here she fights with the temptation instead of immediately giving in to drink and all the consequences. Polly is, however, unable to abstain forever, and thus she ends up on the East End streets for Jack the Ripper to find.

Polly's husband identifies her and is reported as making his oft-reprinted statement of forgiveness at the time, despite how long it had been since the pair had lived together. He has apparently not forgotten all that had gone between them, however, because his attitude was far less forgiving when he took the witness stand. Whatever kindness or empathy was expressed—or perhaps fabricated—earlier is washed away, and there is no strong compulsion for him to present his deceased wife in a more favorable light. Death is no kinder to Polly than life was.

Annie Chapman is not anchored down by a husband who is still living, although having once been married to an army pensioner who also happened to be a veterinary surgeon in Windsor was not much to help to her in the end. Cullen explains that no reason is given for "why she had left her good provider,"[12] whom she apparently often raised to the level of doctor in her recollections. These reminiscences, however often they came, were spoken solely to the annoyance of her fellow prostitutes. Apparently it would have served her better to have only gone down one rung of the ladder instead of having descended from on high and ending up their equals. It is puzzling, though, why the marriage failed, since she is not painted as being either a drunk or shrew, and little enough is known of her husband. Cullen speculates he was much older than she was, and leaves it at that, though a mere mismatch in age seems to be of little consequence in comparison to life alone in the East End.

She seems to get on well enough alone in Whitechapel for as long as he paid her a weekly allowance, but her husband's death ended this weekly payment. Annie's health began to fail around this same time. Dizziness and fainting spells are not conducive to any manner of work, whether this meant the small sorts of trades Annie is said to have cobbled together for herself or, when that failed, prostitution. Her problems went beyond what the infirmary could do for her, even if she could have afforded better care, since Annie had tuberculosis. On top of this, she was slowly starving to death, especially without the help her estranged husband had once provided.

Cullen recognizes Annie's dual character, both at the time of her death and in the Ripper texts that have discussed her since. He puts his foot down, stating flatly that "to insist she was not a whore is to take the romantic view"[13] and lamenting that previous authors had been fooled by Annie's tales of her past. Even if she had once been respectable, by the time she landed in the East End, she was far from it. Whatever small things Annie did in an attempt to make a living, from selling matches to cheap sachet, it would not have been enough, and she clearly supplemented this pitiful income with prostitution. There is a similarity, however, between this literary treatment of Annie and the responses at her death, since her contemporaries also waffled between condemnation and public tears.

However much Annie—or authors prior to Cullen—was moved to turn her past into a golden recollection of a better age, she is bested by Long Liz Stride, a "born actress"[14] who narrated her life in such a way that she became the center of a tale both tragic and romantic. In Cullen's version, Liz's *Princess Alice* story was inspired by the fact that her carpenter husband had helped to build at least one ship. One variation says that she herself was involved with its creation, or at least the cushions and salon fittings, but the timeline says she would have been only fifteen at the time and still in Sweden. This Liz, like many others, does not let the facts get in the way of a good story.

In this variation she does indeed have nine children, two of whom died with their father during the disaster. A new detail is added in that Liz, in the process of saving herself—instead of being rescued—was kicked in the mouth, resulting in the loss of two of her front teeth. Cullen is quick to point out, however, that Liz's post mortem does not support the claim of such an injury, even though Liz was indeed missing all of her lower teeth. It seems that this Liz has not only come up with an explanation for her position as a single, childless woman, but also for the state of her mouth, all of it combined into a narrative that was clearly a tragedy with Liz in the coveted position of sympathy at its center.

Cullen treats the *Princess Alice* recollection with the same sympathy as he does the question of whether or not Liz was actually indeed drunk each time she was brought before the court on such a charge. Liz, the actress and heroine of her own life, would protest that she did not drink, but had fits. When she demonstrated—or rather, was overtaken by such a fit in front of the judge—more often than not she was dismissed. The frequency of her success perhaps led Liz to continue on drinking, often and to excess, since she was so often able to get away with it. Where she got the money to do so, considering the fact that, *Princess Alice* or not, her husband was not around, was through prostitution. At the very least she was living with Michael Kidney off and on for three years before her death, so John Stride was presumably out of the picture by then. What Kidney did for a living, if he even had a semi-regular position, is not mentioned, and their relationship is also not examined. With this bare description, it is however possible for readers to assume that he did not have a calming influence on Liz, who apparently needed one.

John Kelly fares better than Michael Kidney in this narrative, since he is given both a job title—market porter—and his relationship with Kate, whether her last name was Conway or Kelly that day, is established straight off: his description of her clothing includes that of "a hole in her boot which he himself had mended with a piece of leather."[15] He had been living together with Kate for the past seven years, and though they were not married, she often adopted his last name, the way she had adopted the last name of her first common-law husband. Kelly is not only able to narrate

Kate's biography, but the fact that he had mended her boot for her shows a degree of care, no matter how small.

This is, perhaps, undermined by Cullen's next paragraph. He shows Kelly moving from his long viewing of Kate's body to the table with her clothes, no longer concerned with her boot but with her hat. He checks the inside of the hat band because she kept her money there, although he found none. This is offered as a simple action with no explanation or clarification. Was Kelly himself penniless at the time? Did he send Kate out to earn some money through prostitution? Was he hoping that she might have done so behind his back, if only to leave him the money for a bed that night?

It seems strange that the couple should be penniless, since they had taken the typical East Ender holiday of going hop-picking. Kate was quite ill, with Bright's disease found during her autopsy, but they had gone to the country all the same. They made an early return to London, not waiting out the season, because Kate wanted to earn the reward money for identifying the Ripper. Apparently she told Kelly that she thought she knew him, but did not pass on her suspect's name. They bought a train ticket to return to the city and spent the rest of their money, however much it was, on gin.

During the final days of Kate's life, the couple routinely met up and parted again in London, looking for money, earning it, pooling it, and spending it more on drink than food or a bed. The night before her death Kate told Kelly to pay for his bed while she took one in the workhouse. This is apparently an entirely practical decision, considering the sort of work the workhouse demanded of men as opposed to women, and not a show of devotion on Kate's part. Jobs the following day did not come easy, and the last time Kate and Kelly were together, they were "too miserable to look each other in the eye."[16] This couple of seven years, all of those spent in the East End, has reached such a low in their final moments together that they are too ashamed to even look at each other.

If Kate had come to claim the reward for identifying the Ripper and they were so constantly penniless, why had she not tried to get it? Her straw bonnet had no money to hide and could have been pawned, but it does not seem to have occurred to them. This pair decides to part, Kelly with no clear plans and Kate to attempt to find money from her daughter, with no mention of pawn shops whatsoever. And, despite the lack of money for food, Cullen suggests that their failure to find work is due to their visibly being the worse for drink. Not as far gone as Kate is discovered to be later, when she is arrested for being a public nuisance and locked up until she is sober enough to be released.

Unlike Liz, Kate does not romanticize her life story, and she does not need to. Unlike Polly, whose husband had no compunction about speaking ill of the dead, Kate underwent a transformation. Cullen reports that so many witnesses at her inquest could only speak well of her, and suggests that, were Kate still alive, they would not have been saying such lovely things. There was even resistance to the idea that Kate had been a prostitute and not a morally pure woman struggling along as best she could, even though the police officers who knew her declared her occupation without qualification.

Despite the myths that Liz propagated during her lifetime and that sprung up after Kate's death, it is still relatively simple to separate fact from fiction. The same cannot be said for Mary Jane Kelly, who told legends and fairy tales of her own life that have no corresponding reference in recorded history and thus cannot be proven or disproven. The extent to which she presents herself in different ways, and indeed the way various others relate her story with differences, means that Cullen can only conclude two things about her: "she was a striking-looking woman ... and she loved her gin."[17]

Cullen reports as fact her birth in Limerick and her marriage at age sixteen that only lasted a year or two before her husband's death in a mine explosion. By the time Mary was paid compensation, she had already been driven into the streets. Not only was the money delayed, but it was a pitifully small amount, and a young, striking girl needed an income. He does not believe that she spent any time in the West End of London, much less that she ever set foot in France. This Mary was on a quick downward trajectory that ended with her death.

On the last night of her life, Mary was desperate for money, out and about and in search of any potential customers. Here the maritime language resurfaces: "It was among such flotsam that Mary Jelly drifted ... borne along by the tide, yet remaining aloof, as befits an Amazon Queen."[18] Flotsam by definition floats aimlessly, being the wreckage of a ship or its cargo, and thus the others in the East End are the aftermath of some calamity that has left them unable to choose their own course. Mary drifts as well, but the Amazons in Greek mythology were warriors. Cullen's Mary is a bit of a terror when she defends her own turf and is thus perhaps a warrior, but it is difficult to imagine an Amazon, let alone an Amazon Queen, in the East End. A woman would not have to be as elevated as a queen to stand out among London's poor, and to be queen of the East End would mean very little. Cullen's queen is borne along by the tide just as the flotsam around her, and perhaps even fares worse than the others, since, despite her looks and stature, she cannot find a customer.

This Amazon Queen is not above stealing from her customers, and Cullen even reports that Mary has been known to rush into a pub and swap shawls or other outer garments with another prostitute so that she might escape identification. Now, if Mary is a queen and all others are flotsam, it hardly seems that the changing of a shawl would hide her hair, her figure, or attitude that it seems a queen must have. For a queen, though, she is well liked, although this may have little to do with her attitude and more to do with the fact that she was "as open-handed with money as she was with her other favors"[19]—again, not the behavior usually associated with a queen.

Despite the similarities in her biography Cullen claims as truth for Mary compared with the other women, he remains determined to separate her from the others. They are bound together in the location in which they lived out the ends of their lives, as well as in the violence of their deaths, but no other woman is such a queen. Cullen includes one final summation in which he refers to Mary Ann, Annie, Liz, and Kate as "bundles of rags,"[20] removing Mary Kelly because of her youth and the fact that she had retained her looks, but this hardly seems worthy of an Amazon Queen. In the end, Mary Kelly is a prostitute who was all too fond of gin and, like the others before her, crossed paths with the Ripper while looking for customers on the street.

It is important for Cullen, as it is for many authors, to stress the similarities between the Ripper's victims rather than their differences. Authors must do this in order to explain why these women—and only these women, whether they choose to add to the victims or disregard Elizabeth Stride—were killed. This not only allows them to point to their choice of identity for Jack the Ripper, but also to reassure audiences that the danger of the East End is not one they themselves ever need to fear. If the Ripper could kill Amazon Queens along with the other flotsam, then hardly anyone could be safe. If, however, that Amazon Queen was simply a younger and prettier version of the flotsam, but of the same class and occupation, then her death can be equated with theirs and just as easily dismissed.

Situated Empathy for the Dehumanized

Robin Odell's 1965 book *Jack the Ripper in Fact and Fiction* contains a wide array of terms to describe those living in the East End, and especially the prostitutes themselves. At times the prostitutes—along with pickpockets and other low members of society—become strange hybrids, "human vultures who preyed on honest men's money."[21] They are not only animals, but those who simply wait and watch for others to die, seeking out weakness and thus needing no real power of their own. Alternately, prostitutes are "on the prowl after midnight,"[22] now stalking a more active prey but still being associated more with animals than humans. In more modern crime narratives, it is the serial killer himself who stalks his prey, but in this case the victims—these prostitutes—are somehow seeking out those even weaker and lesser than they are. Odell continues the previous theme of calling them "broken wrecks of women,"[23] although he does not rely nearly so heavily on seagoing metaphors in the process. Once again they are no longer women, but some form of remnant of a woman, no longer complete or whole. All of this comes along with the usual terms of unfortunate, street-walker, lady of the pavement, harlot, and prostitute of the lowest kind.

Who does Odell suggest murdered and butchered the women who fit all of these phrases? Like Stewart before him, Odell names an occupation rather than a specific name, although his choice is that of a Jewish slaugh-terman or *shochet*. He explains that a *shochet* would have the rough anatomical knowledge apparently required for the mutilations performed by the Ripper, and explains how the kosher slaughter of an animal must be performed with a quick slice of the throat and followed with an inspection of the animal's internal organs to be sure that it is fit to eat. What Odell does not explain is why a *shochet* would choose human vultures, broken wrecks, and ladies of the pavement, since it seems doubtful that they would pass the same inspection given to the animals. After all, one of the Ripper letters claims that a piece of kidney from Catherine Eddowes was fried and eaten.

Odell takes more time to describe the general condition of the East End to his readers, both to situate the victims clearly and to show how a *shochet* would have been a respected, trusted member of society who would not have aroused their suspicions. In fact, he suggests that the women would have been amused at a *shochet* who sought their services. He considers that these women were neither foolish nor willfully stupid when they continued to ply their trade even during the heyday of the murders, explaining that desperation would have driven them to the streets to find money for their beds simply because they would not have been allowed to remain indoors without the coins they earned. Odell reminds readers that "the East End streetwalkers of that time cannot be measured in present-day terms of human conduct"[24] because the conditions in which they lived were so far removed from those experienced by contemporary readers.

Against this background, a Mary Ann Nicholls who was estranged from her husband and living in various doss houses is in a position to be more sympathetic than a Mary Ann Nicholls who is given no historical placement. Her progression from the wife of William Nicholls, who is only able to forgive her when he looks down upon her mutilated corpse, indeed becomes a "tragedy of a broken life"[25] and not a woman to be scorned. Part of this tragedy is indeed her drinking, but Odell does not dwell upon the breakdown of her marriage or even mention any children. Polly is simply murdered for the sad—yes, tragic—reason of not having the pennies to buy a bed for the night, with no judgment being passed as to why she found herself broke. She simply drifted from doss house to doss house until she met the Ripper and, being the first victim, would not even have known that there was such a man to watch out for.

Annie's biography is similarly brief, but not quite so positive. While nothing is mentioned about how Polly was treated by her fellow East Enders, Annie received a poor reception, Odell argues, because of her middle-class background. Annie was a woman who had once been respectable, married to a veterinary surgeon, and had wound up in the East End after what Odell describes as a slow decline. This may have taken as long as the four years between her separation from that husband, who presumably has the last name of Chapman but is not given a first name, since only the end points of this descent are given. What happened to her three children is as much of a mystery as what happened to her husband.

Odell states that Annie's "intemperate habits and ill-health made her look ten years older"[26] of her actual age of thirty-seven, although he does not go into details of her health. Her drinking, however, is a continual problem, since she was turned out of her lodging house on her last night because she had spent her final pennies on drink. She is perhaps even foolish enough to have gone from pub to doss house hoping that she would be allowed to say even without the coins in hand. Annie, despite living in a similar predicament as Polly, has her drinking emphasized. This, along with the fact that she did not seem to have many friends—and had even had a violent quarrel with a fellow prostitute shortly before he death—makes her a less likable character.

"Long Liz" is indeed sympathetic despite her descent into prostitution because Odell relates the sinking of the *Princess Alice* as an understandable reason for it. When the ship sank, it took her husband, a carpenter with whom she had previously run a coffee shop, and three children. In this case there is no mention of any other children and thus Elizabeth appears to have lost her entire family in a single day. As "one of the few rescued"[27] she could be understandably wracked with guilt and grief. The deaths of her husband and children could easily explain why she walked the streets of the East End.

In spite of her occupation and her emotional state, Odell does not depict Elizabeth as a drunk. He even states that she was sober the last time that Michael Kidney saw her. Presumably she had some money on the night of her death, since she had done some cleaning in her lodging house and been paid for it. Despite her position in life, Elizabeth still seeks out work that does not involve walking the streets, although it seemed to do her no good. Odell does not tell us whether she tried to find a room for the night, so we do not know if she was also kicked out for a lack of money or if she simply had not decided to turn in yet. He mentions that she was seen in the kitchen earlier in the evening, but it is not certain that she went out with the intent of seeking a client—even though witnesses report her talking to and kissing men. Still, Elizabeth's loss of husband and children was out of her control and she is simply doing what a widowed Victorian woman must do to survive.

Catherine Eddowes's relationship status is more questionable. Although she had been living with a man named John Kelly, he knew her as Kate Conway, presumably married to—or having once been married to—a man named Conway. Conway himself does not surface and this relationship is not explained, although Conway must have presumably been out of Catherine's life before she took up with Kelly. Why he remained with her for seven years when she was clearly addicted to drink and looked seventeen years older than she really was is left open to interpretation. For Odell, Kelly and Michal Kidney are side characters who barely deserve a mention, much less a motive or deeper consideration. Even their reactions upon finding out that Elizabeth and Catherine were murdered go unrecorded.

On the last night of her life Catherine was arrested for being incapably drunk and, upon being released, almost immediately crossed paths with the Ripper. Here Odell makes an interesting example of her character. He points out—quite reasonably—that readers may wonder why a woman would willingly go with a stranger to the darkest part of a square, especially in the wake of previous murders. Catherine would not have known of Elizabeth's death, since it happened so shortly before her own, but Mary Ann and Annie had been fully discussed in the daily newspapers. Odell argues that readers should not label her as foolish, but instead should remember that "East End prostitutes were not motivated by ordinary standards of conduct and judgment."[28] He judges that, for Catherine, this was not a time for caution but one of desperation. Although it is not stated whether she had any money on her that night, Odell decides that she must not have, because only a great need for coins would have driven her to go with a stranger. Catherine is, after all, a known prostitute and drunkard, but she was not a known half-wit.

Mary Jane Kelly's age and looks are duly noted, but she, too, is a known prostitute and drunkard. Like Annie, she is "alienated from her fellow whores"[29] due to a history that did not begin in the East End. Mary wandered from her birthplace in Ireland to Cardiff, the West End, and France, and it was only in Ireland—likely due to her young age—that Odell does not mention her work as a prostitute. Like Elizabeth, she turned to the trade after the death of her husband, but she began it in locations that were clearly higher class. This Mary—or Marie Jeanette, as of course she liked to be known—sank quickly from her higher position, helped along by drink and the need to earn money to buy more.

Like Elizabeth and Catherine, Mary had a long-term beau. In this version, she and Barnett live a comfortable life for about eighteen months, with nary a single quarrel until she invited a friend to stay with them. Apparently they did not even argue about her drinking habits, despite the fact that they were meant to have brought her so low. Perhaps Barnett drank just as much as she did, or he may have earned enough so that the pair had enough expendable income to finance her habit. It is unclear whether this Barnett was the sole source of income because she had ceased prostitution as well as drinking, or if she had continued both—and whether Barnett knew or approved of either.

Although this is where Odell ends his retelling of the murders, he continues to speak of the conditions under which these women lived and relate to the lives of prostitutes as a whole. There is the irony of the meat tea the Lord Mayor of London gave on the same day as Mary's murder, feeding "three thousand of the poorest inhabitants in all of London,"[30] an act Odell mocks. As much good press as the Lord Mayor may have gained, this was undercut not only by the reports of Mary's death as well as the fact that he happened to serve the poor a single meal in which portions were clearly limited. Whatever happiness and excess those three thousand experienced, it was only temporary.

Odell once again emphasizes the desperation that he says drove Catherine to walk with a client on the last night of her life, reminding readers that "[t]he necessity of their often impoverished plight forced them to walk the streets even during the terror of the autumn of 1888."[31] Women on their own who did not have the pennies for a bed would have been forced to walk the streets at night anyway, even if this did not mean they were specifically looking for a client at the time. They could hardly have spent the night in a pub, even if one were open, considering the lack of money, even if the presence of so many others would have been safer. It is thus understandable that women would have been out and about, although for Odell, the understanding ceases when it comes to taking such a client into a secluded location if he seemed at all suspicious.

Odell does not make a list of the signs he himself would brand suspicious, but presumably a seasoned prostitute would have her own list and do well to heed it. It is thus understandable for Catherine to have gone with a man upon her release from jail, and perhaps also that she would have sought out the darkest and most secluded corner of Mitre Square with her client, but once again the reader is faced with possibilities. Is Catherine foolhardy—or still drunk—enough that she overlooked or ignored such signals? The East End was poorly lit, so she might have been unable to see any signals that were present. Or, perhaps, most dangerously, there were in fact no signs.

The pursuit of the real name of the Ripper is in fact a quest for signs. There is the belief that a man who would wander the East End streets at night, brutally mutilating the women he killed, could not have been a normal chap. Something in his life must have been noticeably out of the ordinary and, presumably, threatening. If his victims had been given absolutely no warning, then there would have been no way they could have protected themselves or prevented their own deaths. If they were given no warning, then these women were guilty only of prostitution—or perhaps even solely of being on the street alone at night. If there was nothing about the Ripper to have indicated that he was different from any other man, then there would be no way in which women at the time—or even women today— might be able to identify and avoid the threat. If the Ripper is simply a nobody sort of man, then the threat could be anywhere.

There is, perhaps, a bit of hope, because the women in question were indeed prostitutes. As Odell explains, "All men were the same to them."[32] With a sigh of relief, readers can argue against the theory that Mary Ann, Annie, Elizabeth, Catherine, and Mary must have missed the signs. Perhaps they were not in the practice of carefully scrutinizing the faces of potential clients, in case that might drive them off. Any skittish behavior might have been interpreted as a reaction to negotiating with an East End prostitute, an act which many men might not wish to draw attention to. If these women simply accepted all men as the same and failed to look for any difference in this particular specimen, then the blame is once again back on their shoulders and any reader would be safe as long as she took a moment to look fur such deviant signs herself.

Doctor, Lawyer, Shochet, Ripper

Unlike the Ripper narratives of the 1920s and 1930s, these books do not repeat the same suspects except to disprove them. Matters and Woodhall both argue for a Dr. Stanley whose selection of victims led him closer to the one woman he sought. He murdered prostitutes in the East End because he was searching for one of them and did not wish to leave a trail that would alert her in advance. Stewart's Ripper, while lacking the pseudonym, continued the theme of revenge. His midwife Ripper had herself been wronged by an East End prostitute, and thus the victims she sought were women of the same class and profession who sought her care. These Rippers chose their victims for these very specific reasons.

It is difficult for a suspect who is mad to be shown to so carefully choose his victims, as in the complicated tale of McCormick's Pedachenko. Even the figures of M. J. Druitt and Odell's unarmed *shochet* are not necessarily sane, nor driven by something as relatable as revenge. It is perhaps understandable enough when violent crime is enacted against the very people who wronged the criminal, the same way children will lash out at those who have hurt them. These directed acts of revenge have their limits and their reason. Madness has no reason.

Mary Ann, Annie, Liz, Kate, and Mary Jane are now no longer representatives of the person who harmed the Ripper, but become victims because of their occupations. These Rippers do not wish to kill East End prostitutes specifically, but have chosen East End prostitutes because of the ease of getting them alone in a secluded area. There is indeed media attention in the wake of the killings as newspapers compete with headlines and details in order to sell more copies, but the Ripper has indeed chosen people near the bottom rung of society, and it is difficult to be entirely sympathetic to women who sell their bodies and then spend those few coins on drink instead of a bed.

Whatever public reactions happened during the murders, it was not enough to stop the Ripper until he quit of his own accord. There was no easy solution to keep such women off the streets—indeed, there were not enough lodging house beds to hold all the homeless in the district—and, as we can see, there was difficulty in explaining why such women would still be out and about even during the height of the murders. Those who never had to contemplate spending the night without a bed could not understand why such women would apparently make the choice to spend their money on the apparent luxury of alcohol instead of the necessity of shelter. The East End prostitute was far removed from the general population in her own time, and has since become even more distant from the contemporary reader. Distance is a barrier to empathy.

These Ripper narratives of the 1950s and 1960s suggest that the Ripper's victims were not chosen for a specific reason other than the ease and lack of consequence of murdering them. There is no theme of revenge of the earlier decades, and no overarching conspiracy theory that follows in the 1970s. It is simply that the lives of East End prostitutes matter just enough to make headlines if their corpses have been mutilated properly, but not enough to inspire identification between them and a reader who would then fear for her own life.

• FOUR •

Royals, Freemasons and Schemes

Presenting Victims
in the Conspiracy Theories
of the 1970s

Ripper authors of the 1970s found themselves with a new focus that very nearly took attention away from the Ripper himself, much less his victims. In November 1970, an article appeared in *The Criminologist* in which Thomas Stowell, CBE, FRCS proposed his own theory about the Ripper's identity. Although the article itself refers to his suspect solely as S, Stowell provided numerous details about his suspect to the point where others loudly identified him. Stowell died within days of his article's publication, denying these accusations.

It seemed to many readers that Stowell had identified His Royal Highness Prince Albert Victor, Duke of Clarence and Avondale, as Jack the Ripper. Stowell himself denied this in a letter that was published the day after his death, and his son then burned his papers so there was no proof either way, but the damage was done. The 1970s opened with an accusation of a man who had born heir to the British throne and the question of whether or not "Eddy" was indeed the Ripper or otherwise involved with the Ripper murders continued long past the end of the decade.

Naming "S"

In 1972, Michael Harrison wrote the first book to respond to Stowell's article and gave it the evocative title of *Clarence: Was He Jack the Ripper?* The short answer, falling in line with Stowell's own protestations, is no.

According to Harrison, Eddy had nothing to do with the murders. He simply happened to be tutored by the man who committed them.

Harrison's argument is that "S" could not have been Eddy, not only because the events Stowell describes in his biography of the killer do not match those of the Duke of Clarence and Avondale, but also because Eddy's name is not at all related to the letter S. Later authors point out that Stowell used "S" because his editor had requested something beyond the usual "X" and had thus chosen his own initial. In 1972, however, Harrison does not consider this option and instead fixates on James Kenneth Stephen, the prince's tutor.

Since the bulk of the text is devoted to the prince's biography—and indeed seems to focus more on his mother, Princess Alix, than the prince himself—very little space is devoted to the identity of the Ripper. The biography is meant to show how Eddy could not have been the Ripper, not only because his life does not match up with the life described by Stowell, but also because of who Eddy was as a person. Indeed, Harrison chooses not to discuss the crimes themselves at all, suggesting that readers consult the main works of the previous decades in order to acquaint themselves with those "ghastly details."[1] Harrison chooses not to write about the murders at all.

The oddity, perhaps, is that Harrison does not discuss the women's deaths even to show how Stephen would have been capable of causing them. He does not concern himself with their wounds and whether or not Stephen exhibited the appropriate anatomical knowledge, or whether Stephen's schedule shows him to have been available on the given dates. In fact, the victims—the women without whom there would have been no Jack the Ripper—barely exist at all.

He does acknowledge their profession, if only to make the argument that it was indeed believable that no one would have noticed any of them talking to a strange man, but this is only to explain why J. K. Stephen was never identified or brought under suspicion. Harrison cites Stephen's own poetry and love of misogynistic pub songs as suggestions of why he might have chosen women from this specific class without giving further information about the individual women themselves. To Harrison they are a group bound by their deaths—at Stephen's hand, no less—and not worthy of individual scrutiny. Perhaps he agrees with Matters and his lack of detail is a more convincing argument that, to him, these women are all the same. Harrison does not even engage in the customary separation of Mary Jane Kelly from the others.

It is, perhaps, merely a reflection of what Harrison meant his book to be. He poses a question in the title, follows the life of the accused prince, and is able to give an answer without delving into the sordid details. Indeed, if Eddy can be proven to have not been able to be in Whitechapel on the given dates, then there is no need to go into the details of the Ripper murders at all. He never crossed paths with Polly, Annie, Liz, Kate, or Mary Jane, and thus they have no role in a biography of the Duke of Clarence and Avondale.

What is out of the ordinary, however, is the fact that Harrison does indeed turn his attention to accusing a man of being the Ripper, but manages to do so without recalling the crimes themselves. Perhaps he only anticipated readers who were already familiar with the Ripper story, or perhaps he had entered into a deal with previous authors such as Odell, Cullen, and McCormick in an attempt to boost sales of their own works. In a narrative that accuses a man of murder, even one that attributes this to a head injury that exacerbated his history of mental instability, it seems odd to brush off the telling of those murders while attempting to make this accusation stick. Harrison's main purpose, it would seem, was to clear the name of the Duke of Clarence and Avondale once and for all—naming another possible suspect was purely secondary.

Ripperologists, however, were far from done with Eddy.

Victims of Conspiracy

Stephen Knight did not go so far as to accuse Eddy himself of being Jack the Ripper, but, unlike Harrison, he did not remove the Duke from all semblance of blame. *Jack the Ripper: The Final Solution* (1976) lays the groundwork for numerous conspiracy theories to follow, many of them including the Freemasons, although the main cast of characters—and the assignment of guilt—fluctuates over time. Although Knight reports the narrative as it was told to him by a man calling himself Joseph Sickert, Knight even changes the situation from what Sickert told him.

Joseph Sickert, claiming to be the illegitimate son of artist Walter Sickert, first related his tale during a segment of the British documentary *Jack the Ripper*, aired in 1973. After many meetings with Sickert, Knight is able to piece together the story in chronological order, and even to fill in the gaps he found to be missing. Sickert's story is the one his own father told to him, one that Knight thereafter investigated. This begins a long tradition of accepting Sickert's tale as mostly intact and mostly truthful.

Apparently the painter Walter Sickert was asked to be a companion for Eddy, who needed both to be removed from public life and to nurture his artistic side. Thus the Duke of Clarence would change carriages and his clothing for romps with the older man in the area around Cleveland Street, where he met a shopkeeper whose name was either Annie Crook or Annie Cook. Sadly, Annie happened to be Catholic at a time when the crown could only find a spouse among the Anglicans, but the heir did not let that bother him. She was soon pregnant, and the couple married in secret after the birth of their daughter. Whether or not this marriage would have stood up to legal questioning is in doubt.

The couple employed a nannie to look after their daughter, a young woman named Marie Kelly, and even took her to France with them on a trip. When the marriage was discovered, the daughter was with her nanny and thus was not removed from the family's room at the time when Eddy and Annie were forcibly separated. He had to return to his princely life; she was sadly relegated to asylums and workhouses for the rest of her life, at first under observance of the queen's own physician, William Gull. They had to ensure that Catholic Annie would not spread the rumors that she had married the heir to the throne.

Although the child was not considered to be a threat, the nanny, Marie, certainly was—or made herself to be. Knight declares that she is "no hapless harlot who happened to run into Jack the Ripper"[2] and that the only woman undeserving of the Ripper's knife was Kate Eddowes. Marie, having known about the affair and the child and having witnessed the marriage, knew that the Duke of Clarence had taken a bride and was thus in possession of knowledge that might, perhaps, topple the crown. Silly thing that she was, she even took three other women into her confidence. When Marie related this story to Polly, Annie, and Liz, they encouraged her to blackmail the crown. William Gull, a coachman named Netley, and a third mystery figure—Knight puts the blame on Walter Sickert himself—all conspire to murder the meddling women in order to keep them quiet.

As factually questionable as the narrative may be, it is of interest that Knight presents an explanation not only for why the murders stopped after Marie Kelly, but also why she was the most horrifically mutilated. Instead of speculating that it was because she had her own room and thus the Ripper could take his time without fear of being spotted, Knight deals concretely with the question of blame. Had Marie kept her mouth shut and told no one of what she had witnessed, she would not have been talked into using what she knew. Had she not attempted to use this information as blackmail, she, her co-conspirators, and Kate Eddowes would not have been killed.

Interestingly Knight makes it clear that this blackmail was indeed the idea of the women Marie shared this story with and not Marie's alone. His presentation of Marie is indeed almost sympathetic, especially as he recounts her early life and the reason she ended up in London. Knight recounts her marriage and descent into widowhood, accompanied by the lack of money that put her at her low point and drove her to London in the first place. This Marie, unlike most previous iterations, does not immediately resort to prostitution in order to support herself. She seeks shelter in a convent and then finds her position as a shopkeeper in Cleveland Street, where she met Annie and then Eddy and Walter Sickert.

When Marie is finally presented as a prostitute, it is after the raid that separated Eddy and Annie. Marie is said to have fled from Cleveland Street to the East End, although she did manage to return the child to Walter Sickert by some means Knight does not explain. Even though she herself is living a terrible life in the East End, she does not drag her friends' daughter into it. When Marie does resort to prostitution, Knight tells us that it is only because she would starve without the profits, which makes her situation sound quite desperate. It is perhaps then not much of a stretch to imagine that a woman in her position would think of blackmail, or apparently allow others to persuade her into considering it.

Knight adds to this sympathetic portrayal when he explains the discrepancy in her name, telling the tale of how, when Walter Sickert was looking after Annie and the girl, their nanny went with them to France. Knight explains that Kelly developed a fondness for the language, and "laughingly insisted ever after"[3] upon being addressed as Marie Jeanette instead of her given name of Mary Jane. This is an aspect of Marie/Mary that is often presented in a negative light, as though she were putting on airs and separating herself from the women around her to make herself look better. This tactic is generally used by authors attempting to explain Marie's difference as a victim by investigating the small known facets of her life, and usually by authors who make sure to emphasize her youth and beauty. None of the other victims went around asking people to call them foreign versions of their names—their nicknames were simpler.

Knight, though, presents his readers with a Marie Kelly who fought against the misfortune of being a widow before age twenty and who may have been unable to resist the siren call of London, but managed to keep herself off the street. She is a respectable shop assistant who turns nanny when her friend needs her and is not above accepting a holiday in France when it is offered to her. Further, she adopts the name she is buried under as a bit of a joke, something that makes her laugh. This Marie, it seems, does not take herself too seriously.

All of this is related within the first two chapters of the book, before Knight moves on to discuss the crimes themselves. Readers are given that single sentence condemning Marie and giving her responsibility for the deaths that will follow before being taken through the rather positive biography of Marie up until the start of the murders. Knight seems torn between placing the blame firmly on her shoulders and wanting to keep her as a lighthearted young woman making the best of her situation, someone who is indeed better than her surroundings, not yet done in by drink and prostitution. This is a Marie whose death is not described, since Walter Sickert had known her, and "even after so long the memory was too painful for him"[4] to relate to his son. It is also a Marie who stands in distinct contrast with her fellow conspirators and fellow victims.

It is not that the other women's biographies are less kindly worded than Marie's, but that they do not exist within the text. Reports of their deaths, written at the time of the murders, are printed so that readers may experience the discovery of their bodies and read the description of the injuries done to their corpses, but otherwise information about the women who talked Marie into blackmail and unwittingly signed their own death warrants is scarce. Mary Ann Nichols is given a name, the title of first victim, and a location of death. Annie is not identified in Knight's text at all, and given the identified of "the widow of a coachman named Chapman"[5] in a report written by Inspector Abberline. Long Liz is simply "a gangling Swede"[6] but Kate is presented with a comparative wealth of information: she is "a pathetic little woman"[7] who looked more than fifteen years older than her actual age, and who was reported as having a rather cheerful disposition despite her lot in life.

There is a distinct dearth of information about the women who plotted the downfall of the crown. Kate, who receives the attention of two complete sentences, was not one of them—since she had given the false name of Mary Kelly upon her arrest the evening before her death, she was presumed to be the Mary Kelly that the murderous trio was looking for. Kate is therefore the only murdered innocent, at least of this crime—in a parenthetical whisper she is later revealed to have been an alcoholic.

Liz was also drunk, and therefore she was a difficult victim. Gull is meant to have invited the women into his enclosed carriage and fed them drugged grapes before committing the murders, at which point his coachman, the faithful Netley, would drive to the proper location and arrange the body. Knight suggests that Liz, being drunk, was immune to the "appeal to her vanity"[8] that Gull had made to the other women with more success. Apparently being invited into a fine coach, the likes of which would have seemed out of place in Whitechapel, would have made the women grateful to be treated like human beings instead of arousing their suspicions. These women died, then, not solely because of their blackmail scheme, but because they were so flattered that they could not resist a carriage ride and a treat of grapes.

The blame, then, is multifaceted: Marie is at fault because she could not keep her mouth shut. Mary Ann, Annie, and Liz are at fault because they encouraged her to make use of her secret knowledge. Mary Ann, Annie, and Kate are at fault because they willingly got into the carriage of a strange man and ate the grapes—although this is rather weakened by the fact that Liz refused but was murdered all the same. And finally, Marie is at fault for having been drunk enough to invite Netley into her room, where she was then murdered.

But what of Eddy and Annie Crook, who made the possibility of blackmail in the first place? Under the "care" of William Gull, Annie was certified as insane and subjected to treatment that changed her personality. Although her daughter was conceived and born out of wedlock, she did indeed marry her child's father and was never recorded as working as a prostitute. Annie is therefore presented kindly enough, a woman whose daughter and husband were taken from her. And Eddy himself? The Duke of Clarence and Avondale is a victim of love and circumstance, a tragic romantic figure who was prevented from rescuing either his wife or his daughter, helplessly caught up in the consequences.

Victims of the Crown

There is one more book from the 1970s to focus completely on the question of whether or not the Duke of Clarence and Avondale was involved in any way with the murders, and Frank Spiering's *Prince Jack: The True Story of Jack the Ripper* (1978) comes to a very different conclusion than Harrison's earlier text. Perhaps the title makes it clear why the book was published in America but not in England, since Spiering leaps wholeheartedly to the same conclusion as Stowell's readers had at the start of the decade. For Spiering, Jack the Ripper is also known as Eddy.

This Eddy is not a very likable man. In fact, his own family has very nearly abandoned him, leaving him without parental influence or approval. J. K. Stephen is not just his tutor but his lover, with no room for misinterpretation of a close friendship, although Stephen did participate by writing the various Ripper letters. Eddy's victims are chosen simply because of their occupation, since this version of the heir to the throne has contracted syphilis from his dealings with prostitutes and wishes to seek revenge. This is helped along by the fact that his syphilis is quite advanced and is thus affecting his brain.

Spiering's Eddy thus does not specifically seek out Polly, Annie, Liz, Kate, Marie Jeanette, and sixth victim Frances Coles specifically. There is no conspiracy theory among the women, who may in fact not even know each other. They have not bought and paid for their gruesome fates the way Knight's conniving band of prostitutes did, but Spiering shows them to be responsible for their own deaths all the same.

Even though there is no underling thread of conspiracy, he takes more time with the individual women than Knight did. There is an air of fancy about his narrative, which, after all, is "a reconstruction of what *I* feel did happen"[9] and not necessarily a reproduction of contemporary reports. In taking his time to set the scene before each murder takes place, Spiering outlines each woman's history to show how she managed to end up on the street in the middle of the night, crossing paths with his syphilitic killer.

Instead of Mary Ann Nichols, nicknamed Polly, Spiering introduces his first victim as Polly Ann Nicholls, utilizing one of the many spellings of her name put forth in contemporary papers. The reader comes upon her drunk and penniless, shortly to be denied entrance the lodging house in which she had been staying, not trusted for credit. He declares that "[p]overty and gin had marred any attractiveness she might once have had,"[10] painting the picture of a short woman aging poorly. Spiering is almost sympathetic to Polly, saying she began to drink due to loneliness even in her marriage. When he reports that her husband blamed her for desertion, it is formed as a claim and not a statement of fact. This Polly may have been alone even when she was surrounded by family.

It is a mark against her that, when she left, she abandoned her children as well as her husband, but perhaps Polly was unfit to be a mother. This escape certainly seemed to help her in the right direction, since she found employment and the time to write of it to her father, but this situation, like her marriage, did not last. Once again Polly escaped an arrangement that was not to her liking, and Spiering indicates that, in this case, the problem was the fact that her employers were teetotalers. Certainly Polly appears drunk on the last night of her life, having apparently spent all of her doss money on drink before earning it again and losing it the same way.

Despite her drunken staggering, Spiering allows Polly a moment of hesitation and indecision when she spies a shadowy figure who turns out to be Eddy. This moment is overshadowed by her desire for money and a warm bed, however, and in the end she gestures to the man who ends up being her murderer. Having squandered her money on drink, Polly ends her final night alone and on the street, ostensibly through no one's fault but her own.

Annie is not given this same order of introduction, biography, and then death. She is encountered, nameless, upon the street, where Spiering gives the reader a brief description of her appearance through Eddy's eyes. Although she, too, has clearly been drinking—gin, by the smell—there is something about Annie that makes Spiering describe her as attractive. Her hair, at least, is still brown and not Polly's almost entirely gray.

Her past is solely investigated through the death inquisition, and then only reaches back less than a week. Whether Annie was married, to whom, and if there were any children is never discussed. It is enough for Spiering to inform readers of a fight she had gotten into with another prostitute— thus indicating Annie's profession once again without saying it outright— as an explanation for why Annie had not been feeling well during her last night alive. Because she had been so drastically injured in a fight that was said to have been over a piece of soap, she could not work and had not been able to earn any money for food or her bed. Like Polly, Annie was turned away from her usual lodging house and forced into the street in the wee hours of the morning.

Thus the woman who is so often portrayed as the most sympathetic, having done her best to engage in and sell handicrafts instead of resorting to prostitution, is given a somewhat confusing and abbreviated background. This Annie is a woman who will engage another fiercely in a physical fight to the point where she must nurse her injuries for days—a rather short-sighted battle, considering how it left her unable to pay for her own basic needs. Is this Annie hotheaded? Was she drunk then, as she apparently was on her last night, despite her inability to pay for a bed? And the fact that this brawl was apparently over soap—what are readers meant to make of this? Is this part of what Eddy found attractive about her? As the sole report of a living Annie, this incident conjures up more questions than answers.

Liz is introduced prior to her death in a manner similar to Polly, and Spiering perhaps sums it up best when he says "Liz Stride played many roles."[11] He relates the story of the *Princess Alice* sinking—in this version a single child drowns with the father—and describes how Liz would protest any charges of drunkenness against her by feigning a fit in court to prove that it was this condition and not drink that had led to her arrest. Spiering does, however, allow that all of this fantasy may have helped Liz save face in front of her friends and companions, since she had to explain why she was no longer with her husband. Perhaps Liz, apparently childless in reality, also felt she had to turn herself into a mother of deceased or absent children—she claimed nine—instead of a widowed woman with none. The position of a mother whose children predeceased her would have earned her marked sympathy.

In an encounter that is too perfect to be anything but apocryphal, Spiering relates the tale of a doctor who had visited the East End and overheard a number of prostitutes discussing Annie's murder. One of these women happened to have a Swedish accent and she, if no one else gathered there, had been drinking. This woman makes the dire prediction that any one of them around that fire could be next, and indeed, she was. Perhaps Spiering's dismissal of Liz's penchant for storytelling is undercut by the fact that he felt the need to relate this one.

Again like Polly, the reader is introduced to Catherine Eddowes prior to her encounter with Eddy. Her past, unlike Annie's, is discussed, from her long-term relationship with Thomas Conway that resulted in three children but not marriage, to her current relationship with John Kelly. Catherine may have practiced monogamy, but it was serial monogamy outside of a marriage contract. Spiering does nothing to hint that she engaged in prostitution, but he makes it clear that the couple did indeed drink, wasting their last coins on gin in a familiar story. Catherine in fact wakes up for the last time in a jail cell, coming out of a drunken stupor.

She is evicted from this cell instead of from her lodgings, but Catherine still ends up alone on the streets in the wee hours of the morning, and is apparently still drunk when Eddy meets her. In her last moments, Catherine is described as "small, thin, and alone"[12]—clearly she has not been eating well, preferring to spend the money on drink instead of food, and although she has a steady man in her life, he is not with her then. Catherine's death is not a result of prostitution but clearly the result of a woman being alone on the streets at night. Other authors choose to blame the policemen, who should have followed the woman they say was a known prostitute, but Spiering's Catherine is not such a woman. Catherine was not looking for a man or for her doss money, and yet she died all the same.

Marie Jeanette Kelly appears in a chapter entitled "The Birthday Gift," since her death corresponds with the birthday of the Prince of Wales, Eddy's father. It is perhaps worth noting that objects, not people, are generally given as gifts, although whether this objectification is of Marie Jeanette's corpse of her as a human being is unclear. As is fitting for the youngest and most attractive victim, more time is spent on her physical appearance, although Spiering insists this was not the most striking thing about her. Marie Jeanette, like Liz, tells stories about her life.

Spiering's Marie Jeanette speaks of French parents, although he immediately cuts this down and proclaims the plain Mary Jane from Ireland. This Marie Jeanette was forced into the streets immediately after the death of her husband, without any struggle or apparent search for other work. She did not do so poorly for herself, however, since she occupied a small room of her own, which she shared with her long-term companion Joseph Barnett. Lest anyone wish to equate this relationship to that of Catherine Eddowes and John Kelly, Marie Jeanette discovers in August that she is pregnant and knows that Barnett is not the father. As expected, this revelation causes quarrels and puts a strain on the relationship, resulting in Marie Jeanette being alone in her room on her final night.

On par with the tale of Liz Stride predicting her own death is Spiering's declaration that "there was no woman in Whitechapel more frightened of Jack the Ripper than Marie Jeanette."[13] He makes no connection between this fear and the prostitute Marie Jeanette allowed to stay in the small room, leading to the final straw for Barnett, which would indicate an empathy and concern for life beyond her own. Despite this fear, the stresses in her life drive Marie Jeanette to drink, very much like the other women before her. A woman so terrified of the Ripper is now walking the streets drunk instead of remaining in her own room after dark, and she has driven out the man who would mean both protection and an income. Does this mean that risking the Ripper was preferable to spending another day with Barnett? They were in arrears for a surprising amount and Marie Jeanette was said to be out on her final night looking for customers so she could pay some of her rent. What would have driven her to kick Barnett out if staying alone meant she was solely responsible?

Although Spiering does go further than Knight in exploring the lives of these women, the details he presents remain disconnected and confusing. At times he seems at least partially sympathetic to their plights, but it is always a combination of drinking and a lack of money that leads them into the waiting knife of his syphilitic Prince Eddy. These are women who have left their men—husbands, if they even bothered to get married—and have abandoned any children they bore. Two are known to have turned their pasts into obvious falsehoods grander than anything they had ever experienced. All made the mistake of being a woman who had sex outside of marriage, whether or not they were paid for it, and even those that were squandered that pay when four pence would have bought them a bed for the night and kept them from becoming famous in their deaths.

Not Joined by Royal Blood

There is, however, one book from the 1970s that is willing to commit to the identity of Jack the Ripper without pointing in the general direction of the Duke of Clarence. Dan Farson's 1972 book *Jack the Ripper* reintroduces the idea of a young lawyer named Montage John Druitt as his suspect, based on notes composed by Sir Melville Macnaghten. Granted, Macnaghten joined the force the year after the murders; his notes, while not fully accurately representing Druitt, also lists two other possible suspects; and Druitt committed suicide sometime after the murder of Mary Kelly without actually confessing. Little enough is known about Druitt, and certainly not enough for Farson to find any glaring evidence that he could not have been the Ripper. But does an accusation of common blood in the Ripper have an effect on his presentation of the women who were killed?

Farson, like Spiering, does not think that the Ripper chose his victims for any specific reason, although he takes this a step further. This Ripper does not have a grudge against prostitutes in general, either, and simply finds them to be "the easiest prey."[14] The East End itself was dangerous enough that cries of "Murder!" were common and the women walking the streets were generally left to themselves, not overseen by brothel matrons or even presumably by their common-law husbands. Farson is, however, one of the few to realize this aspect instead of turning the victim choice into a personal crusade involving some form of revenge.

His attention to the women in question, on the other hand, is minimal. Although Farson does indeed set the scene for each murder, he does so with a bare sketch of the woman as she was that night, hardly touching on any biographical information. Again, this brief information comes across as contradictory, since readers are presented with a Mary Ann Nicholls who "was a pathetic creature.... But she had spirit."[15] This spirit might be embodied by the bonnet she wears, the one she indicates before being thrown out of her lodging house for the night. Farson suspects that Mary Ann did not mean to sell the bonnet in order to make her doss money, although he does not indicate whether she might have been able to pawn it at that hour. It would seem that any other woman out and about would be in the same situation and not have any money to pay for it, but Farson concludes that she did not mean to sell it since it was still in her possession when she was murdered.

Aside from being irresponsible enough with her money to be forced out into the streets in the middle of the night, Mary Ann was clearly too drunk to have been expected to fight for her life. Aside from her bonnet, if she had indeed purchased it herself instead of having been given it, she had enough money for drink. In case any reader would wonder if this was a singular incident, testimony from her father later on cements the fact that Mary Ann was indeed prone to drinking. Whatever negative emotions her death stirred in her father, her husband, who is mentioned only at the end of Farson's discussion of Mary Ann, offers a blanket forgiveness for what his wife had done to him. What that is, exactly, is never mentioned, but leaves the reader to wonder how many sins can be forgiven in light of a brutal murder.

No father or husband comes into Annie's story, although, since Farson indicates she had known better days, at least one must have factored into her past. This Annie is simply "another pathetic old prostitute"[16] who ends up turned out in the middle of the night. She is allowed the explanation that her lack of money stemmed from having been in the infirmary— instead of having squandered her money on drink and a new bonnet, Annie has been too ill to earn it. This is her valedictory, since Annie's next appearance is after her death.

Farson reverses Liz and Kate, presenting them in the order of identification instead of the order of their murders. Kate "fitted the pattern of the other woman,"[17] referring to her preference for alcohol and the fact that she looked years older than her age. Unlike Mary Ann or Annie, Kate has the benefit of a long-term male companion in John Kelly, although the pair seems little better suited to keeping track of their money than the women before them. Once again a woman who has no money for a bed is found drunk, and Kate was locked up for a few hours, presumably to sober up.

Acknowledging the fact that she must have heard about the two murders that occurred prior to that night, Farson notes the fact that Kate may have gone willingly with her killer into Mitre Square. He admits that she may have been suspicious of the man accompanying her, but she needed money. Farson's tone in this matter is a bit flippant, since he declares that "she went readily to her death"[18] that night without acknowledging the struggle she and Kelly faced over the previous span of days that led to their return to London, ostensibly in search of the reward money for identifying the Ripper. Their desperate situation is covered quickly in such a way that yes, Farson might express incredulity at the risk she presumably took with a customer.

Liz's life is confined to a single paragraph. In it Farson mentions her Swedish origins, her marriage to an Englishman, her arrests for drunkenness, and the every-popular account of the *Princess Alice*. Liz is reduced to being a pathetic foreigner, living in an area well known for housing prostitutes even if he will not commit to calling her a prostitute outright, and one who played up the sympathy of those around her with her fictitious tale of the sinking. As a drunken attention-seeker, Liz is perhaps considered no great loss, even if she had managed to avoid of a life of prostitution. She, like those before her, found herself alone on the streets at night, and though Farson does not indicate that she went in search of money, readers are still left to wonder why she might have been so desperate to risk it. Liz was, after all, not specifically denied a bed, and it was still comparatively early.

The need for money makes a reappearance with the figure of Mary Kelly, whom Farson first places apart from the others through her age, attitude, and looks before shrugging those off and declaring, "Otherwise she was a drunken prostitute like the others."[19] Despite the fact that she alone was said to have begun her career in the West End and had gone to Paris with a client, there is nothing in her life to raise her above meeting the same gruesome end. Unlike the others Mary had her own room, but she was behind on the rent. There is no mention of Joseph Barnett or his recent departure—Farson's Mary has been keeping this room on her own, although clearly not very well. During her last day, many reported seeing her in all kinds of comings and goings as she sought money, and these various ventures eventually led to the Ripper joining her in her room.

In a final dismissal not only of these women but all of those in Whitechapel, Farson mentions that they "were so indifferent to their fate"[20] that they joked about the Ripper and their chances of being next. It is his interpretation of their reaction as one of "indifference" that is jarring. Although his narrative does not go to lengths to explore these women's backgrounds or even the position of a woman without a husband during this time period, apparently their attempt to make sense of the situation through black humor instead of finding themselves respectable jobs so that they might afford their beds each night makes them indifferent. Perhaps a better assessment would be "trapped, and doing their best to confront the realities of the situation." At any rate, Farson does not make a suggestion for what these women should have done to protect themselves.

Still Unnamed

The remaining books from the 1970s do not champion a particular suspect but rather hint at what is to come by reviewing previous theories—and rejecting them all. Although these narratives are not informed by a leading theory of the Ripper's identity, they still offer some unique perspectives worth noting.

Richard Whittington-Eagan's 1975 *A Casebook on Jack the Ripper* largely ignores the victims after presenting them in a list on page 2. The information is limited to date, name, and location of the murder—so limited, in fact, that nicknames of the victims must be clarified in footnotes on later pages. Otherwise they do not appear as individuals in the text. Whittington-Eagan's introduction and epilogue, however, are noteworthy in their generalizations.

He declares that the story of the murders, even almost ninety years removed, is still enough to procure feelings of empathy and pity—although there is little indication where these emotions can be found in writing. These women are deserving of such a reaction because their "small shortcomings in life were surely redeemed by the enormity of their deaths."[21] It is almost a throwaway comment, a token acknowledgment that the women in question were indeed drunks and prostitutes and an emphasis on how terrible their murders were, but it deserves some attention.

The mere fact that Whittington-Eagan believes these women to have been in need of redemption comments on their lifestyle as though it was indeed a choice and a willing descent into sin. This lack of background of the individual women and lack of situating them within an East End world that was by 1975 truly foreign allows this judgment to be passed simply and universally. There is no discussion of what these women may have done in order to be in need of redemption, and likewise no acknowledgment that prostitution was the last resort of the desperate and not an easy answer. The Ripper, meanwhile, becomes the one dispensing redemption, assuming the role of a priest or other man of god while he wields his knife. True, Whittington-Eagan admits that none of these women deserved to be carved up, but the statement still remains: their terrible deaths redeemed them when it seems nothing in their lives could.

He comes full circle in his epilogue when he returns to this idea of these deaths as somehow a positive event, claiming that the women "share an uneasy immortality that has been envied to the worthier majority."[22] Their deaths not merely redeemed them but made them immortal. It is true that the names of Mary Ann, Annie, Elizabeth, Catherine, and Mary

Jane would likely never have been recorded if not for their deaths, and how many people are still discussed nearly a century after their lives ended? It is this idea of envy that should be more complicated than Whittington-Eagan makes it seem.

Those who envy their notoriety should also remember the deaths that led to it and the lives preceding. Whittington-Eagan does little to remind his readers of what life was like for women without husbands in the East End during the Victorian era, instead focusing on this jealousy-inducing legacy. Their struggles in both life and death have been minimized and dismissed, because they have been redeemed and remembered. They are no longer women but symbols, and their status has somehow been catapulted into one that others wish to obtain.

Donald Rumbelow's contribution comes in the form of *The Complete Jack the Ripper*, also published in 1975. His addition to the growing Ripper library stems from his occupation as a police officer, and the main focus here will be his assertions involving Mary Kelly, her landlord John M'Carthy, and her common-law husband Joseph Barnett.

Although it is well known and often repeated that Barnett had moved out of the room he and Mary rented from M'Carthy, Rumbelow proposes a reason that would also explain why M'Carthy had allowed Kelly to fall so far behind in paying her rent. Despite the fact that M'Carthy testified he did not know that Mary had been a prostitute, Rumbelow adds that most, if not all, of the other women in Miller's Court were prostitutes and suggests that the term "M'Carthy's rents" did not in fact refer to the rooms in Miller's court, but to the prostitutes he controlled.[23] In Rumbelow's narrative, Kelly is indeed pregnant, again likely not by Barnett, who tries to keep her off the streets due to this fact. Barnett is thus the sole breadwinner, and Rumbelow suggests that he gave the rent money to Mary so she could pass it on to M'Carthy.

The fight before Barnett left Mary is thus not necessarily over the prostitute she had invited to stay with them in their room, but over the fact that he discovers she has been drinking the rent money and they are far behind in payments. M'Carthy has been allowing the rent to pile up at an alarming rate for an East End landlord because he knows it will give him more control over Mary, who is of course working for him as a prostitute, presumably behind Barnett's back. When Barnett discovers this, he abandons Mary to fend for herself and attempt to make up the amount in spite of her pregnancy and the accompanying morning sickness.

This Mary is just as far in arrears as her previous iterations, but while other versions might be able to blame Barnett's lack of work on her inability to pay bills, Rumbelow's Mary has no one to blame but herself. She has managed to get herself pregnant by someone other than the man who has been living with her as her husband, and has then drunk away the money he had set aside for their rent. Although readers might question why M'Carthy would have said nothing to Barnett about the rent as it piled up, Rumbelow's explanation of M'Carthy as in control of the prostitutes living in Miller's Court would mean he would not want to change the situation if he could see it working out in his favor.

Mary is thus deceptive and underhanded as well as shortsighted and possessing poor money management. Her relationship with Barnett comes into question despite the length of time the pair had spent together. Her pregnancy and deception would indeed explain why he would not have wished to move back in with her once the fellow prostitute—the ostensible reason for his departure—had left, but he was still on record as having visited her since their final fight. Does she still hold sway over him even once the deception has been revealed? What sort of woman must Mary Kelly have been in order to deceive the man she lived with—the one who had done what he could to keep her off the streets? Rumbelow does not provide enough information for readers to conclude whether Mary's deception comes out of desperation or whether she might have an understandable, relatable reason for her actions.

Arthur Douglas' 1979 book *Will the Real Jack the Ripper* very nearly waxes lyrical about the killer in question, especially when he proclaims the Ripper to be "the one man in all England who, by his deeds, called a whore a whore and not a fallen angel."[24] Apparently the act of recognizing a whore leads not only to murder but to mutilation, which means that the people of the East End were ignoring the identity of tens of thousands of women. If every man had taken up the avenging role of Jack the Ripper, there is a question of how many women would have been left.

It seems in contradiction with previous authors that Douglas even suggests that prostitutes were seen as "fallen angels." True, many of the women who became victims of Jack the Ripper were said to have known better times and to have descended into the East End instead of having been born there, but no author has been so charitable as to refer to any of them as an angel. With this single sentence Douglas sets up all women to be one or the other, a madonna or a whore—and a whore is punishable by brutal murder.

Douglas, it seems, might perhaps agree with Whittington-Eagan's assessment that redemption was necessary for these women, even if he would not think that the Ripper would have been so kind as to give it. For

Douglas the Ripper represents a moral cause, pulling back the curtain on the conditions of the East End while at the same time eliminating those whose lives offend. The Ripper is indeed praised, and in this case outright instead of sotto voce, for performing his role in cleaning up the streets.

Preparing for a Long Look Back

The 1970s represent an eclectic mix of theories surrounding Jack the Ripper, introducing the notion that the women—or at least one woman in particular—called their own deaths down upon them for reasons beyond that of simple prostitution. Even in the midst of these conspiracy theories the lives of the women in question do not demand further investigation. It is enough that they find themselves in possession of information that could be used to hurt the crown and decide to use it for their own gain instead of remaining respectfully, and wisely, silent. Even the notion that they must have known each other needs no further evidence beyond the fact that all were prostitutes in the East End, and thus apparently must have crossed paths.

The utter lack of attention to the victims, or even the crimes themselves, in a number of these volumes turns out not to be a deviation from the norm, but a forecast of Ripper narratives to come. As little as is shared about Polly, Annie, Liz, Kate, and Mary Jane in the books of the 1970s, even less is revealed in the multiple retrospectives that populate the 1980s.

• FIVE •

One Hundred Years Later
Writing for the Anniversary
of the Crimes

The 1980s was a landmark decade for books about Jack the Ripper, not in the least because it marked one hundred years since the crimes. Numerous authors took this occasion to write reflections on the preceding century, proposing new suspects and rejecting many past theories. They focused intently on identifying the Ripper himself, utilizing new information that had emerged on the subject of serial killers and serial murder.

First, the term "serial killer" was itself introduced to the reading public. There is debate as to when the term was officially coined and by whom, in English as well as in German, but its common use can be traced to the 1980s. This was also the decade of the American true crime boom which flooded the market with gruesome tales. Ann Rule's inaugural book, *The Stranger Beside Me*, was first published in 1980 and discusses serial murderer Ted Bundy without ever using the term. America first found itself face to face with Bundy, the killer "boy next door," and then was given the language to identify and categorize him. Rule herself testified before the senate about such killers, given her experience of having known Bundy prior to his identification as a criminal.

This classification applied to Jack the Ripper, as well, although numerous differences separate the two, not the least of which being that Bundy was caught and identified. Bundy was also interviewed extensively while he waited on death row in an attempt to learn about what would make a man murder a series of strangers. These interviews, and interviews of other such killers, were of interest to the FBI's Behavioral Science Unit for the identification and classification of criminals. It was the BSU that first used criminal profiling, which itself exploded into popularity with Thomas Harris'

Silence of the Lambs, first published in 1988. Bundy was a major influence for more than one aspect of this novel, shaping both serial killer Buffalo Bill and Special Agent Clarice Sterling's interviews with one killer—Hannibal Lecter—to catch another. The idea of the serial killer as a type permeated both crime fact and crime fiction.

Supervisory Special Agent John Douglas of the BSU was even asked to profile Jack the Ripper for a television special to commemorate the century mark of the murders. Douglas, who has since retired and published numerous books about his work as a criminal profiler, used the skills he helped develop and perfect on contemporary cases to take a closer look at the Ripper's identity. Douglas "was provided basic background to each case,"[1] although of course forensic techniques of the 1880s were hardly comparable to those of the 1980s. Douglas uses the language the BSU curated in order to discuss such cases, and his section on victimology is first.

Whereas the entire document is a profile of the Ripper, victimology is the profile of the victims. Douglas classifies these women using the FBI's term "high-risk" based on their occupations and drinking habits. Risk, when related to a victim, is the chance of that person becoming a victim of violent crime. Because prostitutes regularly go to secluded locations with strangers, and because these women in particular seemed unlikely to be sober and completely aware of their surroundings, they were therefore placing themselves in danger. He also mentioned the fact that many Victorian prostitutes worked on their own instead of under a pimp who, according to Douglas, would offer the benefit of protection in the form of strict control.

In one of his later books[2] Douglas clarifies that identifying victims as either high-risk or low-risk is done with the same purpose as the rest of the profile: in order to identify what sort of criminal would have committed this crime. This investigation into the life of the victim is meant to show the profilers how much of a risk the criminal himself was taking. If the victim leads a low-risk lifestyle, then the crime itself is high-risk for the criminal, and vice-versa. Because Jack the Ripper chose female prostitutes of the lowest class, he murdered them with a very low risk to himself. They would not be noticed to be missing immediately, because their absence would have been more of a comfort to "decent" citizens than their presence. There was also less of a risk because of the conditions of the Victorian era itself—the newness of the police was only one factor working against the women of the East End.

Although Douglas insists that the purpose of this high- or low-risk label of the victims is purely to point toward the identity type of the killer, this classification is uncomfortably close to the more popular judgment of victims as deserving of their fates or even as complicit in their own demise. This is indeed what Douglas is describing: the lifestyle of these women, often perceived as a deliberate choice, put them in the position where the Ripper could kill and mutilate them. It is somehow not the fault of the Ripper for murdering these women, but the fault of Polly, Annie, Liz, Kate, and Mary Jane for having put themselves in his path.

It is also intriguing that Douglas felt it was worth noting that "[t]hey were not particularly attractive"[3] women, aside from Mary Jane Kelly. This is perhaps more of a note of absence than of presence, because presumably a killer who only preyed upon attractive prostitutes would direct Douglas toward a different profile. So often the appearance of these women has been exaggerated to the extreme, to present them as truly the lowest of the low. Prematurely gray hair, missing teeth, and emaciation all play a role in the presentation of these women as victims deserving of their fates but not of sympathy. For decades authors have been pointing out that these women had been leading high-risk lifestyles that wreaked havoc on their bodies, and now, it seems, the FBI—the leading authority on serial killers—is agreeing.

With this introduction of expert knowledge and expert language coming from the FBI and specifically from the unit directly concerned with serial crime, it seems that the long-standing conceptions of these women are endorsed and certified. Specific terminology had been created to label exactly what had been being discussed. The victim of a serial crime is now officially examined solely for the clues she can provide to the identity of her killer, and her own actions are used as an explanation for her death.

This is not to say that every book written in the 1980s minimizes the identity and biography of these women because the authors saw this enacted within the FBI. Rather, it serves as a point of comparison. Whether books about Jack the Ripper feed off the FBI or the FBI reflects the culture of the books, these two distinct entities working for different audiences and different purposes agree on many points. It is not a perspective solely dis-seminated by the self-selecting readers of Ripper narratives alone, but is now being proclaimed to the government and to the public, couched in language specific to an elite discourse community as an authoritative assess-ment. As we move through the 1980s, the women themselves almost cease to exist, although their corpses remain to be picked over for the latest fad theory.

Corrections and Collusions

In his 1987 book *The Crimes, Death, and Detection of Jack the Ripper*, Martin Fido makes his assessment of the murdered women clear. He summarizes their situations by lumping their pasts together into a single pattern: "respectable working men found drunken wives intolerable, and after separation the women changed their names and sank to the streets."[4] The women in question must have at one time been respectable themselves, since it seems unlikely a respectable man would take a wife who was not, but by the time the women encounter the Ripper they have sunk far. Due to their drinking they have forced good men to part with them, men who clearly could have supported them due to their jobs. Drinking turned respectable wives into women so terrible that they lost all means of support, and even their good husbands could no longer endure their behavior. Because it is drinking and not, for example, illness, this behavior was presumably a choice and could have been controlled. It is therefore the women's fault that they tested the patience of their husbands beyond its limit.

Despite the statement about name changes, Polly Nichols is still Polly Nichols even after she has left her husband. Polly not only spent her husband's money on her drinking habit but also managed to alienate her father so that all men in her life were glad to be rid of her. When Polly tried to work as a maid, a low but still respectable enough position, Fido declares that this "bored her."[5] This Polly apparently craved the excitement of life on the street, coupled with the uncertainty of income and whether or not she would have a place to sleep at night. Being bored seems like such a trivial assessment of the situation when the alternative was prostitution and death. This apparent boredom may have sprung from the fact that Polly was working for teetotalers, since the overall assessment was that all of these women shared a fondness for drink, but really what it means is that Polly is easily dismissed as she meets the Ripper's knife.

Annie Siffey at least occupies more space on the page. She has indeed changed her name since parting from her husband and Fido refers to her as Annie Siffey even though the chapter title presents her as Annie Chapman, still using her husband's name. At the time of her death even Annie Siffey is passé, since she was no longer living with a sieve-maker. Instead Fido makes sure to point out that there was more than one man in Annie's life: one who paid for her bed at the weekends and one who apparently enjoyed her favors when the first was not around. Lest readers feel sympathy for the men, it would have been hypocritical for them to expect monogamy from Annie when each of them also went with a second woman—and the same other woman, to boot. Although Polly may have engaged in prostitution, she at least refrained from two-timing a long-term relationship.

Like Polly, Annie was separated from her husband, although she had managed to live well enough on the allowance he paid her until his death. Fido does not make it clear whether Annie had her concurrent relationships while her husband was still alive, or if she only relied on those men after her payments ceased, but he does argue that she managed to refrain from prostitution until her husband's death. However bad their marriage had been, and however acrimoniously it had ended, he still supported her. Perhaps because of this income, or simply to make her past seem more appealing, Annie was apparently fond of telling people that her husband—a coachman—had been a veterinary surgeon, and that they were parted because of his death. Granted, for the last eighteen months or so of her life, Annie was indeed a widow, so the last may not have been a lie, but she certainly seems to have romanticized their time together.

Whatever Annie's fantasies may have been, Long Liz Stride topped them all. Fido makes quite a list, from the *Princess Alice* disaster story to her supposed nine children—seven living and at school thanks to support from the church—to her speech impediment and soft palate injury supposedly incurred during the sinking. Fido, following in the footsteps of Dr. Bagster Philips at Liz's death inquest, picks through and dismisses these tales completely. Liz was married, yes, but separated from her husband and also childless. She, unlike Annie, was not only an occasional prostitute. Indeed, Fido describes Liz's final hours as "a busy night of professional whoring."[6] Her husband had died—of illness, not drowning—in 1884, and there is no record that he had given her an allowance prior to this. Liz Stride was a foreign woman left on her own in the East End to make whatever living she could manage.

Because he declares Liz to be a working prostitute, Fido dismisses any claims that she might have spent the last night of her life with just one man. He finds it almost laughable that other authors have taken witness descriptions and declared that, in each instance, the witness was describing her with the same man. After all, a prostitute is only paid for her favors, and in the hours she supposedly spent with this mystery man she could have—as Fido suggests—serviced two or three. The reason why there was no money found on her body was because the man witnessed attacking her stole it, and here we see another side of Liz: Fido has her marking the man so that she can identify him to her boyfriend later, with the intention that

Michael Kidney and perhaps some of his friends would then beat him up. There is a shrewdness as well as a fantasy to Liz who, while she might lie about her past, displays a realistic and perhaps ruthless assessment of the present.

Catherine Eddowes, whose current situation could be seen as worse than Liz's, maintains a vastly different outlook nevertheless. This Catherine is a "perky little streetwalker ... [with a] cheeky outlook which belied"[7] her situation in life. She was short and thin, with no fixed address and no steady income with which to feed herself. Once again her initial long-term relationship ended when her common-law husband left her because of her drinking habits, since he was himself a teetotaler. Perhaps it is her alcoholism that allowed her to always be in such good spirits, since her attitude is mentioned multiple times. Her relationship with John Kelly was impacting by her drinking, but apparently only rarely, and although it led to quarrels the couple had remained together for years. Catherine is perhaps a sprightly, less fanciful version of the women who went before her.

Marie Jeanette Kelly, on the other hand, gives Liz's tales some strong competition. Fido's main contention is of how many previous authors seem to have accepted Marie's autobiographical narrative, filtered through her boyfriend Joe Barnett, as truth. He remains skeptical of much of her tale, especially her time in France, and suggests that the more elaborate version of her name was given out of "pretension."[8] Granted, this pretension might have come from an actual trip to France and a true past in a brothel of the West End, but it seems to be more likely just another aspect to make Marie stand out from the others, such as her age or her looks. Her name was simply something she had control over, the same way she had verbal control over her past. In Marie's case, however, there was not enough evidence, either at the time of her inquest or discovered since, to concretely prove her tale to be false.

Fido thus draws a line between himself and previous Ripper authors, at times agreeing with what they have said—marking all of these women as having drinking problems—and at others declaring the popular image to be false, such as when he makes the point that "[t]hey were not, as is usually stated, prematurely aged harridans."[9] He walks that line and feels that tension between what others have said before him and some new declarations, many of them made to correct past false beliefs based either on new information or on Fido's own new approach. It is a struggle between what so many authors have claimed to know and what it is possible to prove, or to see in a new light, that many latter Ripper authors have faced and attempted to confront themselves.

Enter the Black Magician

In 1987, Melvin Harris published his *Jack the Ripper: The Bloody Truth* and put forth a new name for the Ripper: Doctor Roslyn D'Onston, whose hobby of dabbling in black magic might explain the ritualistic nature of the murders. D'Onston himself only appears in the final chapter of the book, occupying less than twenty pages. Harris uses the majority of his text to examine and reject a number of other theories. After a brief introduction, all five women appear in a single chapter totaling fifteen pages. As little attention as Harris gives to his star suspect, he makes the five victims share even less space.

Chapter 2 is given the title of "The Bundle at Buck's Row" and headed with the date Friday 31st August 1888.[10] There are no other headings throughout the chapter listing the other dates on which the victims' bodies were found, and nothing to separate one from the other, even though Mary Ann Nichols was the only one found in Buck's Row. Due to this compression of all five murders into a single unbroken narrative, it is therefore unsurprising when little information is given about the women themselves.

As befitting this lack of information, Mary Ann—subject of both the title and heading—is "unremembered and unmemorable."[11] She is lucky not only because focus is lent to her through these titles, but because two entire paragraphs are devoted to information that would not have been in the coroner's report. Her husband left her due to her drinking habits, presumably taking their five children with him, and in the three years since he had had contact with her, those drinking habits had apparently not improved. A friend who encountered Mary Ann after she had been ejected from her lodging house for lack of funds reported that she had been too drunk to walk properly. And that is the sum of information about the woman nicknamed in the chapter title. Intriguingly, Harris refers to her as Mary Ann when referencing her past life, but on the streets of the East End, she is Polly.

Annie occupies a single paragraph on the facing page. She is a widow. There is no further discussion of her marriage—her husband's name and occupation are not reported, and there is no information about the possibility of children. As a widow she turned to prostitution, but there is no suggestion of wither her occupancy of the East End predated her husband's death or represented part of a downward slide. Like Mary Ann, she was out on the street because she lacked the coins for a bed, and, also like Mary Ann, Annie was "sozzled."[12] She had somehow managed to attain this state even though she was unable to pay for a place to more safely spend the night.

Catherine likewise has her biography in a single paragraph, although she is introduced as "the most tragic"[13] of the women. She did indeed spend her last evening locked up for being drunk, and the police who regularly patrolled those streets were used to finding her that same way. Drink would also have helped contribute to the fact that she is presented as looking twenty years older than her actual age, although it might also have been simply life on the street that aged her prematurely—or that drove her to drink in the first place. In this version Catherine must be a loner, and the only part of her life given any attention is that last night, from her arrest to her death. The only mention of John Kelly comes after Mary Kelly's death when it is pointed out that Catherine gave his last name instead of hers at the time of her arrest, and much is made of the coincidence of two of the victims having used the last name of "Kelly."

As little as that is, Elizabeth fares worse. She receives no biography. There is some discussion of whether or not she was indeed "Long Lizzie," since a woman came forward and claimed that the victim was her sister, but in the end "the original identification of Swedish prostitute Lizzie Stride was then shown to be correct."[14] That is the sum total of information provided about her: that her name is Elizabeth, her nickname "Long Lizzie," and her address Thrawl Street. Perhaps she, unlike the others, had not been drinking on the night of her death, and thus it was not worth mentioning. If that is the case, then there was a lot of information not worth mentioning.

Strangely enough, despite her usual position of attention as being the final victim, as well as the youngest and the best-looking, Mary Kelly does not fair much better. She is "young, spirited, attractive"[15] and behind on her rent. Aside from the descriptions of her mutilations, there is little to distinguish her from anyone else. Granted, she had a rented room and was not a frequenter of the doss houses like the other women, but age and residence do not paint a very full picture of a person.

Despite his introduction of D'Onston as the true identity of Jack the Ripper, the real purpose behind Harris' book seems to be to summarize the century since the crimes and not to focus on the crimes themselves. His arguments against previously proposed Ripper suspects focus more on the information discovered about those suspects and not on relating them to the specific victims. In fact, Harris does not relate any of the possible killers to the specific victims. D'Onston is performing ritual murders in which the locations apparently matter—Harris provides a map that depicts the locations of the murders as a cross—but the women themselves were inconsequential. Their deaths were needed for his ritual, and in fact Harris proposes that the murders stopped because D'Onston did not see the magical results he searched for. The women thus not only died randomly, but also in vain.

More Poetry, Less Sympathy

Nineteen eighty-seven was a banner year for Ripper books, and the next was Martin Howells and Keith Skinner's *The Ripper Legacy: The Life and Death of Jack the Ripper*. Although the narration of the murders does take place over three chapters instead of Harris' one, those three cover a total of 36 pages. Indeed, there are few points to make as notable among their short descriptions of these women. The main interest lies in the more enveloping statements.

Howells and Skinner use the term "nefarious transaction"[16] when discussing what brought Mary Ann Nichols to Buck's row on the night of her death. Although there is little argument that a prostitute seeking to exchange sex for money could call that a transaction, "nefarious" is a term more often suited to the villain—in this case, the Ripper himself. It is not his nefarious scheme to get a woman alone so that he might murder her and mutilate the corpse, but her nefarious actions meant to earn her the coins for the night. She has, after all, been kicked out onto the street and can have no shelter unless she can pay for it. True, the act of sex outside of marriage and specifically for money has long been considered sinful, but in the comparison between prostitution and murder, it seems a bit harsh to use such language for the former.

In their discussion of the items each woman had on her at her death, Catherine Eddowes' lengthy list of belongings proves to the authors that she "was rich by comparison"[17] when her belongings are placed alongside those of the other women. Granted, Mary Jane had her own room and thus didn't need to carry around every single thing she owned—however little it was—but Howells and Skinner's list of Catherine's possessions hardly makes her well off. Some items, like a pipe, matches, and handkerchief, seem to be quite common to be taken along. Perhaps they think she is rich because she could afford a packet of tea and sugar that hadn't been drunk right away. Or perhaps it merely is "by comparison," a simple counting of the items and nothing more. There is certainly no consideration that Catherine's lifestyle may have been more itinerant—or rather, no consideration at all. Just a list of items and this declaration, as though it is possible to declare any woman of the East End to be rich.

The authors do, however, seem to at least be aware of the fact that such comments about these women can be flippant. In the introduction they observe that "[o]ur interest in the death of five Victorian prostitutes has become a curiously antiseptic and painless experience"[18] and, in the course of the book, go on to prove just that. There are few details given about the victims, but also no acknowledgment that they realize they are participating in distanced reaction, or even whether this happens to be a good or bad thing. It is simply an observation, and then perhaps not even entirely true. If it has become antiseptic and painless, then there is the assumption that, at one time, it was the opposite. At one time, the deaths of these women must have inspired sympathy and been more personal instead of distant.

Granted, this was likely true at the time of the murders, for the population that was at the center of the crimes, but it is difficult to stay whether anyone who was not living in the East End in the 1880s was ever given the opportunity for such a reaction. Contemporary newspapers certainly wrote extensively about the murders, although their purpose was to sell more copies. Attempts to present these women in a way that was not antiseptic and painless have been few, if they exist at all, and Howells and Skinner do not attempt to make their book one of the minority. They might use more poetic language to describe what was happening, such as when they say that, using losing her husband, Liz "became vulnerable to the evils that formed the very fabric of life in Whitechapel,"[19] but that fabric is neither nuanced nor described in detail. This statement becomes a way of glossing over what happened to Liz, either because of a lack of information or a lack of interest, and moving from her brief history to the one part of her life that mattered: her death. The metaphorical language conjures up a certain image of both Liz and life in the East End while at the same time offering little of substance.

Howells and Skinner employ a similar technique after the double murders when reporting the words of a prostitute in the East End who had spoken to the *Pall Mall Gazette*. Although they do not give the context of the original piece or the questions that prompted it, this unknown woman says, "I only have to die once, and I'd not mind being murdered by Jack the Ripper if it led to the brute being caught."[20] She goes on to add that she is well aware of how kindly people—all people, from all walks of life, many of whom had their words recorded in print—talk about the victims. It is her opinion that a quick death would be better than starving, although she does show an awareness of the brutality of the crimes, since she acknowledges that having her corpse desecrated would be worth the beautiful eulogies.

Howells and Skinner place this quote near the end of a chapter and use it to direct their narrative toward the intrigue and mystery surrounding the Ripper. They therefore ignore the implications surrounding it. Clearly this woman believes that nobody speaks well of her now, and that they would not after her death unless she were to meet not only a violent end, but an end that involves the Ripper. It has already been shown that the Ripper's crimes earned a place in the newspapers above and beyond the usual murders of the East End, and thus simply being murdered, while a realistic death for an East End prostitute, would not have been enough for those sympathetic words.

She dreams not only of having her death turn her into a figure worth sympathy, but also of being the final victim because it would mean the Ripper was caught. Since she was speaking to a newspaper, it is difficult to see how this mystery woman could have missed that the Ripper murders were widespread news. Certainly she must have heard about the crimes, if not read about them herself, because she knew how others were talking about the victims. Is it possible that, in her quest to escape her current situation and have nice things said about her, she was also aiming to find herself a place in history as the names and carefully scrutinized final victim of the man formerly known as Jack the Ripper?

Finally she compares the death that would await her at the sharp end of his knife with starvation. Presumably from her current position, starvation seems to be likely, if not imminent. Being murdered in a strange alley, however, has more perks than starving, not only because it would be quicker. The one common wound between all five women was the fact that their throats were cut, presumably before further injury took place, and thus this mystery prostitute could assume that she would not be conscious—or even still alive—when the mutilations that made the Ripper crimes stand out were then enacted.

Howells and Skinner have found an East End prostitute who, rather than staying off the streets had night, has expressed the desire to be the next of her kind to encounter the Ripper, but they do not use this sentiment to direct the conversation toward conditions in the East End and the lives Mary Ann, Annie, Elizabeth, and Catherine must have been living up until that point. What might this mystery woman have known about them that would lead her to assume the large gulf between what she read or heard about them after their deaths and the lives they had lived previously? Was it simply the fact that they, too, had been prostitutes that made her come to what, to her, was an obvious confusion? And if it was so obvious, then what does this preference for being murdered really say about the East End and the lives of the women who lived there?

They do return to the idea of the worth of a life of an East End prostitute later on, although there is no connection made between the previous mystery woman and their discussion of the law. According to Howells and Skinner, women "who took to the streets deserved everything they got—though even the most ardent retributionist would have drawn a line somewhat earlier than Jack the Ripper."[21] A woman's worth was strongly connected to men, first through her father and then through her husband. She was expected to pass from the first protective non-sexual relationship directly into her first—and only—sexual relationship, where she had little to no say over her own body. Engaging in sex before marriage interrupted this order and made a woman unfit to assume the role of respected wife and mother, whether or not that sexual activity involved the exchange of money.

Only one of these five women connected by Jack the Ripper has ever been accused of having been a prostitute before marriage. Mary Ann may not have been a fit wife because of her penchant for drinking, and some versions indicate that she might not have been loyal to her husband before they parted, but she did not turn to prostitution until she was turned out. Annie faired even better and managed to avoid the label until her husband's death ended her weekly allowance. Although Liz had gone on record as having been a prostitute in Sweden prior to coming to England, Howells and Skinner make no note of this. Catherine is likely to never have married Thomas Conway, despite their years together, and Mary Jane married at a young age and also turned to prostitution after widowhood.

A further complication is that women who turned to prostitution for their livelihood did not necessarily do so of their own free will. It is not as though these women threw themselves into having casual sex with random strangers wholeheartedly. There are many situations in which a woman might willingly engage in intercourse before marriage without being coerced or being on the receiving end of violence, but being an East End prostitute is not the same as being a kept woman or even living in a brothel in the West End. These women who "deserved everything they got" were homeless, at the mercy not only of their customers but of the roving gangs, and forced out onto the street at night if they did not have the money for a bed.

The final point is how the expectation of what these prostitutes deserved is "somewhat earlier" than the fates that actually befell the Ripper's victims. Apparently the cost of prostitution lies somewhere between a day to day, hand to mouth existence that waffles between doss houses and work houses, a life accentuated by drink when there was money to be had, with the threat not only of robbery but of disease, and a brutal death. A woman without a man in Whitechapel seemed to have a very narrow range of experience to look forward to.

Just as Howells and Skinner turn the previous quote from a mystery prostitute to a discussion on the mysteries of the Ripper, these observations about women and women's bodies turns in the next sentence to speculation of what Victorians might have done with another sexual deviant: the homosexual. Their candidate for the Ripper's identity, Montage John Druitt, is speculated to have been homosexual, which would have indeed placed him in a difficult position in life. Whether it was more or less difficult than the average East End prostitute is up for debate.

The authors suggest that part of the reason Druitt would have murdered East End prostitutes is the fact that he would have had to pass through the East End on his way to visit his mother, who was in an asylum from the summer of 1888. They add together the puzzle pieces of sexual frustration, a mother who has secretly been locked away, this constant sight of women "who were reaping the harvest of their poverty and vice,"[22] and throw in layers of secrecy and conspiracy in order to explain why Druitt did not simply keep continuing to kill victim after victim in a growing frenzy. Their choice of Ripper becomes difficult when comparing theories to known facts and records, but they still decide that the choice of prostitutes was not necessarily because of the ease of encounter, but because there was something about this particular sort of woman that set him off.

Despite the lyrical language and metaphors Howells and Skinner use to discuss some aspects of the Ripper's victims, and indeed life in the East End in general, the end result is not in fact one that inspires empathy in the reader. Empathy would involve a personal recognition between reader and subject, a way in which the reader could see herself in the shoes of one of these women. Part of this difficulty comes with being one hundred years removed from Victorian Whitechapel, although clearly contemporary readers were confronted with similar distances in class and circumstance.

Like many authors before them, Howells and Skinner continually and routinely turn the focus of their book back to the Ripper himself. It is, after all, a quick summation of the salient facts of the crime meant to lead into various theories developed in the years since, ending traditionally with the suggestion of the "real" identity of the Ripper. Further investigation into the lifestyle of East End women or questions into what, exactly, some of these provocative quotes and statements reveal would just distract from the main focus of this and every Ripper text: the killer himself.

"Not so pretty"

Terence Sharkey's book, *Jack the Ripper: 100 Years of Investigation*—also from 1987—takes a rather mathematical approach of rating the likelihood of various proposed Jack the Rippers by percentage. The various theories themselves are presented in a chapter he entitles "Identity Parade" and then rated in the next, "Pick Your Ripper." The most likely, according to the rankings, is Montague Thomas Druitt—presumably the same man others name as Montague John—who is assessed at 75 percent. The pseudonym of Dr. Stanley and known criminal Fredrick Bailey Deeming are each rated at 0 percent and thus entirely dismissed, but, as far as Sharkey is concerned, the rest have at least a small chance of one day being fully proven.

Because of this approach, he does not set out to prove a single theory. There is therefore no need to link the murders or victims, and he presumably does not need to discard details that would disprove his favorite Ripper or to emphasize small points that would otherwise not deserve such attention. He even allows each woman her own chapter, with four of them titled with her accepted nickname: Dark Annie, Long Liz, Kate, and Mary. Chapter 2, however, is entitled "Not So Pretty Polly."

Polly is, of course, already the nickname of Mary Nichols, and she is not said to have been known as anything with a further description, pretty or not. And pretty she had indeed once been—it is the reason Sharkey gives for her marriage to William Nichols and their five children. It is perhaps then no surprise that William eventually left her due to "her drinking and general slovenliness."[23] If nothing but Polly's looks had attracted William to her in the first place, then excess drinking could have indeed led to a decrease in her attractiveness, as well as simple aging and motherhood. There is no indication as to why Polly would have started turning to the bottle or caring less about her appearance, and no suggestion that her husband might have done anything to lead to her alcoholism or apathy.

Sharkey overemphasizes the fact that being without a husband in the East End made Polly turn to prostitution, stringing together a number of euphemisms that leaves no doubt as to her profession. Her last night finds her ejected from the lodging house, boasting about her bonnet, which he derides. Clearly he interpreted her comment as indicating that this bonnet would help men find her attractive, a prospect Sharkey clearly doubts. Even then he follows this dismissal with commentary by Polly's friend, Emily Holland, who notices something wrong with Polly aside from her drunkenness. Apparently Polly was usually quite cheerful and pleasant to be around, even when drunk, and thus this lack of spark caught Emily's attention. Polly was, however, too drunk to listen to her friend's concern, and is next seen after her death.

This assessment of her personality is really the only positive thing to have been said about Polly. The rest of her life seems to be failure: as a wife, as a mother, as a respectable working woman, and even as an attractive prostitute. Her one redeeming feature was her cheerful personality, and even that was missing on the night of her death. In case readers are influenced too strongly by the opinion of Emily Holland, William Nichols is given his valedictory when he views the body of his wife in the mortuary. It is not her personality that causes him to forgive her, but the gruesome state of her corpse. Nothing Polly has personally done could have redeemed her to him, it seems, but Jack the Ripper's knife managed what she could not.

Annie Chapman, given the nickname Dark Annie, suffered a similar descent in her life, although her position as a married woman may have placed her higher than Polly. She had lived with her husband in Windsor and, according to Sharkey, Annie had been the one to instigate their separation. He suggests that it was her drinking that caused her to leave, although it does not seem she abandoned any children. These had already been sent away, and her husband died not long after she had left him.

Aside from her drinking and the usual life associated with women living on their own in the East End, Annie is known to have been involved in "frequent brawls—she presented no attractive sight."[24] In spite of both her apparently incendiary personality and her less than beautiful appearance, Annie clearly found work as a prostitute. Witness after witness at her death inquest confirmed this, and even those who did not know her personally but had merely seen her on the night of her death described a procession of men.

In the face of such testimony, Sharkey does not even mention any other means by which Annie may have been making a living. She is given no steady man and no steady income, since she was on the street that night because she had no money for a bed. Apparently, again in spite of her looks, she may indeed have found a client before meeting her fate with the Ripper, since Sharkey reports that coins were found near her body. If they had belonged to Annie and had not been left there by her murder, then she must have earned them recently, both because she had not had them to pay for her lodging, and because she had not spent them on the gin of which she was so fond.

Liz was different in that she was neither drunk on the night of her death, nor had she been kicked out of her lodging house for being penniless. She also had the support of the clergy—at her death inquest, the pastor of the Swedish church suggested that she made her living by means other than prostitution. His testimony to this matter ends up being disregarded, since a number of men turned up at the inquest to say that they had once lived with her, but Liz is the only one of these women to have been associated with a church at all.

She is, of course, Swedish, although she had been living in the East End for nearly two decades at the time of her death. Her last name is the result of a marriage, although Sharkey does not know what happened to John Thomas Stride. What he does know is that the *Princess Alice* story, once again related here, was shown to be false during the inquest. Any sympathy Liz might have gained by either being widowed during the sinking or because she earned her living through sewing is ultimately denied her. There is no series of people to prove that she was not a widow because of the sinking, but this story is dismissed all the same.

Thus most of the information given about Liz is shown to be a lie, or perhaps a fairy tale meant to present her in a better light. Sharkey does not even indicate whether the pastor may have lied because he was honestly unaware, or if he meant to give Liz a better public reaction in death than she had been given in life. When she crossed paths with the Ripper—it is not clear if she happened to be looking for a customer at the time—she "moved silently and swiftly from the obscurity of the ill-lit East End streets to national and lasting fame,"[25] although whether or not fame might have been worth the price of her life is debatable. Unlike the claims that Liz was not a prostitute and was widowed by the *Princess Alice*, this one goes uncontested.

Kate fairs a bit better since John Kelly is present and accounted for to tell more of her story. He is described as her "'latest' husband in common-law,"[26] indicating that there must have been more before him, even if they are not named or even numbered. Sharkey informs readers that Kate had indeed been married, and the relationship was important enough to her that she had her husband's initials tattooed on her arms. None of the other women were said to have tattoos, and there is no discussion of how common this might have been, or what the contemporary reaction would be to a woman with tattoos, no matter what their content. Unfortunately Thomas Conway abandoned his wife and she was left with this reminder long after he had gone. There is no indication that Conway was upset or at all impacted by Kate's death.

In contrast, when Kelly takes the stand at her death inquest, he is emotional. Clearly he cared about the woman he had lived with for seven years, and their relationship is not questioned even though Sharkey states that Kate was a prostitute. The police knew her to work in a certain area, and if she had refrained from prostitution the entire time she was with Kelly, it is unlikely that they would have remembered this seven years on. And, even though she was a prostitute, somehow she and Kelly spent their last days virtually penniless, spending what they earned on drink first, with food and lodging only as afterthoughts. Even their annual hop-picking did not earn them enough money to pay for everything.

The picking was cut short not only because Kate was feeling unwell, but because she told Kelly that she wanted to return to London to claim the reward money for naming the Ripper. This tale, unlike Liz's concerning the *Princess Alice*, is not declared an outright lie. It is simply surprising and left at that. No one seems to have pestered Kelly to learn whether Kate had told him the name, or even to ask him why she had not claimed the reward sooner. The legend of Kate knowing the Ripper has reached the level of supreme acceptance, unquestioned at the time and unexplored in the years since. If nothing else, with this depiction, Kate would have done her best to secure the reward so that she could keep herself in gin, weakening the support for this story.

When confronted by the rumors and tales surrounding Mary's past, on the other hand, Sharkey sidesteps them by listing the locations in which she was supposed to have lived before coming to the East End but not discussing them further. It is almost easy to overlook the fact that she was ever anything but an attractive East End prostitute in a sea of drabs. She is given a place of honor, not only in the relative length of her chapter but also because Sharkey opened his book with a discussion of her. His Mary "shone like a beacon"[27] and thus attracted, and was deserving of, attention. Whatever bad things may have been said about her—things that Sharkey has said about the other women, for example—he argues that there must have been something good about her, something appealing, if only because she had managed to charm her landlord into letting her owe weeks' worth of back rent.

This charm also extended to her relationship with Joe Barnett, since she was walking the streets behind his back. Although they had been together for almost two years and he was meant to support them through day labor, Sharkey tells a different story. His Mary spends her day in prostitution and then meets up with Barnett when he finishes work, he being none the wiser, and the pair would then drink together until bedtime. Mary, of course, had been drinking all day, and perhaps this is where her money went, since it clearly had not gone to paying rent. Sharkey also has to mention that there were rumors that Mary might have been a lesbian, in case Barnett needed another reason to garner sympathy at having been duped by a pretty face.

Unless, of course, he was simply too dull-witted to have realized what Mary was pulling one over on him. After Barnett left Mary, Sharkey pictures her simply waiting for him to come back, certain he will return. As conniving and deceptive as she might be, though, Barnett earns sympathy in the end when he gives evidence at the inquest despite a stutter and his tears. Through both the fact that he was not aware of Mary's daytime prostitution, intending to support the pair of them on his own, and this emotional reaction, Barnett is shown as a devoted man who happened to pick an East End woman singular for both her looks and her connivance.

The doubt and negative comments that Sharkey expresses have been embedded in Ripper narratives for a century at the time of his writing and thus should not be surprising. Dismissals are common and do not need explanation beyond the fact that the speaker was making an attempt to present the subject in a positive light. Aside from Mary Kelly, who has issues of her own to counter this, it is rare to find anything redeeming about these women, and Sharkey does his part to continue this representation.

Ghosts, Psychics and Suspects

In Peter Underwood's 1987 book *Jack the Ripper: One Hundred Years of Mystery*, he claims the description of being "possibly the first to consider paranormal aspects"[28] of the murders. He does not consider black magic and does not name Doctor Roslyn D'Onston as one of his suspects, even as one of the theories to be dismissed, but Underwood does involve Robert James Lees in his accusation of Sir William Gull and devotes a chapter to the discussion of ghosts encountered at the murder locations. It was only Gull's connections to the royal family, Underwood points out, that saved him from a more public accusation, and thus it is high time for the Ripper's name to be known.

Underwood groups the murders into a single chapter, but does allow each woman her own heading. He opens the section on "Mary Ann 'Polly' Nichols" with a narrative of the woman in question, describing an almost whimsical account of her final hours. His Polly has indeed been evicted from her doss house for not having the money, but she has since been lucky with two clients. "[A]lthough the second one had been a sadistic slob of a beast, he had plied her well with gin beforehand and she had survived"[29] and was presumably on her way back to her lodging house with coins from two such encounters in her pocket.

This version of the tale clarifies how Polly could have been drunk when she encountered the Ripper after having been evicted for being penniless. The gin came from one of her clients—the second she had met that night. If lodging houses required four pence for a bed, and Polly allowed herself to be plied with gin by the second man, the question occurs: how little was she charging per encounter? If the first man had given her enough for a bed, why did she need a second client? While it is true that East End prostitutes could not charge a fortune for their services, does this mean that Polly had been desperate enough to accept an offer for less than four pence in the hopes that she could then make up the difference? And was it desperation that led her to accept the offer of the sadistic second customer, or love of gin?

The irony, of course, is that Polly survived an encounter with this second customer only to encounter someone who better fit the definition of "sadistic." In Underwood's version, she does not willingly go with the Ripper as a client, but is instead surprised by the Ripper. He is aided by her drunkenness, and perhaps by this point Polly was also relieved to have earned her money and was not as inclined to pay attention to any man she saw. Then again, Polly is not found with any money, which is what has led most authors to conclude she either could not find a customer or had bought her own drink that night.

This opening scene makes way for very little information about what Polly's life had been like up until that last night. Her estranged husband is mentioned, but no children, although Underwood allows for the conflicting reasons of who ended the marriage and for what reason. He recounts how she failed at both living with her father and working as a maid, and the repetition of her drinking habits, even though not explicitly linked, provides readers with an explanation for these shortcomings. The tale then circles back around to its opening scene, with Polly on the street and looking for money for her bed. After all, for all of these women, their importance always returns to their final moments.

Annie does not receive such a romanticized opening of her last night, although she is given more background information, as well as a middle name. Underwood introduces her as "Annie May Chapman," using a middle name that seems to belong to him alone. As a young woman, around the time she met her husband, Annie is described as a "slim, dark ... impressionable and attractive girl"[30] who finds herself utterly taken with soldier-about-to-turn-veterinary-surgeon Fred Chapman. It is unknown how long her slenderness lasted, since she was not described as such at the time of her death, and Underwood does not explain the effects Chapman had on his impressionable young wife. Was she impressionable because she was swayed into marrying him? Underwood connects the idea of Chapman being an honorable man and his marriage to Annie, allowing for much speculation about the reason behind their marriage, but he also comments that the marriage itself was happy.

Three paragraphs later, however, the marriage has crumbled for no concrete reason. It might be the birth of their children—mysterious figures both—or outside influence, but Annie and Fred agreed to part. Underwood even states that Fred visited his estranged wife in the East End from time to time, as well as giving Annie a weekly allowance until his death. He even reminds readers that Annie did not change her name after the split, although he never mentions her birth name. She is Annie Chapman from the heading of her story until the end.

What confuses Underwood is whether or not Annie was a prostitute after her husband's death. On page five he derides authors who have been fooled by her friends' comments that she had other ways of earning a living, accusing them of being led astray as well by Annie's rose-colored description of what her married life had been like. However, when summarizing her murder ten pages later, he declares that "Annie was not a regular streetwalker."[31] Does he mean that she did not walk the streets as frequently as Polly had? Underwood indicates her poor health as a reason she may not have been able to work, whether he meant as a prostitute or as a seller of trinkets.

He makes it clear in the preceding pages that Annie had become a prostitute. No longer thin but still able to attract men, she had taken to selling herself for money simply because she needed necessities like food and shelter. These are regular needs and thus Annie would be in search of more regular employment. She was certainly penniless on her final night, and Underwood presents her as in search of a customer, so perhaps it is Annie's happier past that prevents her from being a "regular" prostitute and not any events that happened since her husband's death.

Elizabeth Stride is introduced as being half of the hard-working couple running a coffee house in the dockland district. Her Swedish heritage was almost an afterthought. Apparently their coffee house was known for the cheerful demeanor of the owners and they way they would not tolerate the tougher customers, an interesting prospect. It would seem that cheerfulness might have helped Liz later on in her life, when she worked as a prostitute, but her ability to refuse customers service might not have carried over.

Thomas and Elizabeth Stride have three children in this version, and apparently the coffee house was not enough to support a family of five, since Elizabeth also took work on pleasure steamers. This, of course, led to the entire family being aboard the *Princess Alice* on the day it sank, and Elizabeth lost all four members of her family. Underwood reports that, when the ship began its sudden sinking, Thomas went to look for the children while Elizabeth "dived into the water to wait for them."[32] This gives Elizabeth multiple points of guilt: not only was she reason that her husband and children were on the ship in the first place, but the fact that she jumped into the water while her husband went off into the ship is the sole reason she survived. Presumably she had previously learned how to swim, because Underwood describes her as having been in the water for quite a long time, looking for her family, before she was recused. Now widowed and without her children, Liz could no longer run the coffee shop, and this is what drove her to the streets.

Like other authors before him, Underwood promptly undermines this sympathetic tale by reporting that the *Princess Alice* part of it was inaccurate. He cannot trace her husband—but suspects he was still alive in 1888—and wonders if she might indeed have had nine children, all of whom outlived her. Even her long-term relationship with Michael Kidney is thrown into doubt, since Liz is painted as having lived with a string of men. Not only did she drink with them, but she supported them through prostitution. If Liz had done this with previous men, and if Kidney were only the next man in line, then there is reason to suspect that she had been supporting him, as well. If this were true, then she not only lied about her past to gain sympathy, but Kidney is responsible for the fact that she was on the street that night.

Clearly her men would have wanted a relationship if she were supporting them, despite Underwood's disparaging comments about her looks. But what would Liz get from them? She was not in these relationships for the money, if she happened to be the one providing it. If Liz could take care of two people on her income, surely she could have managed by herself. But Underwood gives her the basic human need of companionship, of having someone to distract her from her past woes and dismal-looking future. As pathetic as she may have been, Liz was still seeking out human comfort, and her *Princess Alice* story may well have been a way of ensuring that received just that.

Michael Kidney, who had lived with her on and off for three years, certainly would not admit that he was using Liz for her money. Underwood pushes him even further to the point where Kidney is presented as being willfully unaware—that is, even if Liz came to him with coins, he would not think about how she had obtained them. It would seem either that Kidney was able to fool himself about Liz's activities, or that he wanted others to think him so naïve so they would not judge him harshly. Further, his testimony at the coroner's inquest was far from straightforward, and he is not shown to have known much about Liz's past. With all of these factors, it seems likely that he may have been using her for money, after all.

John Kelly at least has the honor of being known as Catherine's common-law husband, and he is not presented as having no idea that Catherine was a prostitute. This couple cobbled together a living between his casual laboring and her selling: her body at night and trinkets during the day. Apparently this still was not enough, since Underwood says that Catherine never had a full meal and looked both ravaged and aged.

The two should have had at least a slight change in fortune before her death, since they had been out in the country hop-picking, both working hard. Underwood reports that their money was stolen after they had used some of it to get drunk, but does not explain how they returned to London. At any rate, they arrived penniless, and any money earned over the next few days was quickly lost to drink. Once again Catherine ends up locked away because she had achieved enough alcohol on her last evening to be rendered senseless, and Underwood laments the fact that she was released in the middle of the night and not followed, as the police had apparently been ordered to do with known prostitutes.

Catherine went from her cell to die in the darkest corner of Mitre Square. For Underwood, "it says little for Catherine's common sense or awareness"[33] of the previous murders that she so willingly went with a stranger and probable client into such an isolated place. At least he then acknowledges that there are reasons beyond blatant ignorance or stupidity, admitting that it might not have been a stranger; that there might have been nothing about a stranger to make him seem like a threat; or that she might still have been drunk enough that she was not aware of the danger. It is more empathy than he affords the other women, and he shows it in the way he allows for variances within the situation. In truth there is no evidence as to whether Catherine went to Mitre Square to meet someone, went there with someone, or happened to there for another reason, only to be ambushed. It is unusual for authors to admit that they are uncertain of the exact way these events unfolded, since most of them must present the murders in a single way in order for their pet theories to hold true. Underwood's uncertainty in this case admits that we know very little of Catherine and her habits.

Even less is known for certain about Mary Jane Kelly, although she is presented as a "fascinating puzzle"[34] that is worth a bit of time and effort to examine. Underwood, like others, points out that Mary Kelly—often mentioned with her first and last name, while the other women are referred to by their first names or nicknames—seems to have taken a nosedive at top speed from the West End and France to the East End. Since so much of Mary Kelly's past is a mystery, Underwood suggests that perhaps a certain rumor is true, and that she did indeed have children—perhaps during those two years that are so mysterious. Since these possible children do not appear in the East End with her, their absence, either due to death or her inability to care for them, could be a plausible explanation for her drinking.

Mary Kelly keeps up a string of relationships in the East End, apparently going from man to man as she was continually abandoned or kicked out due to her drinking. Underwood even has her repeatedly make visits somewhere near Elephant and Castle, possibly to visit the child or children she had to give up for adoption. Stability only comes in the form of Joseph Barnett, who stays with her until shortly before her death and does not report being abandoned at any time before then. They did argue, though, following the traditional issue of Mary Kelly's drinking, "but sometimes, no doubt, about her child, if she had one."[35] Mary Kelly might not even be a mother, but Underwood has her possible offspring coming between her and Joseph Barnett.

The final blow is, of course, when Mary invites another woman to stay with them in their small rented room. It seems as though Underwood can think of no reason she would do so, outside of a possible accusation of lesbianism. It is also this specter of lesbianism that might had led to Barnett's departing, although he seems more inclined to think it was the fact that Barnett found out Mary Kelly had been prostituting herself behind his back. The threat of Jack the Ripper that made Catherine Eddowes a complete idiot to go with a stranger in the middle of the night has no bearing on Mary Kelly's decision to allow a friend to spend the night with her. Apparently this Mary Kelly has no room for empathy.

She does, however, stand out in any way possible from the other women in the East End. Her personality, her looks, her past, and her education may not have been exemplary elsewhere, but they were certainly of note in Whitechapel. Instead of being labeled a snob, she is instead popular, presumably friendly instead of distant. Mary Kelly could easily have stood out in a negative way, driving the others way instead of drawing them to her, especially because she could be "a little more selective"[36] in how she earned her drinking money, or with whom.

Despite all these positive attributes, Mary Kelly may in fact have been the least fortunate the Ripper's victims. One of the two new suspects Underwood presents, although he personally campaigns the Robert James Lees story, is Joseph Barnett himself. Ostensibly he committed the murders in an attempt to keep Mary Kelly off the streets. She would have heard about an earlier murder and, upon seeing her reaction, Barnett would have decided that this would be the way to make sure his girlfriend stayed indoors, especially after dark. When things did not turn out in his favor, he ended his crime spree by killing Mary Kelly herself. This would explain both the increasing violence of the crimes—with the exception of Liz— and the fact that Mary Kelly was both the last and the worst.

There are times when Underwood shows compassion and insight into the lives of these women, admitting that many facts are unknown and some oft-repeated sentiments may indeed be untrue. Unfortunately these moments then highlight the places in which details are glossed over instead of being examined. The inconsistency in his representation of these women makes their narratives vastly uneven. For example, although he starts with a dramatized narrative of Polly's final hours, he does not follow through with this method for the other women. In fact, it is Catherine's final moments that lead to one of the segments in which Underwood admits uncertainty and allows himself to flesh out the many possibilities that exist without the anchor of certain fact. In the face of a century of declarations as though they were the truth, made to support an ever-changing array of Ripper identities, perhaps the more surprising segments are not those in which Underwood backs away from these details and questions, but those in which he engages.

Judge and Jury

In one last book from 1987, Colin Wilson and Robin Odell present themselves as lawyers in the case of the identity of Jack the Ripper. *Jack the Ripper: Summing Up and Verdict* presents readers with the details of the murders and then moves through the various Ripper identity proposals in chapters headed with general professions that are, at times, associated with specific names. Their conclusion is perhaps no conclusion as they inform the readers that they must acquit all proposed Rippers in the face of such a lack of evidence, although Wilson and Odell do remain hopeful that there will be others advanced to their fictitious courtroom to stand their own time of trial.

The murders are discussed together in the first chapter, "Ripper at Large," a title which at least does not discriminate or direct attention toward a single woman. It is even the longest chapter in the book, being fifty-one pages. Granted, covering the time period between August 31 and November 9 means discussing the police case, the inquests, and the Ripper letters as well as the women themselves, but at least Wilson and Odell do not attempt to condense this information into the twenty or thirty pages of their other chapters. The amount of space devoted to each woman, however, does not necessarily expand to help fill this space.

Polly's life is discussed on a single page, starting with the identification of her body and briefly recounting the apparently relevant information that led up to her death. Wilson and Odell begin with her name, age, and occupation: Polly is, without question, a prostitute. The authors focus mostly on the Polly who was murdered that night, and thus their relevant information is that she had become a prostitute was because her marriage had ended five years previously due to her drinking. Any details of her childhood or even of her marriage are irrelevant, since she was only on the street because that marriage was over. It was over because of gin, which is also relevant to the fact that she was drunk on the night of her death. Gin was also the first thing Polly is meant to have bought with any of her earnings, the second being a bed for the night. Food is not mentioned.

This is the entirety of Polly as they see fit to present her. She crossed paths with the Ripper because she needed money to pay for her bed; she could earn that money through prostitution; and she had to work as a prostitute because she was no longer with her husband. The narrative line, as always, points toward the Ripper.

Annie receives a similarly brief description with few variations. She, too, had been married, and had "been separated"[37] from her husband for four years before his death. There is no blame in this phrasing—unlike Polly, she is not shown to be an alcoholic. Instead of going straight to prostitution, as Polly seems to, she tried to live with another man for a time, and was assisted by the allowance from her husband. When he died that allowance stopped, and this was the reason Annie found herself in the East End.

It is only at this point that Annie's children are mentioned and placed in homes. They had not made prior appearances and had likely stayed with their father during the separation. Annie is left widowed, childless, and at some point without the man she had been living with, since she is forced to fend for herself. Still, she makes a good try to stay off the street with her crochet work and selling flowers. Annie fights every step of the way before "she lapsed into drunkenness and prostitution,"[38] having resisted both conditions for so long. It does not matter how long she worked as a prostitute, and Wilson and Odell do not say—it could have been her very first customer she met early on the morning of September 8, because she was surely looking for such a man to earn money for her bed.

Elizabeth, on the other hand, may not have been seeking a customer and may indeed not have been a prostitute at all. She was Swedish but had been in England for twenty-two years at the time of her death. Once married and now on her own—although not widowed by the *Princess Alice*, since that tale is again reported as being false—Elizabeth had been living off and on with Michael Kidney. Like Polly, she would turn to drink, and this was the cause of the breakups. Apparently Kidney took her back regularly once she had sobered, although she had left him again a few days before her death. Wilson and Odell do not discuss what she did for money when she was on her own, or what she might have been doing out and about the night of her death, although half past one in the morning might not really be all that late for the East End. The authors make no note of this—it is enough that she was indeed out, a woman on her own because she was separated from her husband and had recently also left her current companion, and that was how she met the Ripper.

Kate, like Elizabeth, was also not out looking for a customer when she was murdered. In fact, John Kelly reported that he had "never heard of Kate walking the streets for immoral purposes"[39] in all seven years they were together. Although Kelly is not the only man she has had in her life, it seems that Kate lived for quite some time with the first one, as well, and there is no list or even hint at a list of names between the two relationships. Unlike Annie, Kate seems to have been able to make her living well enough hawking goods on the street, and of course she had the benefit of Kelly's income to supplements her own.

This Kate does drink, but rarely too much, and she was well-liked by those who knew her. Her sister, her lodging house keeper, and Kelly himself having nothing bad to say about her, although they could simply wish to not speak ill of the dead. Still, their reports, and the picture painted by Wilson and Odell, present Kate to be about as respectable as an East End woman could get.

Mary Jane Kelly, often referred to as Mary Kelly but at least once simply as Kelly, receives the most attention, both in this first chapter and then in the rest of the book. Because she is central to many past theories of the Ripper, she is mentioned and discussed again, especially under "Doctor Ripper," "Royal Jack," and "Jack of all Trades." This last includes her most recent companion, Joseph Barnett, as a suspect, with Barnett committing murder after murder in "a losing battle to steer Mary Kelly away from drink and prostitution."[40] There is no question, then, about Mary Kelly's habits or her means of earning a living. She, like Polly, is flatly declared to be a prostitute and denied even Annie's efforts to slow her slide into such a position.

Much of what Wilson and Odell report about Mary Kelly comes from the man who, in at least on version of the tale, ended up murdering her. Her travels from Limerick to Wales to the West End to France to the East End are mentioned, but not questioned, and there is no speculation about the speed at which she "degenerated."[41] She may have returned from France, asking to be called Marie Jeanette, the day before she met Kelly—the timeline is left unclear. Like Annie, however, Mary Kelly is suggested to have come from a much better situation and landed in the East End as a last resort.

She is still singular among these women, being young, but her attractiveness and magnetic personality are not emphasized as much as they have been by other authors. Her looks are lamented as lost after the mutilations that accompanied her death, but not stressed beforehand. Really, anyone's looks could have been lamented, considering the fact that Wilson and Odell point out that the body buried in her grave may not even be Mary Kelly, due to the difficulty of identification. They do mention multiple times that Barnett's reason for leaving may not have been purely because Mary Kelly invited her friend to stay with them, but because Mary Kelly had dropped him for one of her female companions, although this is not the usual level of universal appeal Mary Kelly seems to exert. As much as is said about her, she is still an unexplored mystery.

The task of declaring suspects innocent because of a lack of proof is easier than attempting to link a single specific man to all of the Ripper murders, and Wilson and Odell are thus perhaps not as concerned with details as other authors might have been. As long as they are aware of what these women were doing in the last moments of their lives, they have enough information to draw conclusions about the Ripper. Even though their chapter covering the murders encompasses more pages than some of the other instances of 1987, tidbits of information on the women before they became victims frequently occupies a single page—or a single paragraph. Only Mary Kelly, the darling of so many pet theories, stands out.

"A sort of immortality"

Perhaps not wishing to crowd one more look back into 1987, Paul Begg's book *Jack the Ripper: The Uncensored Facts* was published in 1988, 100 years after the canonical murders. It is his observation that, though there have been multiple books about Jack the Ripper, few actually discuss the case itself. As we have seen, many books focus on the identity of the Ripper and proving their own pet theories, or at least disproving the theories of others. Begg therefore sets out to provide such as book as has been missing.

His chapter order includes five titled with the women's names, interspersed with those devoted to the events between the crimes. Discussions of police reaction, suspect accusations, and the letters and other newspaper coverage, when not related to a specific victim, happen in these dated chapters. Although the chapters on the women cover their murders and inquests, they do open with a biography of that specific woman that covers more than just the last few years of her life.

Before venturing into the crimes and these biographies, Begg observes that "[i]t is little consolation that Jack the Ripper bestowed upon them a sort of immortality, but it is a consolation nevertheless."[42] Who, exactly, is meant to be consoled? Anyone who knew the victims personally would not be alive at the time of Begg's writing, and it was forty years after the crimes when the first book was written. A single book is hardly proof of immortality, and those who had been reading the newspapers during the crimes themselves would have witnessed a distinct cessation of reports shortly after Mary Jane Kelly's murder. The women, of course, were dead and past any means of consolation, and no mention is made of whether their children, if they had any, had grandchildren who might have been in need of comfort.

Begg seems to insinuate that part of this comfort comes from the fact that some of the women—not all, but some—were given funerals grander than they could have hoped for, and that their names are known while richer contemporaries have been forgotten. Somehow this consolation seems to be tied in with money and class: how the have-nots, though dint of being murdered and mutilated, were given the chance at a fancy funeral and city-wide mourning without having to pay a penny. The price, of course, was their lives, not just then but in a century of being overlooked and passed by in favor of concentrating on the person who killed them.

Mary Ann's early life, between her birth and marriage, is still scarce on details, but once she left her husband and two children there is a thorough list of the workhouses where she lived. This includes an interruption during which time she was living with a blacksmith named Drew for a period of four years, a relationship not mentioned in other accounts of her life. At that time Mary Ann Nichols is thought to have been doing quite well, since she was respectably dressed at her brother's funeral. The couple has parted by October 1887, although Begg only provides a reason for this separation on the next page when he states that "Nichols was almost certainly an alcoholic, two men having let her because of her drinking habits."[43] On her own again, Polly is in and out of workhouses and makes her failed foray into honest work as a servant. Then it is back to working houses and a lodging house that was known to allow men and women to share beds.

But was this Mary Ann a prostitute? This last statement concerning the White House on Flower and Dean Street is the closest Begg comes, since it was one of the few to allow men and women to share a double bed. On her final night, when she is turned out for not having money, she does not make her customary statement of having had her doss money multiple times and spent it already—she simply points to her new bonnet and laughs off the concern of getting the money. Begg does not discuss how Mary Ann earned a living, or how she expected to find the coins so late at night. She simply has nothing and reels out into the darkness, cheerful and perhaps already drunk.

Along with not being a prostitute, this Mary Ann Nichols happens to look almost ten years younger than her given age. Begg points out that, while the movies always make the women younger and more attractive, books have had a tendency to add ten or twenty years to their appearance. East End prostitutes in their forties must have been terrible hags, and the Ripper certainly did not pick them because of any sexual attraction—at least, that is how the books have continually worded it. From derelicts to bad drawings of human beings, the first four women have never had a break. But Begg refers to newspaper reports of the day. His Mary Ann had been attractive, and not just when she was younger.

Annie Chapman's life is likewise blank between birth and marriage, although this time her husband is a coachman and valet. In a vague statement passed on throughout friend via the deputy at one of Chapman's lodging houses—Begg at times refers to the women by their last name when other authors reserved the last name for their husbands—we learn that John Chapman lost this valet position "because of his wife's dishonesty."[44] Perhaps the vagueness is due to the fact that this information comes thirdhand, if not fourth, but even the fact that John Chapman had ever been a valet seems to be in doubt.

Begg covers the couples' two children and their locations at different homes, although he does indeed place them there before the separation. He then undermines his own statement about how no reason was given for this by providing information from a police report tying their parting to her drinking. It would seem that Annie Chapman managed to get her alcoholism under control, because the deputy of her lodging house thought it was out of character that she had been the worse for drink on the night she was murdered. Begg insists that her drinking was limited to Saturday nights and that she, unlike Mary Ann Nichols, was most certainly not an alcoholic.

During Annie Chapman's fight to stay off the street after her husband's death, when she was forced to get on without a weekly allowance, Begg traces her through relationships with two men. One, with a sieve maker, was serious enough that she was known as Annie Sivvey as well as Annie Chapman, while the second was a more recent relationship. This man was present at her inquest, although mostly to give an account of himself so that he would not end up a suspect. Even with this relationship, Annie had to resort to prostitution to survive, so it would seem that he might have been with her more for his benefit than for hers.

Elizabeth Stride is also a prostitute, although Begg has managed to find more information between her birth and marriage. When she first went to work in her home country of Sweden it was as a domestic, although five years later she was registered as a prostitute. A year after this she moved to London, where, according to two slightly conflicting stories, she came to work for a family. Presumably this position ended when she married John Thomas Stride three years later, since she moved and told people the two of them had owned a coffee shop. Begg takes issue with the factual details provided, but not nearly as many issues as he does with the *Princess Alice* story. Instead of dying as a result of the boat disaster, Begg has come up with a death certificate for John Thomas Stride from 1884. Presumably he and Elizabeth Stride had parted on or around 1878, when the *Princess Alice* sank.

Her relationship with Michael Kidney began in 1885, and on the Tuesday night before her death "[h]e had expected Stride to be at home when he returned from work, but she was not there. He was not particularly alarmed. Stride had gone off before."[45] Their time together is summed up in this brief description. During their three years as a couple he had been used to finding her waiting for him at the end of the day, although it was not entirely a surprise when she was not. He was accustomed to Elizabeth Stride going off on her own when she went on a drinking binge and then returning to him when she was through. Kidney denied rumors that he and Elizabeth had fought before she left that last time, which is an understandable protest. First, if he allowed that they had parted on bad terms, he might be accused of having murdered her as a result of their argument. Second, if he cared about Elizabeth Stride, he would not want to recall that they had fought the very last time he had seen her. Begg does not provide enough information about Kidney or his relationship with Elizabeth Stride for any firm conclusion to be drawn.

The place where Begg does show consideration and contemplation surrounding Elizabeth Stride's movements on her final night. Again, this is meant to tally with witness reports in order to determine who, if any of them, may have actually seen her with the Ripper so that Begg may then compare witness descriptions to possible suspects. It would seem from witness statements that Elizabeth Stride was with a number of different men in a surprisingly short amount of time, although Begg proposes that it might be the fault of the witnesses for not being properly observant. He suggests that she may indeed have been with the same man for at least an hour that night even if she had been soliciting and compares this situation to that of Martha Tabram, who spent even longer in the company of a soldier on the night she was murdered. Further, Begg does not believe that Elizabeth Stride was really out that night out of desperation, "for she could always have returned to Michael Kidney and his bed for as long as she wanted to stay."[46] However, Elizabeth had clearly chosen not to go back to him.

If Elizabeth Stride left Michael Kidney so she could go on a drinking binge, it would not be surprising if she had already run through whatever money she had with her from that Tuesday. Surely a couple who lived in lodging house was not well enough off to have gathered a nest egg. If, for whatever reason, Elizabeth Stride was reluctant to return to Michael Kidney, then she may indeed have been looking for money for a bed of her own. Begg seems to assume that Michael Kidney served solely as a source of income for Elizabeth Stride, and this statement also supposes that their last parting was not as the result of an argument. There may have been reasons beyond money for the couple to have stayed together, just as there may have been reasons that drove Elizabeth Stride to both drink and leave him on occasion. She is not allowed to be this complicated.

This same lack of inquiry or analysis is applied to Catherine Eddowes, who ran off with an older man when she was in her early twenties and was thereafter refused entry into her family's home. This meant in fact her aunt's house, since she had been orphaned somewhere around the age of ten. Catherine Eddowes thus had no parents, and she had no family to turn to once she had been with Thomas Conway for some time and had already had a child by him. Was she returning simply for a visit, to show off the child, or was she experiencing problems in her relationship and seeking advice and comfort? Thomas Conway was much older than she was, and it seems the couple never married—perhaps more fodder for her family's locked door. According to her daughter the couple had a relationship along the lines of Elizabeth Stride and Michael Kidney, in that they came together and parted routinely without spending more than a year in each other's company. Again, drinking was given as the reason for these partings.

Although the effect of Catherine being turned away by her family does not receive scrutiny, the parting of Catherine Eddowes and Thomas Conway is at least allowed two possibilities. Thomas Conway, of course, referenced her drinking, but Catherine Eddowes' sister accused Thomas Conway of abuse. Begg acknowledges that, although she might just be defending her sister, it was highly unlikely that any man would have admitted that he beat his wife when he was drunk. Now we have a Catherine Eddowes who has lost her family either through death or shunning and has also parted from the man that was the cause of that shunning. She has parted from her children, as well, since they do not move into the lodging houses with her. At this point Catherine Eddowes is completely on her own.

Shortly thereafter she meets John Kelly, whom Begg describes as sickly but dependable. He worked as a day laborer where he could and reported that, to his knowledge, Catherine Eddowes did not work as a prostitute. Granted, since he was working he would have been gone for hours at a time, but Begg paints a favorable picture of John Kelly. He was not stupid and would have known the signs.

In this version the couple indeed goes hop picking, but they leave because they "didn't get on too well"[47] and started walking home. There is no mention of illness on either side, and this Catherine Eddowes is apparently not going back to London to claim the reward for identifying Jack the Ripper. The couple is broke before reaching town and has to walk the entire way, where John Kelly earns enough money for him to have a lodging house bed while Catherine Eddowes goes to the workhouse. Oddly enough it is the casual ward deputy who reports that she spoke of earning this reward. Begg at least considers this claim of identity questionable and says that he cannot find any evidence of John Kelly supporting the superintendent's statement. Begg is further confused when Catherine Eddowes told John Kelly she was going to see her daughter, naming a town where her daughter no longer lived. Now Begg is the one asking the pertinent questions: if Catherine Eddowes often went begging her daughter for money, wouldn't she have enough known that her daughter had moved? Did she purposefully lie to John Kelly? And, since her daughter did not see her that day, where did she go? For once these questions are actually in the book and not left for readers to compose on their own.

Although there is no evidence that Catherine Eddowes was a prostitute, she somehow found money after parting from John Kelly on the last day of her life, or at least found someone to buy her drinks, since she is next seen drunk, immobile, and being taken to a police station so she can sober up. Soon after she is released in the wee hours of the next morning, she is murdered.

Begg introduces Mary Jane Kelly with a couple of questions, observing that she is often given the most attention of any victim. This is, he concludes, because she is generally considered to be the last victim, and the questions he asks as an introduction actually center around the Ripper. Did he mean to kill her for a personal reason, and this was why the murders stopped, or was he locked up or otherwise incapacitated after her death? It is really this first question that has led to so much attention being given to her, since the Ripper might then be identifiable through something within her past. The problem, of course, is finding a reliable telling of that past.

He finds more information about Mary Jane Kelly's childhood than has previously been mentioned, including seven or eight siblings, one of them a sister. Instead of having made a clean break, she sometimes received letters from Ireland, from either her mother or one of her brothers. Apparently her childhood was rather privileged, considering her perceived level of education. This is meant to have even included the fact that she was a good artist, although there is no mention of her preferred medium or how anyone in the East End would have seen her, for example, paint. Although other authors have accused Mary Jane Kelly of making much about her past, Begg argues that "[w]hat is said of her life cannot be proved, but neither can it be disproved,"[48] much the same way that many Ripper suspects must remain simply probable.

Begg even says that he found supporting evidence for Mary Jane

Kelly's tale that she had once lived in a West End bordello and had been to Paris for two weeks. The evidence is, however, highly circumstantial, starting with the fact that Mary Jane Kelly repeated this story and ending with witnesses who came forward years later, after her death, thinking they recognized her description. It seems that Begg is only leading with this lesser information before bringing up the practice of *placeurs* who would seek out likely women and entice them into high-end brothels in their home countries before transporting them across the Channel. If Mary Jane Kelly had indeed been seduced by such a woman who first placed her in a high-end bordello before moving her to a far lesser position in France, then she is likely to have escaped that situation. She may also have felt very much the country mouse, having gone to the big city in order to make her way in life and been fooled so easily. It is an explanation that would both allow for Mary Jane Kelly to tell the same tale every time, since the locations were true, and would also explain why she did not seem to give anyone further details.

Another possible reason for her silence on her past is suggested when Begg questions whether the body found so terribly mutilated at 13 Miller's Court was, in fact, hers. Joe Barnett's testimony, especially concerning why he may have fought so terribly with Mary Jane Kelly before they parted, mentioned multiple prostitutes staying in the room. Begg allows that two have been named, but wonders if there might have been others, and if it is one of them whose body was buried under Mary Jane Kelly's name. Begg wonders if this lack of information about her past hides someone who might have wanted to harm her, and the reason for this silence. If Mary Jane Kelly returned to her room to discover that her guest had been murdered there, she then quickly slipped away and managed to hide her true identity for the rest of her life as the story played itself out with her as the victim. Then again, after this supposition that seems less likely than many previous ones, Begg does admit that "[i]t is easy to build complex theories on very slender evidence."[49] He is, of course, not the only one to have done so, though most authors confine their wilder tales to the identity of the Ripper.

He does manage to rather undermine his own theory with his points that Mary Jane Kelly was weeks behind in her rent, meaning she would have had to strike out penniless with only the clothes on her back, and that she was so striking. A woman with her looks, her education, and her apparent pretensions would likely have a difficult time hiding in the East End, especially when her name and description had been in the newspapers. Granted, she may have also had a number of things working in her favor.

If she had only been hiding in the East End because of a threat, then that threat was neutralized and she might have been able to move on and elsewhere. Secondly, since the inquest into her death only lasted a day, the story disappeared from the newspapers rather quickly. In the end, though, this theory seems too much like a fairy tale, especially since variations have been used in fictional accounts of the murders.

Like Wilson and Odell, Begg begins to ask questions at certain points in the narrative, seeking answers or explanations that have been ignored or overlooked throughout the previous century. Certain assumptions are allowed to continue unquestioned, and Begg may not have picked the most obvious places to start with his questions, but at least they are present. He shows that he is capable of critically considering the gaps in the narratives and acknowledging that more than one explanation could lie behind them. It is the continuation of these questions, adding more to those Begg, Wilson, and Odell have already presented, that would increase the understanding of Jack the Ripper's victims as women.

Beyond the Anniversary

The 1980s saw many advances in the knowledge about serial killers such as Jack the Ripper, and this, along with the centennial anniversary of the murders, led to narratives that tended toward summarizations of the event itself and of the investigation over the previous hundred years. It was not necessarily the goal of these authors to prove the identity of the Ripper, although some new names were put forward, but rather to take the long look at the crimes. The question of how far we have come in the investigation into such serial murders was tempered by the fact that no one name has been accepted to replace the sobriquet of "Jack the Ripper." Any attempt at putting this new knowledge about serial killers and psychopathy to use are tempered by the fact that any such diagnosis must be made long-distance and based only on the documents that have survived for contemporary perusal.

The 1980s continued the swell in publications seen in the 1970s, now not focused on whether or not the murders could be tied to the royal family but more concerned with the passing of time. Although it can never be firmly declared that the reading public has access to every single document or file recorded at the time of the murders, any new information would be discovered by luck. These authors could not manufacture that luck, but they could make use of new information surrounding killers like the Ripper, if not new information about the Ripper himself. Because 1988 marked the hundred year anniversary of the killings, the focus of this decade was more on using this new knowledge to take a more general look at the case itself. The term "serial killer" and the language presented by the FBI was still new, although it became more common and widely known due to the general true crime boom of that decade. The anniversary seemed to be a time for reflection; any new accusations, relying on this advancing field of specialty, would come later.

Six

More Than a Century Later
Discussing Murder in the 1990s

Initially the police files concerning Jack the Ripper were meant to have remained unseen until 1992, one hundred years after they had initially been closed. Access was instead allowed to researchers as soon as the 1970s, and even then many of the files had been greatly weeded or even lost, due to accident or perhaps souvenir seekers. Thus the anticipated information boom that was originally meant to have occurred in this decade did not in fact come to pass. Researchers had to continue to make do with the odd now-and-again discoveries that seem to have peppered the history of Ripperology. Some of these discoveries are more hotly contested than others, as shall be seen below.

With the centennial mark of the murders behind them, authors seemed freed to build upon various cases for the Ripper's identity, and the books produced in this single decade nearly outnumber those all of the years leading up to it. This explosion of texts brought with it expanding ideas, topics, and even authors. The first female writers penned books about the Ripper in the 1990s, still very much in the minority. Authors found new ways to place blame on Mary Jane Kelly. Others declared that the Ripper was actually a killer duo consisting of homosexual young men. Some authors set out to increase the attention given to the murdered women, declaring it bluntly and then declaring their intention to give as much attention to the Ripper's victims as to the Ripper himself. Still others continued much in the same vein as the previous decades, largely ignoring the victims and making fuller use of the information about serial killers that emerged in the previous decade. The 1990s thus presented readers with a vast array of titles and ideas, seemingly enough to satisfy any prejudice or theory.

New Authors, New Voices

Along with the other changes, the decade of the 1990s brought the first female authors to the Jack the Ripper narratives. Jean Overton Fuller's 1990 book *Sickert and the Ripper Crimes* takes up the story that began in Stephen Knight's *Jack the Ripper: The Final Solution*, although Fuller rejects the idea of the murders being Masonic in origin. Instead, she places Sickert at the center of the crimes as the lone murderer, forced to kill because of the actions of Mary Kelly.

Because the story centers around Mary Kelly through the reminiscences of a friend of Fuller's mother, the other four women receive little mention. Fuller does inform readers that these women "were elderly and weak,"[1] in stark contrast to Mary Kelly. When discussed they are named as Mrs. Nichols, Mrs. Chapman, and Mrs. Stride, tying their identifies to those of the husbands they had left, although they were at least legally married. Catherine Eddowes is indeed always Catherine Eddowes and never Mrs. Conway, presumably because her relationship with the father of her children was common-law. Catherine Eddowes is allowed the individuality of her first name rather than being presented as the female half of a married couple. Previous authors—all male—have tended to use the women's last names in order to refer to them, allowing them variations depending on the presence or absence of a common-law husband.

Oddly enough Fuller makes the observation that these women "are usually just referred to as prostitutes.... To the public they are hardly individualized."[2] Granted, this comes at the end of her narrative, after she has presented her readers with a very individuated Mary Kelly, but she does not spare this time or attention for the other women herself. In fact, the morgue photographs of Elizabeth Stride and Annie Chapman are mislabeled, switching the women's names.[3] The first four women remain grouped together under blanket statements about East End prostitutes, or as the friends Mary Kelly confided in. Their deaths are also no fault of their own, but caused by the distinct, highly colorful figure of Mary Kelly.

Fuller's Mary Kelly was a strong-willed, good-looking woman who found herself keeping a shop with one Annie Crook. Annie caught the eye of a young man brought around by the artist Walter Sickert, giving birth to this young man's child and eventually marrying him in a secret ceremony. That young man was of course Eddy, Queen Victoria's grandson, and once Eddy was removed from Cleveland Street and Annie properly disposed of, Mary Kelly found herself in possession of knowledge that could threaten the crown. She shared the knowledge of this marriage and child with her friends, and this was what caused all of them to be murdered.

This Mary Kelly is disillusioned with life in London, having come from a previous position washing floors at an infirmary in Cardiff in search of something better and perhaps more glamorous. Fuller reports that Mary was "not a happy girl,"[4] which seems like a bit of an understatement. Although presumably prettier than Annie, and better educated—Fuller mentions that Mary Kelly could sign her name, which was apparently beyond Annie—it was Annie who caught Eddy's eye. Despite the fact that both women lived in the same neighborhood, the one had managed to ensnare a prince and the other, highly dissatisfied, left her shopkeeper's position in search of something more to her tastes. It is this departure, possibly made in jealousy over Annie's fortune and not due to circumstances beyond her control, that led Mary Kelly to prostitution.

Fuller seems determined to ensure that Mary Kelly, as individual and separate as she may be, is not a sympathetic figure. Her descent into Whitechapel is the result of multiple failed attempts to reach for a better life, one presumably beyond her abilities and status. Although she is Mary Kelly throughout the narrative, accorded both a first and last name, Fuller makes it clear that "[i]t was just plain English Mary, and one Christian name only"[5]—even Mary Jane Kelly is a fantasy, much less Marie Jeanette. Although Fuller does allow Mary Kelly trips to Dieppe with Walter Sickert, and questions whether this meant Sickert had taken her as a lover, she is firm in her assertion that any name beyond the simple Mary Kelly is an invention of the woman herself to put on airs.

Even in the East End Mary Kelly continued her search for what had supposedly been her lifelong goal: a man to support her, even if it could not be a man of royal blood. Joe Barnett is this man, and apparently quite a decent one for the East End, treating Mary Kelly better than any man before in her life—including Sickert and the prince. Barnett, however, does not feel the same about Mary Kelly's prostitution as the woman herself, since Fuller has him moving out because he does not wish to live off her earnings. From her shopkeeper's assistant position alongside Annie, Mary Kelly moved directly into prostitution, apparently of her own free will. Mary Kelly is clearly willing to sell her body to make a living, and apparently preferred it to her other options.

Fuller does take some time to discuss what it meant to be a prostitute in Victorian England, arguing that the vast majority of women in that position were forced into it, with the alternative being starvation. She seems sympathetic, at least to the other four Ripper victims, since they fall into her category of women who, for one reason or another, find themselves without a man or other means of support. Fuller even points out that many East End prostitutes had steady men who "forgave"[6] them for their prostitution, presumably as long as it was the result of desperation and not personal choice. Mary Kelly had a steady position that had kept her off the streets, even if she had felt the work was beneath her and she had to jealously witness the love affair of her coworker. The sympathetic prostitutes of the East End were forced to sell themselves in order to stay alive, and Fuller even sympathizes with those who used that money to buy alcohol instead of food or shelter, since their situations were so dire. It would seem that Mary Kelly's situation had no need to be so dire. Presumably Fuller is able to "forgive" the other prostitutes, as well, as long as their profession was forced upon them and not a true choice.

The most unforgivable about Mary Kelly, though, is the fact that she shared her secret with her friends. If she had not done this, then Sickert would have had no reason to murder any women outside of Mary Kelly herself—and indeed, he would have had no cause to murder Mary Kelly had she not written to him demanding money in the first place. Granted, Fuller admits that Mary Kelly had to "have been in dire straits"[7] to make the demand at all, but in this narrative it is Mary Kelly alone, presumably out of jealousy, that sets Jack the Ripper in motion. Mary Kelly is responsible for the murders carried out by Walter Sickert. While a man may have ripped, it was only because of a woman.

In her narrative Fuller makes one reference to her gender identity as being essential to her interpretation of facts. When discussing the report that Mary Kelly's clothes were found neatly folded on the day her murder was discovered, Fuller observes, "Perhaps because I am a woman, it is these I think about, and the circumstances in which she took them off and folded them."[8] While other authors have pondered the folded clothes, using them to conclude that Mary Kelly must have taken them off herself, unhurried, since they were not bloodstained and it was unlikely the killer had folded them neatly at any point in the proceedings, Fuller uses this moment to bring her own gender identity into play. It may come across as an admission: she only focuses on the minutiae of folded clothes because she is indeed a woman, and has thus presumably folded many clothes. They may have no more significance than has already been discussed, but they stick in her mind for reasons she associates with womanhood.

Fuller's identity as an artist has much more influence on the text, especially since both Sickert and her mother's friend, the source of her information, are artists. This leads to various comparisons between artwork and the given situation, at times branching out from pieces painted solely by those involved with the murders. In discussion of a Dali painting, Fuller observes that "the woman is corrupted from within, which is a worse thing than to be murdered by the Ripper, which is only violence from without."[9] Fuller, like many male authors before and after her, appears to take comfort in the fact that being brutally murdered by a strange man has meant that these women's names have been passed down through history. Murder and mutilation in this case are "only" minor in comparison to internal torment. This is an odd diminishing of the consequences of Mary Kelly's actions, especially when Fuller works to present the beautiful, free-spirited Mary Kelly in a negative light. If the consequences to her actions, for herself and four others, was "only" being attacked by Sickert, then it becomes more difficult to condemn her sternly for lighter consequences.

Shirley Harrison's 1993 book, *The Diary of Jack the Ripper*, does not include nearly as much information about Mary Jane Kelly, but Harrison still introduces a new approach to discussions of the murdered women. The focus of her narrative is, of course, a dairy meant to have been written by James Maybrick, confessing to be Jack the Ripper, and thus much of her text is devoted to the origin of the book and various tests and inspections meant to prove its worth. She covers the murders themselves quickly, as points of comparison for descriptions in the diary, and because the diary is only concerned with their deaths and not their lives, Harrison does not need to focus on their biographies.

What she does include, however, is a new way of introducing these women. In her first mention of them, Mary Ann ("Polly") Nichole's is presented with her age at death and the information that she "was a locksmith's daughter."[10] Annie Chapman is "the daughter of a Lifeguardsman"[11] and Catharine Eddowes the "daughter of a Wolverhampton tin worker."[12] Nether Elizabeth Stride nor Mary Jane Kelly is identified by her father's occupation, although Elizabeth is at least presented as being Swedish. Mary Ann, Annie, and Elizabeth's husbands are not mentioned by either name or occupation, and Catharine is meant to have pawned her own boots— John Kelly does not appear in the narrative at all. Only Joe Barnett appears as a player in Mary Jane Kelly's story.

Like Jean Overton Fuller's preference of referring to these women as wives, Harrison's method of identifying these women as daughters situates them according to the men in their lives. Even though the women are grown, with four of them being in their forties, she still turns them into daughters instead of women in their own right. Their choices of husband or personal profession, as well as the general course of their lives up until the nights of the deaths, are ignored, but for some reason their fathers' occupations are relevant to their identities. Indeed, this information is included in their introductions, with no indication of how long it had been since the woman in question lived with her father, or how his position influenced her life.

Even with their new additions of ways to describe the murdered women, Fuller and Harrison still each turn Mary Kelly into a unique figure. For Fuller she is the cause of all the murders, since her decision to attempt to blackmail Sickert drove him to decide that murder was the only way to keep the royal secret. Although Harrison's narrative does not show Maybrick having known Mary Kelly before her death, she does make connections between Mary Kelly and Maybrick's unfaithful wife, suggesting that Mary Kelly's murder was so horrific because she thus functioned as a stand-in for the woman who had angered him. Positioning the last canonical victim at the center of the murders was not new, and it was even repeated with new twists throughout the 1990s.

They All Love Mary Kelly

Mary Kelly has been depicted as separate from the other canonical victims since the time of her murder. The fact that she was killed in her own room and that the Ripper mutilated her body far beyond anything previously seen was part of it, but her youth and apparent beauty and intelligence also tend to come into discussions. If she is seen as the last victim, there is the question of why the murders stopped, and—since the initial narrative of Dr. Stanley—it has been common to conclude that she was in fact the desired victim while the others were stand-ins, obstacles, or mistakes. For two authors in the 1990s, Mary Kelly was the cause of the murders in a new way: the Ripper meant to control her.

In his 1991 book, *Jack the Ripper: The Mystery Solved*, Paul Harrison casts judgment on all of the women involved and not just Mary Kelly herself. When Polly Nichols separates from her husband it is because she "was not up to the permanent responsibilities of a family."[13] Her husband has done nothing wrong—or at least nothing worth mentioning—and Harrison places Polly on the street even during her marriage, drunk and soliciting. It is as though she is already practicing for life on her own in the East End, and the one possibly positive assessment Harrison makes of Polly is that she was hardy enough to withstand life as a prostitute in Whitechapel. He even ends his discussion of her by making the point that, even though she was no longer alive, Polly was making trouble for others, especially her family.

Despite the brevity of Polly's biography, Harrison manages to convey that Polly's death, although troublesome, proved to be no great loss. He condemns her by saying that she "had been given every opportunity to better herself which she failed to accept."[14] Despite the fact that Polly seemed to bounce back every time life knocked her down, Harrison traces each of these instances of failure to her alcoholism. Even when he depicts her as lost in the East End, just one face among many, completely anonymous and overlooked until her death, the cause of her presence there and her situation overall is still her alcoholism. If Polly had been able to triumph over the bottle she might have even recovered from the dissolution of her marriage, since she was given the opportunity to work in a respectable position. Respectability and dependability were apparently beyond Polly, and, no matter how many people reached out to help her, she made a mess of every opportunity.

Eliza Ann Chapman does not fare much better. Like Polly, Harrison's Annie is drinking and going with other men before her marriage is over. Annie even takes it a step further, since she "was prone to throwing anything within her grasp at her better half"[15] during their arguments, many of which were about her drinking. In this case "better half" takes on a deeper meaning, since John Chapman was indeed better than his drinking, whoring, violent wife. This is proven when, even after they separated, he paid her an allowance that was enough to cover her room and board. John Chapman is the wronged party, having done nothing to deserve such a banshee of a wife, and yet he still provided for her after she left him.

Although Annie's allowance was enough to keep her fed and sheltered, it was not also meant to support her drinking habit. Further, when John Chapman died, the payments stopped altogether and Annie found herself in the position of having to earn her own living and keep herself in drink. Since she had already been unfaithful to John Chapman while they were married, it is perhaps not surprising that Annie decided that engaging in prostitution was preferable to remaining sober. Harrison, at least, thinks it was the next logical step for her, as it had been to so many East End women. Despite the troubles she caused John Chapman, however, and the fact that her murder simply added to the mystery of Jack the Ripper, Harrison allows that Annie "slipped quietly from the world in much the same way she led her life with little fuss."[16] In spite of the fact that she was an unfaithful, alcoholic wife who liked to throw things at her husband, Annie was somehow not nearly so much trouble as Polly had been.

There is not much information reported on Elizabeth Stride, although Elizabeth, like Polly and Annie before her, was an alcoholic. A Swede, she came to London after the deaths of her parents and was married for a while before she ended up on the street. Harrison reports that Elizabeth and her husband were meant to have had nine children, ending this proclamation with an exclamation point. His surprise is not that the couple was meant to have reproduced so quickly in such a short amount of time—indeed, the timeline does not arise in this discussion—but presumably that Elizabeth would have allowed herself to have become pregnant so frequently. Certainly none of these children makes an appearance either for her funeral or at the coroners' inquest, so perhaps it might also be surprise that Elizabeth managed to have alienated all nine offspring.

Elizabeth's relationship at the time of her death was an inconstant one, broken up through her drinking and prostitution—which means that her boyfriend, Michael Kidney, presumably disapproved of both. Despite this, he also apparently took her back every time, likely once she had sobered up or earned a suitable amount of coins. Harrison does not mention whether Kidney made use of her earnings or if it was his intent to support her fully without her having to walk the streets. Like many other authors, Harrison does end his discussion of Elizabeth with the judgment that she "was a fantasist who could not contain herself to the truth,"[17] although the lack of evidence for her nine children does allow readers to wonder why Harrison might have believed that particular tale and not others.

Harrison's Kate Kelly follows a similar path as Polly and Annie before her, being accused of "flirtatious habits"[18] during her initial common-law marriage to Thomas Conway. This is interesting on two levels. First, the fact that he accuses Kate of flirtations instead of soliciting places this offense on a different level than that of Polly or Annie. His choice of language seems to indicate that there was not necessarily any physical contact between Kate and other men at the time of her relationship with Conway, and thus Conway might be interpreted to be acting as an overly jealous and controlling husband. Kate's drinking habits are not discussed until later, during her relationship with John Kelly.

The second oddity about this declaration is that Harrison refers to *Kelly's* flirtatious habits. Many authors continually refer to Kate by her maiden name of Eddowes, since they fail to find evidence that she ever married Conway and her relationship with Kelly was likewise common-law. Further, at the time of her relationship with Conway, Kate had yet to meet Kelly. Granted, she did use John Kelly's last name while she was involved with him, as evidenced by pawn tickets and testimony from those who knew her, but Harrison's choice to refer to her continually as Kelly is a strong statement for her relationship with the man and therefore places him clearly in the position of widower, although presumably much more distraught than William Nichols.

When Kate it shown to be drinking it is with John Kelly, who likely joins in. She does not feel the need to leave him in order to do her drinking, the way Elizabeth left Kidney, and she presumably also did not get drunk in order to solicit other men or throw things at Kelly. Harrison is skeptical of Kelly's claim that he did not know Kate was a prostitute, both giving Kelly credit for being aware of their situation and suggesting that Kate would not have been able to keep her activities hidden. The only alternative to prostitution Harrison offers these women, outside of marriage, is when Polly was given work as a maid. There is nothing in the East End that these women could do to support themselves beyond selling themselves, since apparently even having a steady man was not security enough.

Now we come to Mary Kelly, who is at the center of Harrison's narrative. He downplays this at the start, saying she lives "with her lover called John or Joseph or some other similar sounding name."[19] This man is, of course, Joseph Barnett, who had been living with Mary for over a year and whom Harrison never refers to as simply Joe. Joseph Barnett is Harrison's choice for Jack the Ripper.

Harrison's narrative of Mary Kelly is really a description of how she sunk her claws into Joseph Barnett and dragged him down into a life he had been working hard to avoid. This Mary clearly meant to only use Barnett, noting that he seemed more respectable and hardworking than many men in the East End. This was, according to Harrison, Barnett's reaction against the life he had as a child and to what he saw in his parents. Even the coroner at Mary's death inquest commented on how Barnett clearly exceeded his expectations, much in the same way that these comments are often made about Mary herself. This Mary, though, is not nearly as respectable as she appears.

She hides her prostitution from Barnett, knowing his opinion of prostitutes and likely how much his sense of self was bound up in being able to support the two of them on his own. Barnett was "obsessed with her,"[20] likely because of the façade that led others to describe her as intelligent and not of the same class as the rest, and Mary knew this. She was simply a beautiful woman who was not above using Barnett's money not just on herself and on her friends, but on clients, as well. This declaration does, however, seem rather confusing, since it brings up the question of what, exactly, she was meant to have paid for while soliciting. The couple was behind on the rent of their small room, and it was generally accepted that the man in search of a prostitute would be the one giving the coins or paying for a drink. Why would Mary have spent money on the clients who should have been paying her?

In an attempt to control Mary, or perhaps in an attempt to regain the control he thought he had once had, Barnett set about murdering prostitutes in order to scare her off the street. If she would simply give up prostitution, then the two of them would be able to sort things out and make a proper living together. Because Barnett lived in the East End and was known to be living with Mary, he would not have appeared to be a threat to the other women—and further, Mary herself is no longer a complete idiot for inviting the Ripper into her room. If Jack the Ripper had been living with her for months and still coming around to offer her money when he could, then it would make sense for her to have invited him in.

In 1998 Bob Hinton proposes a similar situation in his book *From Hell.... The Jack the Ripper Mystery* although the man intent on scaring Mary Kelly off the street and into his arms is George Hutchinson. Hutchinson came forward after the inquest into Mary's death with a description of a man he had seen go with her into her room on the night of her death—a very lengthy description that raises suspicion because of the sheer amount of detail Hutchinson is meant to have seen during a brief glimpse at night. His testimony is often questioned because he knew Mary personally and must have been exceedingly jealous of the stranger in order to have remembered such an exact description of his clothing. Due to the timing of the death inquest, Hutchinson was never publicly questioned about what he was doing lingering in Miller's Court for so long that night.

Hutchinson as the Ripper is not meant to have murdered five random prostitutes, however. Yes, Polly Nichols and Annie Chapman were chosen as victims because they were indeed prostitutes, thrown out of their doss houses because they lacked money. Since Hinton describes neither of them as being particularly attractive, perhaps Hutchinson was in luck with crossing their paths because they would not have been in high demand, especially not at such a late hour. Polly and Annie are indeed the typical alcoholic East End prostitutes, attempting to support themselves because their marriages had failed, both adhering to the well-known and well-worn narratives of the Ripper victims.

Hinton does not present Liz Stride as a Ripper victim, and thus Hutchinson cannot claim her. The fact that Liz was seen with a man for most of the night of her death, apparently simply walking and talking suggests to Hinton that Liz was not actively soliciting. After all, "[p]rostitutes do not waste time canoodling and talking to their clients,"[21] and any woman who was in desperate need of money would not spend an entire evening with one man when she could have completed multiple transactions in that time. Liz and this mystery man were discovered by Michael Kidney, a fiercely jealous and violent man, and whoever the mystery man was, his departure left a scorned Kidney alone with Liz. Hinton suggests that Liz had been at the receiving end of Kidney's domestic violence before and thus did not make more of a scene because she expected it to take its usual course. Instead, this was the last straw for Kidney, who murdered her and was able to pawn off blame on the Ripper.

Although Catherine Eddowes' friends, like Liz Stride's, argued against her having been a prostitute, Kate benefited from having a steady man who was a loyal "gentleman and obviously fond of Kate."[22] Although her marriage had failed and Kate's drinking was to blame, according to both her sister and her daughter, her relationship with John Kelly was steady and positive. Granted, the observation that Kate was the more intelligent of the pair is more of a backhanded compliment and a reflection of Kelly than of Kate, but Hinton shows the couple obviously working together, especially in the last few days of Kate's life. The fact that they did demonstrate a clear partnership as they managed to get food and lodging for themselves is evidence not only for their relationship, but for the argument that Kate did not work as a prostitute. Again, if prostitution were a common means for the couple to earn money, why would they have done everything else in their power to make some coins and not fallen back on it? Even John Kelly, gentleman that he was, would have been expected to keep his boots and wait for his girlfriend's earnings rather than pawn them and leave himself barefoot.

Therefore Hinton's Kate was not in Mitre Square on the night of her death in order to service a client. Her apparent intelligence, however, must come into question, since Kate managed to get herself released early from being held for drunkenness in order to meet and then blackmail Jack the Ripper. Her claims that she knew his identity were true, since he was a local man, and, being poor, Kate clearly thought that setting up a private meeting between the two of them in the dead of night would be the best way to earn money. Although she had bragged that she knew the Ripper and would earn the reward money, Kate had decided to meet him on her own, without telling anyone what she was up to, and thus found herself to be his next victim. Hinton's scenario helps explain why Kate's body was mutilated to such an extent, because this murder was personal. The Ripper had to kill her in order to retain his anonymity—a tactic that clearly worked, since Hinton is only accusing Hutchinson more than a century later.

It is once again Mary Kelly at the center of this narrative, and although Joe Barnett is perhaps not so honorable as John Kelly, he is not the murderer this time. Instead he is simply a "friend"[23] of hers, willing to live together and fully aware that she was working as a prostitute the entire time. This Mary Kelly does nothing to keep her profession a secret and shows herself to be more than a bit of a user. Current and past boyfriends always seem to hang around, willing to give her money. Barnett himself, although no longer living with her, joined the ranks of those who continued to give her both attention and coins.

Hinton states it bluntly: "She naturally expected the world to revolve around her, and probably because of this—it did!"[24] With her confidence, youth, and apparent looks, she never seemed to lack for anything. He adds that she was described as being stout and thus, along with having money for drink and shelter, she also presumably didn't lack for food. Mary Kelly was a prostitute, but she was not necessarily desperate for clients, since she had a string of men ready to jump at her slightest need. One of these men, at least in the beginning, was George Hutchinson. He is most often known as the man who dallied in Miller's Court and gave a detailed description of the last man seen going inside number 13 with Mary Kelly, but Hinton agrees that this description is entirely fabricated. Mary Kelly the user made the mistake of attempting to capture the attention of George Hutchinson, the obsessive.

Hutchinson became a stalker, brutally murdering any who reminded him of the object of his obsession. Because of the disparity between the appearances and ages of Mary Kelly and the other women, Hinton rushes to explain that this similarly need not be entirely physical. Because Hutchinson was obsessed with—and continually rejected by—a prostitute, he turned his anger on prostitutes. Mary Kelly's habit of using men and stringing them along backfired when she chose to use the wrong man. On November 9, 1888, Hutchinson went to Mary's room and woke her in one last attempt to convince her to run away with him. This was when Hutchinson was finally confronted with the fact that the woman he had thought he could rescue "was a foul mouth, drunken whore, lying in fifth"[25] and rejecting him one final time.

For the second time in his narrative, Hinton invites the reader into the mind of the Ripper himself. The first time was after Polly's murder when he suggested readers place them in the murderer's position when he was in need of escape, perhaps only moments from being caught. In the case of Mary Kelly, Hinton asks readers to imagine his emotions around the time of the murder, perhaps even to justify his reaction. Hutchinson may have been obsessed, but Mary Kelly was the one who led him on. "Put yourself in Hutchinson's shoes,"[26] Hinton urges, because apparently readers need not feel the same obsession to understand his reaction. It is this realization that Mary Kelly is indeed what she has been all along and has never pretended not to be, not even to Barnett: a prostitute. Hutchinson has traveled a long distance and has been standing around in the rain in order to see Mary Kelly, but has been rejected because he spent his last coins to make this journey and has none left to give her. It is in this rejection and this realization that Hinton asks his readers to imagine themselves in his position, asking them to empathize with the killer in his final and most vicious act.

This identification with Hutchinson is reflected as well when Hinton suggests that any effort that has been put into researching the victims themselves has been a complete waste of time: "For example, what is the point in establishing the family tree of the victims? What possible use is it to know where they were born or what school they went to?"[27] What Hinton really means is, how would this information at all help to inform the identity of the Ripper? Indeed the history and biography of these women is generally thought to have little or nothing to do with the Ripper, since the murders are thought to have been committed by a stranger and thus the Ripper would not be found in their past. Clearly, since the reader is meant to empathize with the killer, there is no room left for empathy of the victim—especially when she is a user who brought her own murder and mutilation on herself.

By suggesting that the Ripper killed multiple women because of his obsession with Mary Kelly, both Paul Harrison and Bob Hinton attempt to shift the blame from a man to a woman. If Barnett and Hutchinson had never encountered Mary Kelly, then they presumably would never have gone on to murder a number of women, ending with the subject of their obsession. If Mary Kelly had been a better woman—either rejecting prostitution in favor of living on Barnett's earnings or responding in kind to Hutchinson's attentions even when he had no money to offer her—then her own death could have been averted. Barnett is meant to have killed the other women in an attempt to scare Mary Kelly off the street, so perhaps she should have given in to that fear or, at least, been more suspicious of Barnett and his own intentions. Hutchinson's stalking was spurred on by moments of attention, most—if not all—of which revolved around money, and thus if Mary Kelly had been less obsessed with pennies and had looked past her pocketbook to the man in front of her, then perhaps Hutchinson would not have had to murder, after all. Thus the deaths of these women lie not on the man who slit their throats, but the woman who drove him to it.

A Pair of Jacks

Mary Kelly has not simply been accused of driving the men in her life to murder, but also factors into being the cause of further narratives of two men acting as a team to commit the murders. Although neither of the two men, each presumably a homosexual, is personally affected by Mary's secret, they end up working together in order enact the murders. In John Wilding's 1993 book *Jack the Ripper: Revealed*, the murders are instigated when Mary Kelly visits lawyer Montague John Druitt in order to confess that she has become pregnant by the Prince of Wales and wishes to receive compensation for this. Druitt turns to J. K. Stephen for help, since he and Stephen are both set to hold positions of power once the Prince of Wales's son, Eddy, takes the throne, and the two men embark on a series of murders so that, when it comes time to murder a substitute woman in Mary's bedroom, her own death will go unnoticed.

Initially, however, they were not acting to preserve Mary's life—and the secret of the paternity of her child—but to eliminate it. Mary Nichols' death appears to have been something of an accident. Wilding presents her as an alcoholic who would give or do anything in order to have a drink—indeed, "the power of mother-love was easily defeated by the might of alcohol,"[28] driving Mary away from both her marriage and her children. Even an attempt to make a respectable living as a maid was ruined by her thirst for alcohol. Wilding expresses great surprise—or perhaps scorn—at this, since he suspects that any woman who had been living on the street or in workhouses would have made a better attempt to keep that position. This is a Mary Nichols who would accept any offering that could be converted into drink.

On the night of Mary Nichols' murder, Wilding suggests that Mary Kelly was at home in her rented room and became aware of someone lurking outside. Throwing on a hat and a shawl, Mary Kelly retreated to a public house where she came across Mary Nichols, presumably hatless. Showing off her "cool, calculating nature"[29] and assuming that whoever had been following her had been tracking her bonnet instead of her face, Mary Kelly passed the bonnet off to Mary Nichols, who clearly accepted solely so she could pawn it for drink money as soon as the shops opened. The men who had intended to follow and murder Mary Kelly recognized the bonnet and found their chance to murder the wearer before dawn. Thus Mary Kelly is responsible for Mary Nichols' death, and Wilding suggests she must have been shaken by the news—assuming she read the stories and recognized the woman, or perhaps the bonnet. Although perhaps accidental murder might be forgivable, since Mary Kelly might have merely wished for the stranger to follow Mary Nichols and allow her to slip away. After all, Mary Nichols was nothing but an old drunk.

Annie Chapman, on the other hand, is not presented as an alcoholic, nor a professional prostitute. Whereas Mary Nichols might have been willing to do anything for money for a drink, Annie resorted to prostitution only when her other attempts at earning money failed. She was a sick woman who still tried her best to earn a living despite the lack of a man to support her, although Wilding does also disparage her looks. Annie was "not an alluring woman"[30] and thus would not have likely been mistaken for Mary Kelly, even if she had put on Mary's bonnet. Mary's hand in Annie's death, however, is still present.

After the murder of Mary Nichols, Wilding posits, Mary Kelly returned to Druitt in order to express her fears and concerns, unaware that he himself had been one of the men after her that night. In the course of their conversation she told Druitt that she had given proof of her secret to a friend, and must have named Annie Chapman in the process. This, Wilding explains, was the reason Annie's belongings were spread out around her body: the killer was looking for that evidence. In this instance, Mary Kelly foolishly named her friend and thus condemned her to death.

Unlike the first two murders, Mary appears to have had no hand in the death of Liz Stride. Wilding even makes sure that Liz is painted as being different from her predecessors: she was in better health, contributing to the fact that she was better-looking, and also better educated. He attributes her emigration from Sweden to London, as well as her on and off relationship with Michael Kidney, to wanderlust, and deems her a free spirit, albeit a heavy drinker. Liz's death came about because she recognized one of the killers, explaining why her murder was rushed and in a more public place. The killers themselves couldn't linger, however, since they had a standing appointment to meet Catharine Eddowes.

This Catharine is never a Kate, and she never married. Her relationship with Thomas Conway was perhaps ill-advised purely because of their age difference, and Wilding dismisses any claim that Conway might have beat her, since "Catharine, a much younger person with a fiery temper, would surely have been able to defend herself."[31] It is difficult to say whether Wilding means to dismiss the possibility of domestic abuse due to her age and personality, or whether she should have been physically and mentally strong enough to stand up for herself had it happened. His repetition of the age difference makes it seem like he wants readers to find it laughable that a man would have been able to beat a much younger woman. It is not clear whether Catharine should have pulled herself together and left him if these beatings actually occurred, but she certainly should have been able to weather or even prevent them.

Catharine is still interested in getting money any way she can, although Wilding insists that Conway had initially enrolled in the army under an assumed name and thus retrieved his pension under that name. While other authors have had Conway make the change specifically in order to prevent Catharine from attempting to get that money, Wilding has him using the assumed name before the pair ever met. Instead of having Catharine look for her daughter on her final day in order to scrounge more money, however, Wilding puts Catharine with Mary Kelly. This Catharine is not the persistent scrounger her entire family works so hard to avoid.

Mary Kelly, pregnant and claiming the father as the Prince of Wales, had by now become the subject not of assassination, but protection. It would seem that Queen Victoria herself learned of her pregnancy and had decided that any descendant of her beloved Albert should be protected. This plan involved Mary Kelly "being destroyed then reborn as a new woman,"[32] a prospect that Wilding has Mary Kelly embracing completely. Her life in 1888 was at a low point, since she had fallen from a middle-class background and had been unable to reclaim that position through her own means. Being intelligent, educated, and mannered—at least in comparison to the other East End prostitutes—allowed her a wider range of clients, including the future king. The fact that she was carrying his child, or at least a child who could be claimed to have been his, would have looked like the key to her future and given her a special feeling of place. After the initial shock of causing the murders of Polly and Annie, the protection from Queen Victoria herself would have further elevated Mary Kelly's sense of importance. Catharine's death shows just how much stock she put in her promised future.

During her final afternoon, in which Catharine Eddowes managed to get quite drunk despite having been penniless earlier in the day, she was with Mary Kelly. In order to complete the plan that put Mary Kelly's death as just another in a string of murders, there needed to be another murder, and Mary Kelly had selected the victim. Even though she had chosen one of her friends to be the next to die, Wilding suggests that Catharine's steady drinking was perhaps a sort of apology and that Mary Kelly hoped her friend would be drunk enough to be willing to meet Druitt and Stephen, but not so sober that she would be aware of what happened. Unfortunately the men did not manage to find Catharine while she was so impaired and thus Mary Kelly waited around for her friend to be released from her cell, no longer drunk and incapable but mostly sober and willing to go along to service a good-looking pair of men. If Mary Kelly vouched for them, then Catharine would have trusted her, even at the height of the murders.

Catharine Eddowes was not the only friend Mary Kelly offered up as a sacrifice in order to be born into her new life, although the other woman's name is not known. Once she had helped Druitt and Stephen secure one victim, there was no backing out. Even if the protection and life offered to her had not been enough, the fact of Mary Kelly's guilt would have made her continue. Wilding's Mary is, of course, cool and calculating, and thus she does not hesitate. In order to assume her new life as the mother of a royal child, even if the child's paternity was not publicly acknowledged, East End prostitute Mary Kelly had to die. Once again, Mary Kelly chose the woman to be murdered.

In order to ensure that the body found in Miller's Court would not be identified as being someone other than Mary Kelly, the horrific mutilations were necessary, especially of the woman's face. Being so different from the other women of the East End would have worked against Mary Kelly, since she would have had to find someone who was also young and of the same build. Once her friend was asleep in her bed as simply the latest woman to share the small room with her, Mary Kelly left to wait out the murder.

As cold and calculating as Wilding shows Mary Kelly to be, he suggests that she is not entirely immune to thoughts of what was happening behind her closed door. Although Druitt and Stephen take no issue with seeing these women as objects, Mary Kelly suffers a fit of conscience on the night of her supposed murder and, instead of waiting for the men, spends her time getting drunk. The various reported sightings of Mary Kelly after the coroner's declared time of death are thus the real Mary Kelly, miserable after a night of drinking, before Druitt and Stephen were able to track her down again and spirit her away to her new life. Even if there was a rumor that Mary Kelly was living in luxury with a child, it would be easily put to rest by recalling the gruesome scene discovered November 9. This sequence of murders meant that Mary Kelly no longer existed and could give birth to a royal child in private.

While the duo of Montague John Druitt and J. K. Stephen were given a solid, if slightly convoluted, narrative reason for the murders, the pair of J. K. Stephen and Prince Eddy does not have such a clear cut explanation in David Abrahamsen's 1992 book *Murder & Madness: The Secret Life of Jack the Ripper*. While Wilding's pair of Druitt and Stephen happened to be accused of homosexuality individually, Abrahamsen's couple is indeed a romantically linked pair with a relationship established before the start of the murders. Druitt and Stephen were not boyfriends, but Stephen and Eddy were indeed involved on many levels. Druitt and Stephen acted in order to preserve the reputation of their crown prince, and thus their own futures with the crown prince's son, while Stephen and Eddy came to commit the murders together out of a deep-seated misogyny. In Abrahamsen's narrative, Marie Kelly is just another victim, a pawn "strategically moved about on [the killer's] deadly chessboard—before, during, and after the attacks."[33] For once there is nothing special about her.

Abrahamsen writes from the position of a forensic psychiatrist who offered his opinion on the sanity of David Berkowitz, the self-styled Son of Sam, and thus his insights reflect this background. For instance, he declares that "[t]he eternal wish of every woman from childhood onward is to be taken care of by someone who loves her,"[34] a desire that went unfulfilled in the case of many of the women under discussion. Even when they attempted marriage—and even when Abrahamsen refers to them solely by last name, which is in many cases their married names—their husbands could not provide them with the support they sought.

Mary Ann Nichols, for example, was denied this ultimate satisfaction because of her drinking. Her marriage had ended because of it, and her possible opportunity of employment—being taken care of by a man, at least, in the form of a wage, if not given the desired love—also ended because of her alcoholism. The defining characteristic of Nichols, then, is her love of drink. It explains why she was on the street, not just on the night of her murder but the life that had led her there in the first place, ruining every chance she was given to better herself and her position. Nichols not only lacks funds for a bed but a dependable man to provide that money and security that all women everywhere, not just in the East End in Victorian England, desire.

Annie Chapman fares little better, although Chapman at least received an allowance from her husband after they separated because of their drinking. Chapman is lumped in the same boat as Nichols, since presumably their histories aligned quite closely, and Abrahamsen's killer duo would not have cared why they ended up on the street, anyway, so long as the women made themselves available for murder. What Abrahamsen does ponder, however, is Chapman's age: "she was the oldest of the victims, yet her body held attraction for this murderer."[35] Despite her age and presumably her looks, Abrahamsen's Ripper—a homosexual couple, no less—was in some way attracted to her body. It is perhaps fitting that only Chapman's body is of interest, both for the killers and for the author, since it is her body that has caught the attention of researches for more than a century. The living Chapman, with an alcoholic life that paralleled Nichols,' is of no consequence.

Even with this dismissal, however, Chapman fares better than Elizabeth Stride. Stride is given an age, a nationality, and her nickname before she is merely an interesting corpse.

Catherine Eddowes at least has a bit of an interesting past, involving both her "friend"[36] John Kelly and a husband who only admitted his relationship to her two weeks after her death. Although Chapman's husband was already dead at the time of her own death, neither Nichols' nor Stride's husband earns himself such a mention. Presumably the fortnight between the identification of Eddowes' body and her husband's appearance is a unique and interesting timeline of events, especially since the man had gone so far as to change his name in order to avoid her. It is perhaps a darker mark against her than the stain of alcoholism.

Abrahamsen has Eddowes hop-picking with Kelly, although the story of new boots is a bit muddled. In this version Kelly buys Eddowes some boots out of his own earnings, and it is these boots—not his—that are pawned. Despite the fact that she was presumably picking hops alongside of Kelly, it is his money explicitly that is used to buy her some boots. Whatever money she earned goes missing before they return to London, since those boots have to be pawned—although a list of the clothes Eddowes was wearing when her body was discovered includes a pair of men's boots. The provenance of these boots has nothing to do with the killer, however, so it is not discussed. It is left to the reader to assume that Eddowes' money has gone to drink instead of clothing or shelter.

Marie Jeanette Kelly, on the other hand, of course had her own room, and Abrahamsen is reluctant to tar her with the brush of alcoholism. He goes so far to declare that, "[i]f a caste structure existed among prostitutes, she may have been slotted in a higher status than her more degraded associates."[37] Abrahamsen awards Kelly a sense of self-respect and self-care above and beyond the previous women. Perhaps it is because she is younger and thus less ravaged by East End life, or perhaps her beauty was owed in part to her perception of herself. Although her past is the same mystery filtered through Joseph Barnett—who is not relegated to the same "friend" status as John Kelly—the present Kelly was young, beautiful, and self-possessed until she met the Ripper and his knife.

Because he is indeed proposing that the Ripper was in fact a pair of men, Abrahamsen can relieve Kelly of the idiocy of taking a strange man back to her room in the middle of terror over the Ripper. He suggests that seeing two men, especially since the men in question would have been well-dressed, would have alleviated her fear, since the newspapers accused a lone man of wielding a knife. Indeed, even a lone well-dressed young man would have been more than enough to appeal to the previous victims. Since these women are older, Abrahamsen has them gratefully accepting the attentions of his Ripper, since there are women younger and prettier to be had. He even has the Ripper's offer of payment being more than the going rate, and the women happily anticipate what they might do with the money while unknowingly entering the final moments of their lives. They are either too greedy or too desperate to question why such a man might be in the East End, and why he might be willing to pay more than the usually accepted amount. Abrahamsen does not credit them with much of a sense of self-preservation, especially after the murders began.

In fact, he takes things to the opposite end of the scale: "Some of them harbored an unconscious attraction to the murderer who had been bold enough to kill some of their sisters and then disappear."[38] Although Abrahamsen acknowledges that many prostitutes had to continue to walk the streets at night in spite of the danger in order to provide for themselves, he still identifies a group of women as feeling an attraction to the killer. He does not make it clear whether any of the named women belonged to this group, although presumably his background in psychiatry led him to determine that such women existed. Were this prostitutes attracted to the Ripper in the same way so many authors have been, drawn to the mystery of his identity and fascinated by the fact that he was not caught? Or were they attracted to the idea of their own deaths, quicker—and likely messier—than what could usually be expected? Abrahamsen does not explain this psychiatric mystery, merely presenting it as a fact before moving on.

The final lines of Abrahamsen's book are enough to give pause. He declares that "Prince Eddy and J. K. Stephen were victims but so were those who raised them. In a significant way we are all victims of victims."[39] Indeed Abrahamsen posits that his duo murdered because the way their mothers had treated them led to violent feelings of misogyny, making them victims of their mothers and those who allowed that relationship to develop by removing themselves from the equation—their fathers, for example. The young men are victims of their toxic relationships, and their parents become victims by having birthed and raised serial killers, but what of the women most commonly referred to as victims? Are Nichols, Chapman, Stride, Eddowes, and Kelly included in Abrahamsen's "victims of victims" comment with the rest of us? If the statement was meant to include us all, then certainly they would be included and not held separate. Just as Marie Jeanette Kelly does not occupy a special place in this narrative of the murders, so it would seem that the murdered women do not hold a special place as victims, either.

Seeking Out the Positive

Alongside the books offering something new in the way of authors or suspect types, the 1990s of course presented readers with more examples of books accusing a lone male of being Jack the Ripper. The names offered up to replace the pseudonym ranged between previously mentioned men backed up by new evidence to newly named men suggested by new evidence. Just as in previous decades, these authors also run the gamut as far as how much time and space they wished to devote to the victims.

William Beadle's 1995 book *Jack the Ripper: Anatomy of a Myth* resurrects William Henry Bury as a suspect but also closes with the admonition "Spare no thoughts for him; only for those who did not deserve to die—his victims."[40] The Scottish Bury holds the dubious honor of having been the last person hanged in Dundee, Scotland after having been convicted of murdering his wife. In this case "those who did not deserve to die" encompass not only the women murdered by Jack the Ripper, but Ellen Bury, as well.

From the beginning Beadle takes a sympathetic approach to the women murdered in the East End, declaring that the women "were already victims, used and outcast, doomed to wander blind alleys until they died."[41] He recognizes that prostitution was not a chosen occupation but the last recourse of the desperate, acknowledging that the women in question could not hope to find better positions for themselves. Once women became prostitutes, they were trapped in a cycle of misery either ignored or overlooked by the better off. Beadle does not condemn these women for not being able to raise themselves out of such a position.

His empathy toward the murdered women begins with his descriptions of Polly Nichols. First Beadle wishes to correct the modern conception that Polly was a hag and old before her time, bringing up contemporary reports that she looked at least ten years younger than her given age.

Although yes, Polly was a known alcoholic, he does not place the breakup of her marriage solely on her shoulders. Indeed, Beadle declares the allowance William Nichols gave his wife to be "niggardly,"[42] further presenting him in a negative light when he points out that Polly's family gave testimony that he was lacking as a husband. Between her failed marriage, the breakup of her following long-term relationship with a blacksmith, the dismissal from a short-lived maid's position, and her alcoholism, Beadle presents an unhappy Polly who never quite managed to settle into an expected position. The fact that her husband was less than a perfect specimen did not help. We are left with a Polly whose life might have been wasted, true, but a Polly who endured her share of adversity in the process.

Annie Chapman is likewise defended. Beadle notes that writers often present her as "a drunken sot who slept with other men"[43] before pointing out that there is no evidence to support this. Whereas her estranged husband died of cirrhosis of the liver, clearly from his own drinking habits, Beadle argues that Annie was not an alcoholic. She did enjoy alcohol, yes, but limited it to one day a week, and was likely not drunk on her last night as many have argued. Since Annie was sick and had spent her last week in the infirmary, Beadle makes it clear that it was illness and not alcohol that hampered her.

This Annie is almost a pathetic figure, one who huddles close to the lodging house stove because her dying body was in need of the warmth. She has been sick and unable to earn money, either through prostitution or more respectable means, and it is in this condition that she is tossed out onto the street. Already cold, already dying, with a miserable past behind her, Annie was without the pennies for a bed and in no condition to defend herself against a murderer. She may have even gone with him eagerly, being desperate for money so she could pay for a place to rest.

Elizabeth Stride and Catherine Eddowes share a chapter entitled "The Swedish Femme Fatale & The Little Sparrow."[44] Liz's epithet is confusing, since it is difficult to see how she was dangerous to the men around her. Despite the chapter title Beadle once again comes to her defense, arguing that "[s]he in particular suffered at the hands of myth makers,"[45] being portrayed as both ugly and violent. Beadle's Liz is instead a romantic dreamer who wanted more than a Swedish farming village could offer her. Instead of making her a femme fatale this actually turned her into a target, easily used by men and just as easily abandoned. Instead of the user, Liz is presented as the used, unhappy in her relationship with Michael Kidney and with her life in general. Poor Liz was a victim of her own longings and a time period that would not let women fulfill them long before she was murdered.

Moving on in his defense of the murdered women Beadle comes to Catherine Eddowes, whom he insists on calling Cathy. He dismisses claims of alcoholism and ugliness, arguing that Cathy actually looked younger than her real age despite her hardships and her life on the streets. Although he does not recommend that his readers seek it out, Beadle's personal interpretation of Cathy's mortuary photograph leads him to conclude that she was pleasant and likable. The framing of this assessment is just that: based on his viewing of a photograph of Cathy after her death and not on testimony from those who knew her in life. It is enough for Beadle to continue arguing against any negative representation of Cathy, including the reports that her daughter knew her to be a scrounger. It seems that Beadle has made up his mind to defend the women entirely, perhaps beyond the point of realism and certainly against contemporary reports as well as against narratives that have been formed in the decades since.

Despite the fact that she was locked up for being drunk and incapable on the last night of her life, Beadle argues both that Cathy was not an alcoholic and that she did not pay for those drinks through prostitution. The support for the first comes through the coroner's assessment of her liver, which did not suggest a chronic drink problem, and the second rests on the lengths Cathy and her boyfriend John Kelly went to in order to earn money during their last few days together. The Little Sparrow is "a tiny, inoffensive woman"[46] as undeserving of such a violent death as she is of the various negative tales that have circulated in the intervening years. Perhaps because of his assessment of her character through her morgue photograph, Beadle goes so far as to suggest that Cathy would have been amused by the expense and the expanse of her funeral. It was, after all, the first indication that her death meant more to the outside world than her life, and the beginning of a form of immortality, although the lack of support from contemporary interviews brings the thought of amusement into question. After all, as he later parenthetically declares, "(there is nothing frivolous about the murder of a young woman),"[47] and it seems the same would apply to her funeral. Amusement seems too frivolous a reaction for Cathy to have to her own death.

Mary Jane Kelly, presented with a list of nicknames, seems comparable to Beadle's Liz. She is described as "a rather charismatic young woman— possibly intelligent and talented—who needed more from life than the East End ... had to offer."[48] Mary's past is likewise cloaked in mystery and lacking in detail, especially since what little detail is known cannot be corroborated. Beadle suggests she is as mysterious as the ripper—a title he refrains from capitalizing—and has not been given the credit she deserved. When Mary invited fellow prostitutes to share the small room with her and Joseph Barnett, it was done knowing that he would become annoyed and move out. Instead of charity, it was in fact manipulation in a way that would allow her to continue to take advantage of Barnett if she needed to. By making the situation seem like Barnett had made the decision himself, she was able to continue to use her looks and her intelligence to get what she wanted, the way she continued to use a past boyfriend, Joe Flemming.

Beadle summarizes the position of the murdered women by pointing out the failings of Society that led to their demise. Because these women were prostitutes, they almost assisted the ripper by going alone with him to secluded places, although Beadle does pull back enough to point out that Society—capitalized even when ripper is not—was more than willing to look the other way both during these transactions and during the women's deaths. Yet he remains determined to find the good in the story, ending his discussion of Mary's death by claiming that her legacy is both "an epitaph of sorts and in a way her victory over the man who so fouly slew her."[49] Cathy can feel amusement at the scope of her funeral while Mary can feel victorious because her story has lived on—always tied to the ripper name, of course, but Beadle feels this is a victory nevertheless. It seems that his desire to present these women in a positive light extends past their living selves and includes the circumstances of their deaths.

The Search for Balance

Although authors like William Beadle seem intent on correcting many misconceptions about the murdered women and presenting them in a much more positive light, so many others have fairly dismissed them as nothing more than East End whores. It is much more likely that their true character falls somewhere between the two extremes and that they were neither saints nor entirely despicable. Two authors of the 1990s, Philip Sugden and James Tully, have made it clear that their books were meant to focus just as much on the victims as on their killer, and each has devoted more space on the page to the victims than many.

Sugden's *The Complete History of Jack the Ripper*, first published in 1994, sets out to present a simple history of the murders without an agenda to prove or disprove any specific suspect. His book is often praised for being both comprehensive and unbiased. In his descriptions of the lives of

the murdered women he at times offers contradictions based on given testimony in a way that seeks to find the middle path of a true personality,
and not the saint many people seem to become after death, or the dismissal
so frequently offered to prostitutes.

Polly Nichols, for example, is "frequently drunk"[50] throughout her life.
Her alcoholism is in fact a recurring theme, from the dissolution of her
marriage to her condition on her final night. Granted, Sugden does present
the rumors that Nichols cheated on his wife before they parted, although
the fact that all but their oldest child went with their father after the split
suggests that this was not the only issue in that marriage. Sugden offers
no critique of the allowance Nichols paid Polly, and explains that this
allowance stopped when Nichols learned she was living with another man.
It seems understandable both that Polly might live with another man, considering the time period, and that her former husband would not wish to
keep supporting her if she had another man occupying that place. All the
same, and even though her drinking cost Polly her relationship with her
father as well as her marriage and her children, she managed to "inspire
affection"[51] in those who encountered her in the East End. This might have
been because they were interviewed about her after her death, or it might
have been the honest assessment from a population that held different
expectations of its women. After all, even her husband forgave her after
her death, despite all that he insisted she had put him through in life.

Sugden's assessment of Annie leans more toward the positive, or at
least toward the sympathetic, considering the run of her life: a late marriage,
one child a cripple and one dead of meningitis, the failure of that marriage,
and the loss of both her allowance and her subsequent steady relationship
when her husband died. There is certainly room for sympathy when the
sieve-maker abandoned her, considering he only seemed to form that
attachment because of her allowance, leaving Annie completely alone and
on the street. On the other hand, alcoholism is again a factor. Between
some friends saying they often saw her drunk and others saying she confined her drinking to Saturdays—presumably her best market days—the
actual extent of Annie's alcoholism is up for question, although Sugden
mentions twice that Annie's earnings must have been spent on alcohol
instead of food or shelter. Indeed, this Annie is "a pathetic little woman in
the last extremities of want,"[52] both poor and in poor health when she is
turned out of her lodging house for the last time. She is even industrious
enough, at least when sober, to have her position of prostitute questioned,
since she likely only turned to selling herself as a last report—again, likely
for alcohol. Annie's possible good traits are held in foil against the likely

negative aspects, although neither can be fully proven. Thus the reader is left with possibilities that fall on both sides and might even exist in tandem.

Liz is even more of a question than Annie because of her penchant for telling stories about her life. Since she was born and raised in Sweden, there is no one local who would be able to support or refute her claims—all her friends had were these stories. Sugden dispels the narrative of the *Princess Alice* since there is no support, although he also admits that little was known of her marriage to John Stride. Again there is conflicting information regarding how much Liz drank, with one argument being that her friends recalled her as good-natured and sober, while she made multiple appearances at court for being drunk and disorderly. Her boyfriend Michael Kidney seems to agree more with the latter, since he declares that drinking was the reason for the gaps in their relationship. All the same, those gaps add up to a handful of months out of a total of three years, and thus her drinking seems not to have been constant. Again Sugden points out that one of the Ripper's victims may not have been working steadily as a prostitute—unless Liz needed the money to spend on alcohol, "Long Liz may have only been an occasional prostitute."[53] Again, the uncertainty is there for readers to assess and draw their own conclusions.

Kate Eddowes seems to master the dichotomy of opposing tales. Although her sister says her common-law marriage to Tom Conway failed because he beat her when he was drunk, their daughter claimed that Conway was a teetotaler and Kate the drinker. Kate nursed that same daughter through her final confinement, showing a degree of care, but the daughter moved without leaving a forwarding address since her mother continually asked for money that she either did not have or did not want to give. During the final days of her life Kate selflessly negotiated limited funds with her long-term boyfriend John Kelly, except she somehow managed to find enough money to get drunk with this money that was not shared. Both John Kelly and Kate's sister insist that Kate was not a prostitute, but there is the question of how she was able to find the money to get drunk and what she might have been doing in Mitre Square so late at night. There are simply too many questions to make too firm a statement about the lives of any of the victims, although the broad strokes seem to come through.

Mary Jane Kelly, like Liz, had moved to London and thus was able to tell her own tales about her past. There seems to be little corroboration about the details Mary Jane told her boyfriend, Joe Barnett, and thus her past—from her stint in a West End brothels to a trip with a gentleman to France—remains questionable. Her position as a prostitute, however, seems certain, unlike the previous women. Mary Jane was also apparently fond of drink, having been heard singing drunkenly in her room on her final night alive, although friends reported that she was quite kind when she was sober. This Mary Jane is not nearly such a standout as others, since she does not seem to be so highly intelligent or as upper class as other authors have presented. Being far from home but with few close friends, her story is filtered through Joe Barnett, who seems to be the only one to know it. Mary Jane largely kept to herself in life, and thus became an enigma in death.

James Tully's 1997 book *The Real Jack the Ripper: The Secret of Prisoner 1167* likewise sets out to uncover the real murdered women. In his introduction he declares, "I have paid especial attention to the lives of the poor women who were slaughtered so brutally—to give them the dignity they deserve. They were not merely victims; they were *people* like you and me,"[54] and, as people must have both faults and charms. For Tully these women had ended up on the street in the East End because of circumstances beyond their control, and thus were faced with making the best of the bad situation that was the only one offered to them.

Polly was a drunk who had made the mistake of marrying a "pompous … humbug"[55] of a man who could barely be bothered to care about the mother of his children during their marriage, much less after. Tully has her drinking quite heavily during her marriage and even leaving the home a few times, but later managing to keep her alcoholism under some semblance of control during her relationship with the blacksmith, Drew. Perhaps being involved with a man who was less of a humbug alleviated the need for drinking, although it never left her entirely. Every attempt that Polly made—or hoped to make—at a new or better life was foiled by her love of alcohol, which Tully presents as being an essential part of her personality. It is true that this Polly at least wanted to change, but she lacked the means or perhaps the self control to manage it.

Tully's Annie, on the other hand, confines her drinking to Saturdays even if she might manage to live her life out of direct purview of her family members. Considering the fact that Annie's parents were not married when she was born, it might be expected that they would be more understanding of her situation, but that seems not to factor into things. Annie married late, possibly because of the unattractive features Tully describes, and the marriage dissolves for reasons Tully doubts. He says it was claimed that Annie lost her husband his job through her dishonesty, but there seems to be no proof or even a specific accusation. Alone and on the street, it seems perfectly understandable that she might start drinking, and when her various attempts at earning money failed her and she was in need of another drink, she would turn to prostitution. It is all a downward spiral that illustrates the limits imposed on women's lives. Perhaps the best that can be said for the less than pretty, alcoholic Annie is that she seems to have made the most of a bad situation, even if she might have caused herself to end up there in the first place.

Elizabeth Stride, who spelled her name as Elisabeth before coming to London and changing it to be more British, apparently suffered from the same pressures of family as Annie did. After a number of setbacks, a young Elizabeth chose to come to London because she felt her family would not help her, putting her even further out of their reach than Annie from her family. Part of that situation involved having already become a prostitute, and although Tully makes sure to mention that she was attractive—and certainly more attractive than Annie—it seems that the profession was not lucrative enough for her. Considering the age difference between Elizabeth and John Stride, Tully suspects that their marriage was a "business arrangement"[56] or maybe based on issues of citizenship. Perhaps the fact that this union lasted less than a decade helps support Tully's argument that it was something other than a love match. Due to issues surrounding the identification of her body, Tully even suggests that enterprising Liz lived a double life beginning around 1882. If her marriage was in fact a business arrangement, then this double life may have been, as well, another example of how shrewd Liz might have been when it came to providing for herself. If she managed to pretend to be another woman, that allowed her the benefit of preying on the sympathies of her "sister" as well as relying on her boyfriend or prostitution for monetary support. Granted, Tully later returns to the question of Liz's murder and declares that she must have been killed by "her lover, and probably pimp, Michael Kidney,"[57] whose domineering attitude toward Liz makes it sound as though she were not much in control of her life at the end.

While any indication that Liz was intelligent or independent is roundabout, Kate Conway is outwardly declared as intelligent, as demonstrated by the fact that she and her common-law husband wrote and sold chapbooks for a living. Her childhood was marred by the early deaths of her parents and she had ended up running away with Conway when she was quite young, thus losing the support of her family, much like Liz Stride. Despite the many years and children with Conway, the couple eventually parted, and Kate soon took up with John Kelly. Although not as intelligent as Conway, Kelly proved to be kind to her and the couple seemed to have a good relationship. Perhaps this had something to do with the question of intelligence—although scrounging and drinking are usually used to explain Kate's separation from Conway, there is the question of whether perceptions of intelligence may have come into play and whether she might have been too "uppity" for his liking. Lest anyone perceive an overly positive representation of Kate, however, Tully points out that, in her final days with Kelly, Kelly pawned the boots off his feet in order to get the money because she "was loath to pawn her new jacket,"[58] even though the jacket would likely have earned them more than the boots. Kelly's gesture has often been seen as incredibly selfless and of his own free will, although a Kate who would leave him barefoot on the pavement while she went to pawn his boots, wearing her new jacket, seems cold. It is, however, an argument in favor of Kate not being a prostitute, since Kelly would likely have sent her off to work rather than lose his boots.

Once again an author runs into the problem of having little confirmable information about Mary Jane Kelly, including any reliable description of her looks. Tully does consider that, since one of her nicknames was Black Mary, it was "more likely to have been in reference to her temperament"[59] than to her looks, considering how many variants indicated her hair was light or red. It is rare to have this sort of negative perspective of Mary, who again might be better-looking than the other women, but this might only be due to her youth and the fact that she had not been living in the East End as long. She was also meant to have had an easier life before she turned up in the East End, though the speed at which this change was affected is again puzzling, as is much about Mary. Perhaps her redeeming feature comes in the fact that, whatever lies and fancies she told about her past, she never pretended that she was currently anything but a prostitute. Tully points out that hers is the only death certificate to list it as her occupation and takes it as a statement that Mary Jane made of herself, and not an outwardly imposed concession to the facts.

At this point in time, more than a century after the murders, it seems unlikely that any new concrete information will surface about the murdered women. Sugden and Tully, however, make full use of the information available, from declarations confirmed by outside sources to first person testimony in newspapers and inquest reports. It has indeed become fashionable for authors, like Beadle, to flat-out reject past conceptions about these women, with or without the sources to support this new claim, but Sugden and Tully have chosen to walk a more middle line, acknowledging both positive and negative arguments of the women's lives. This is, perhaps, a difficult position to maintain, and such focus on the victims' lives is wildly unpopular, as can be seen by the following books that have little to say about the women.

Of Little Interest

In stark contrast with authors such as Beadle, Sugden, and Tully, other authors who tackled the Ripper narrative in the 1990s do not set out to direct as much attention to these women as their murderer. Many of these books follow the already established pattern of having little to say about the living women beyond perhaps their names, ages, and dates of death. If any aspect of their identities or possessions might point to the killer, such as the question of Annie's rings, then those might be mentioned. Otherwise there is little sense in reviewing how each of these authors presented all five women and our time will be better spent seeking out any moments that raise above the expected.

In 1994 Melvin Harris wrote *The True Face of Jack the Ripper*, accusing Roslyn D'Onston of being the murderer. He displays perhaps the minimum amount of information about the victims necessary to telling the Ripper narrative, grouping them together in terms such as "tragic, lost creatures"[60] deserving of pity to common terms such as prostitutes and drabs. Whatever pity these women earn it is in their role as corpses, bodies, and murder victims or—on one page, when Harris refers back to the murders—as ordinal numbers. Instead of Polly, Annie, and Elizabeth, they become the first, second, and third victims. Catherine is referred to as "the Mitre Square murder,"[61] giving the location of her death instead of the order, and only Mary Kelly is referred to by name. While the location and number of victims are of importance to a murderer invested in black magic, the biographies of the women killed there are not.

Paul H. Feldman's 1998 book *Jack the Ripper: The Final Chapter* shows support for the theory that James Maybrick was the Ripper and likewise gives little information about the murdered women. Mary Kelly stands out from the rest as being "a little different, a little special,"[62] and worthy of more information than the other four women. Mary Ann Nichols has a name; Annie Chapman's rings are mentioned; Long Liz's nickname is declared; the spelling of Catharine Eddowes' first name is discussed, and John Kelly deserves recognition; but Mary Kelly's story of her own past is worthy of a more lengthy discussion. Feldman is unable to track down any record of her marriage and suggests that Mary first became a prostitute and then invented her narrative of widowhood in order to justify her position. Further, the fact that Mary was willing—or perhaps stupid—enough to entertain the Ripper in her room is presented not as an indication of the sort of person Mary must have been, but to support the fact that the Ripper may indeed have been well-dressed and respectable-looking.

In his 1993 book *Jack the Myth: A New Look at the Ripper*, A. P. Wolf takes an interesting approach in his argument for Thomas Cutbush as the Ripper. Four of the victims receive very little attention indeed, to the point where Cutbush has to clarify who Catherine Eddowes is when he mentions her more than one hundred pages in. The fact that he does not expect his readers to recognize the name of a canonical victim shows how little attention he has paid to them in a text that, oddly, begins each chapter with an epigraph from Winnie the Pooh. Wolf in fact devotes a good deal of the text to exploring the life of Elizabeth Stride, whom he claims was in fact not a victim of the Ripper after all. He declares that Long Liz was only an occasional prostitute, using details from her last day cleaning and charring to support the fact that she "was determined to do anything else to earn a living rather than reducing herself to prostitution."[63] This Liz prettied herself up for a night out with someone who was not Michael Kidney, the jilted boyfriend who thus murdered her out of jealousy. When explaining that Kidney often padlocked their lodging house room door and kept the only key, Wolf once again feels the need to explain the identity of someone he names, this time ensuring that his readers recognize "Stride" as being the same person as "Long Liz." Liz is thus the victim of domestic violence and Kidney escaped the consequences of his actions simply because her murder came in the midst of the others, largely ignored by Wolf.

M. J. Trow has no solution to the mystery of the Ripper's identity in his 1997 book *The Many Faces of Jack the Ripper* and offers few insights into the lives of the women he dubs "Jack's targets."[64] He groups the women together not only through their murderer but through their dependence on alcohol, with few details to individuate them. Polly Nichols, for example, surprised the coroner with "the cleanliness of her thighs,"[65] an oddly intimate detail that has readers once more pondering her body piecemeal. Polly seems to be the focus of the majority of these comments that differentiate Trow's narrative from any other, including the fact that she was "plucked from the obscurity of her life by death,"[66] a statement that indeed applies to each of these women. Otherwise there is little to distinguish one alcoholic from another, outside of the locations of their murders and the amount of damage the Ripper inflicted with his knife.

In *The Ripper & The Royals* (1991), Melvyn Fairclough once again returns to a variation of Stephen Knight's final solution, placing Walter Sickert as the ringleader responsible for the murders in order to prevent Mary Kelly's blackmailing of the crown. Fairclough more than other authors jumps around in the narrative instead of taking a chronological approach, dropping tidbits of information about the murdered women instead of taking the time to focus a paragraph or two on each. Thus what can be learned about them is scattered, and readers unfamiliar with the Ripper narrative might benefit from some clarification of identity, in the vein of A. P. Wolf. Since the blame for the murders is once again placed on a Mary Kelly intent on blackmail, she receives more attention than the women whose deaths she is meant to have caused. Fairclough does introduce the idea that Kelly was only an occasional prostitute and in fact supported herself through the secondhand rag trade, supporting this argument through a diary supposedly written by Inspector Abberline. The 1990s, it seems, was the decade of the revealed diary.

The final book of note is Richard Wallace's 1996 *Jack the Ripper: "Light-hearted Friend"* in which he relies heavily on anagrams and word games in order to accuse Charles Dodgson, otherwise known as his pen name of Lewis Carroll. He has little to distinguish his "'gay' women (meaning women of the streets)"[67] or "lower creatures"[68] from one another, except perhaps his assessment of how wealthy they were. While Wallace attributes the coins found near Annie Chapman to have been given to her by the Ripper, since she would not have possessed money on her own, he also labels Catherine Eddowes as "relatively well off"[69] based on the amount of possessions she had with her at the time of her death, not considering the fact that this meant she had no fixed abode at which to leave many of them while she was out. Further, Wallace shares at least part of his approach with David Abrahamsen, declaring his Ripper to be just as much a victim as the murdered women, albeit largely more sympathetic. This sits in strong contrast to his later musings that "[o]ne could wonder where is the empathy for the poor, nameless women so callously murdered and mutated,"[70] since Wallace himself seems to have expressed sympathy for the murderer and not the murdered. Further, he did indeed name the murdered women—at least, the most commonly named as the Rippers victims—so it seems strange to think of them as nameless, unless he means to indicate further unknown murdered women. Whether they are named or not, the victims of Wallace's Ripper do not receive the same sympathetic attention as Lewis Carroll himself, making Wallace's narrative fail to meet its own call for empathy.

Paving the Way

The focus of the 1990s thus broadened beyond the singular question of previous decades. Authors now no longer had to focus on the killer himself, or even the timeline and minutiae of the murders specifically. They were able to begin exploring other aspects of the Ripper narrative beyond what had been thoroughly—and repeatedly—summed up in the 1980s. Although the question of the Ripper's identity still remained largely at the fore, the answer to that question held new possibilities and new explanations for why that name had been put forward. Some authors continued much in the same vein that had proven interesting and worthy of publication in the past, but others started to expand and explore their options.

This exploration continued with the dawn of the twenty-first century. Again, some authors stuck to the by now expected questions concerning the Ripper narrative, while others took the mystery in new directions. Authors began to make use of more advanced technology alongside the psychology already presented, and others firmly turned their backs on the question of the Ripper's identity in order to pursue topics that they felt had been ignored, either willfully or unintentionally. As much as the 1990s expanded the library of Ripper texts, the twenty-first century saw the number of printed offerings continue to skyrocket.

SEVEN

More of the Same?
An Introduction
to the 21st Century Books

Change does not come easily. Although each new text about the Ripper murders must at least claim to offer something that has not been seen before, at times this can still mean that many aspects of the familiar narrative are simply repeated and not expanded upon. The attempt to find something new may focus authors and their research on specific areas so strenuously that they do not have time—or do not feel the need—to apply that same effort toward others. The desire to clearly show that the chosen man was indeed Jack the Ripper still most often demands that authors make use of the murdered women's dead bodies and not their biographies.

This does not mean that every author represents the murdered women in the same way. Some authors tend toward raising them up, in their deaths if not in their lives, as though murder and mutilation were a small price to pay for the fact that their names are indeed known and repeated. Other authors take the topics of prostitution and murder and use them to question the idea of redemption. Another group of authors perhaps downplay the individuality of the women themselves, lumping them together in a homogenous group in order to remove the sting and stigma of murder. One even owns up to his lack of interest in their lives, though he also does not restrain himself from commenting on how others have presented them. These are the books from the twenty-first century who continue their search for the Ripper's identity and follow more closely along the path that has already been set for them.

Walking into History

In his 2001 book *Alias Jack the Ripper: Beyond the Usual Whitechapel Suspects* R. Michael Gordon sets out to argue that the Ripper was in fact Severin Klosowski, a.k.a. George Chapman. If true, this means that the Ripper switched from murdering strangers with a knife to killing multiple "wives" through arsenic. Gordon also suggests that one of those women, Annie Chapman—from whom Klosowski adopted his pseudonym—was in fact Annie Georgina Chapman, daughter of one of his Whitechapel victims. The younger Annie Chapman was lucky in that she parted from Klosowski while still alive, and thus he took nothing but her name.

Gordon dedicates his book "For the ladies of Victorian London's East End, who so long ago walked into history"[1] and adds that they can now rest, since the killer has been identified. This is perhaps a sanitized way of saying that, through their bloody deaths and horrific mutilations, these women's names are remembered. Had they lived and died without having crossed paths with the Ripper, they would not have walked into history— or rather, walked into the path of the Ripper who forcefully propelled them into the history books. Gordon further argues that, considering the horrific conditions of the East End, death would be looked upon "an escape"[2] instead of being viewed negatively. Death would indeed have meant that the women need no longer scrounge for money in order to support themselves, but these women did not resort to suicide. They had the choice of life over death taken from them, with mutilations and missing organs thrown in on the side. Gordon, like many authors before him, does his best to minimize the suffering and loss of the murdered women so that he might be able to focus on proving the identity of their killer.

Polly is not only an alcoholic and a prostitute, but one who sold herself in order to pay for a drink instead of the bed that would have kept her off the street and out of the path of history. Gordon acknowledges that her marriage was bad for both parties and that their final separation was not necessarily purely Polly's fault, especially since there had been previous partings over their seventeen years of marriage. The couple's oldest son avoided his father at his mother's funeral, once again allowing readers to question whether Polly's alcoholism was the only issue involved. Further, Gordon speculates that Polly's relationship with a blacksmith named Dew was in fact better than her marriage to Nichols, considering how well she was dressed at her brother's funeral. Gordon does not come out directly and state that Nichols could have been a terrible husband, but the hints are there. Unfortunately for Polly, her relationship with Dew came to an end in 1887 and her position as a prostitute enslaved to the bottle was secured.

Annie is also fond of the bottle and, due to nebulous comments made by her siblings, Gordon suspects that it was a "long term drinking problem."[3] Because his source is her siblings, Annie's alcoholism need not have sprung directly from a bad marriage, especially since she married rather late in life. Her alcoholism seems to have been a problem before she ever met Chapman, much less before marrying the heavy drinker. Gordon allows that the couple separated by mutual consent, not casting blame to either party, and Annie is able to support herself—and presumably her drinking habit—on the allowance Chapman gave her. The amount was apparently enough to satisfy her sieve-maker, as well, since he abandoned her after Chapman's death and the cessation of the allowance. Annie may have been an alcoholic, but Gordon suggests that Sivvy only found her tolerable when accompanied by the allowance, when he was able to make use of some of it for himself. An alcoholic Annie without an income, however, was unacceptable, and Annie ended up in the same position as Polly: prostituting herself for alcohol and, if any money was left, a bed. Once again it is alcoholism that led Annie into the history books since she, like Polly, spent her final coins on drink and was turned out onto the street.

Unlike the previous two women, Long Liz is not accused of being an alcoholic, and she was not forced out of her lodging house on her final night. Instead she seems to have gone out of her own accord in search of clients. Even though Gordon faithfully reports that Liz made her living "charring," he adds that "[t]here can be no doubt about her occupation."[4] However much cleaning Liz may have undertaken, it was not enough to support her and she also had to go out soliciting. Her history is cloudier than Polly's or Annie's, and the reasons her marriage dissolved are unknown and perhaps unknowable since Liz herself was known to spin many different tales. Liz might have been a fanciful liar, but at least she was not an alcoholic who died because of her addiction to the bottle.

Catherine Eddowes, on the other hand, has no official evidence of prostitution or continual alcoholism. True, she met the Ripper when she was released after being arrested for being drunk and incapable, but Gordon does not report a history of alcoholism. There may be some hints when he acknowledges her that she had a temper or explains that Catherine had been ejected from the casual ward for "unspecified trouble"[5] but neither is explicitly linked to alcohol, and Catherine might simply have been a difficult person to get along with. All the same Gordon does not blame the breakup of her marriage to Tom Conway on Catherine alone, since there are arguments on both sides, but the fact that Catherine's daughter had moved to avoid her and had had no contact with her mother for two years adds to the suspicion that Catherine's personality was perhaps a bit prickly. Catherine finds herself on the street in the middle of the night after being released from a cell instead of ejected from a lodging house, although she may have been on her way to pay for a bed when she was accosted by the Ripper instead of having gone with a strange in order to earn coins—Gordon does not mention whether Mitre Square was on her way. Simply being a woman alone at night, perhaps not entirely sobered up from her earlier binge, was cause enough for her murder.

Mary Jane Kelly is, on the other hand, clearly a prostitute, having first taken up the occupation after the sudden death of her husband. Gordon explains that Mary made attempts at working in more respectable positions, including scrubbing floors and working as a maid, but her life endured a quick descent that found her in the East End. For a while her boyfriend, Joseph Barnett, was able to support the two of them, but when he found himself out of work, "Kelly decided to return to prostitution."[6] Presumably she had not been scrubbing floors while Barnett worked, or perhaps any money she earned through other means was simply not enough to support them. Gordon does at least ascribe the agency to Kelly herself, since she is the one who decided on this means of earning money, possibly to spare Barnett from accusations of pimping out his girlfriend. She willingly returned to her work as a prostitute and thus willingly took the Ripper into her room on her final night.

These are the women Gordon says may now rest, since the identification of their killer has ended the mystery. Just as he allowed Kelly the agency of choosing her return to prostitution, Gordon ascribes it to all five women: they walked into history, apparently under their own power, instead of being dragged into it. Because they were prostitutes, or alcoholics, or both, they willingly encountered a strange who turned out to be their murderer and thus seem to have invited their own deaths—and their own fame, albeit one that is continually connected to his through their deaths.

Facts and Definitive History

Adding to his oeuvre on Jack the Ripper, Paul Begg published two books in two years in the early 2000s. The first, *Jack the Ripper: The Facts* (2004) is an updated and fully revised version of his earlier *Jack the Ripper: The Uncensored Facts* from the 1980s. Many of the facts he includes about the lives of the murdered women resurface again in 2005's *Jack the Ripper: The Definitive History*, tracing the women's biographies with the use of references and, where possible, multiple points of confirmation. There are, however, variations in word choice between the books that can lead to shifts in focus and perception.

In 2004, there is little known about Mary Ann Nichols' early life, and Begg reports that her husband did not deny having an affair, but denied that his wife had left because of it. Despite her drinking and her difficult life after the breakup of her marriage, Mary Ann still managed to look youthful. Begg's 2005 text adds that this is in spite of "the abuse she had suffered, self-inflicted through the bottle as well as possible others we can only imagine."[7] Some of that abuse may have come directly from her husband, while others were a result of her having left him and struck out on her own. True, by leaving her husband Mary Ann put herself out of his reach, although also into danger since she ended up in the East End—between the choice of two evils, the one she selected ended in her murder. Since her alcoholism was self-inflicted it, too, followed her and is given as the reason she did not have money for a bed on her the last night of her life. Perhaps she should have been able to choose to walk away from the bottle, as well, but proved unable to make that choice. May Ann, it seems, was not able to treat herself any better than anyone else in her life had.

Annie Chapman appears to have faired little better. In 2004 Begg reveals that, while in her early twenties, Annie remained in London and likely worked as a domestic while her family moved back to Clewer. It was during this time that she was to have met her husband. A further discovery of a letter possibly penned by her brother reveals that there were already issues of alcoholism in her family and thus, instead of abandonment, perhaps being apart from her family at that time might have been a relief for Annie. All the same she, like Mary Ann, became an alcoholic, although Begg points out that she seems to have gotten her drinking under control by the time of her death.

Begg's second book does not mention Annie having been left alone in London, although here he mentions that she was likely sent to good schools during her childhood. At the time of her marriage, Begg suggests that her character was already in question, likely due to drinking, but he comes to a more forceful defense of Annie in the last years of her life. While living in the East End, Annie "was said to get drunk regularly on Saturday nights (as many people did and still do)"[8] as opposed to constantly wrestling with alcoholism or going about continually drunk. In both books Begg argues that there is no evidence to show that Annie prostituted herself, either for room and board or for drink, until her husband's death stopped her weekly allowance. Begg clearly resists both the idea that Annie was more than an occasional prostitute and that her alcoholism had gotten the better of her. It may have proven a problem during the years of her marriage, but in the East End Annie seems to have fought against the bottle.

The gaps in Elizabeth Stride's early years are smaller, since Begg is able to trace her movements while she was still living in Sweden. Despite her childhood education, which included biblical knowledge, Elizabeth found herself on the police registry as a prostitute after her parents' deaths. After multiple stays in the hospital having to do with venereal diseases, Begg observes that Elizabeth was removed from that registry, which was only achievable when the woman in question found a husband or a proper paid position. Since Elizabeth did not marry until she came to London, it seems that her removal came from employment. There is indeed a small gap in her history concerning the three years she lived in London before marrying, although the incidents commonly attributed to her life between her marriage and her death—including the familiar *Princess Alice* tale—are in question. Begg observes that, during the inquisition into Elizabeth's death, Coroner Baxter "tried to confirm the tale"[9] of the sinking and Elizabeth's loss. This is a much more positive phrasing than is often given, since Begg does not come out and directly say that much of Elizabeth's personal narrative was a lie.

Jack the Ripper: The Definitive History offers more information about the Swedish system of registering prostitutes. Once Elizabeth's name was recorded, Begg observes, she would have been caught in a system that often labeled women permanently and involved a grueling process to reverse. He further suggests that the employment that allowed Elizabeth's name to be removed was in fact a position in a brothel, which meant no real improvement in Elizabeth's circumstances. Indeed, her only escape came when she finally inherited after her mother's death and was able to emigrate to England—although, after a twelve-year marriage that seems to have marked an upswing in her life, Elizabeth once again found herself on the street. Her poor relationship with Michael Kidney would have likewise worked against her chances at stability and happiness, and she seems to have been parted from him, perhaps permanently this time, on the night of her murder.

Catherine Eddowes is compared to Elizabeth in that Begg finds evidence that they both worked "for the Jews"[10] whenever possible, only turning to prostitution to supplement their income. Catherine, however, unlike Elizabeth, seems to have had a poor relationship with her first common-law husband and a much better relationship with her second. Although Begg argues that Conway need not have been much older than Catherine, despite the fact that he was a pensioner, he marks Catherine's first relationship with alcohol and black eyes—both in reference to Catherine. She was likely feisty, a character trait not tempered by drink, but Conway was not entirely uninvolved in the breakup of their long term relationship.

Lest he seem too reluctant to mention any negative aspects of these women's personalities, Begg does acknowledge that the glowing character traits given to Catherine immediately after her death are tempered by other reports. Although John Kelly may have had only good things to say about the women who had shared his life for seven years, Begg points out that Catherine's own children avoided her. Whether or not she worked as a prostitute, she was still a known drinker and a scrounger, and thus any attempt after her death to only speak well of her had to be taken for what it was: the cultural impetus to not speak ill of the dead. The Catherine who spent so many good years with Kelly was still the same woman who drank and fought with Conway, and even if her relationship was improved, she was still the same fallible woman.

Mary Jane Kelly presents more of a problem for a researcher intent on grounding his representation of the victims on outside corroboration, but even here Begg manages to take the personal history Kelly told her boyfriend and align it with known practices. The fact that she was not originally from England and claims to have come to London to work in a West End brothel—which somehow involved a trip to France—makes Begg question whether "she had fallen into the hands of a procurer."[11] He expands on this idea in *Jack the Ripper: The Definitive History* to explain that said procurer would have been out a great deal of money if Kelly had decided to leave France and return to England. If she had made an agreement with such a person and then not followed through, then the fact that Kelly might have seemed to have been hiding in the East End would be explicable. She would not have been able to return to the West End without being identified, and any comments she made about being fearful of someone might have been connected to this scenario.

Begg likewise suspects Joe Barnett of doing what Catherine's friends did after her death and presenting her story in a more positive light. It is possible that Barnett may have altered Kelly's personal history in his retelling, consciously or not, since even her other friends could not be called upon to corroborate that information. She seems to have kept herself mostly to herself and thus is known more for her youth and her looks than her background, although Begg does point out that her history and lack of contact with her family suggests that her relationship with her parents was not a positive one. No family or friends from outside of London attended her funeral.

In neither book does Begg make an argument for the Ripper's identity, ending *Jack the Ripper: The Facts* with the declaration that "the identity of Jack the Ripper isn't really important. It's the story of these crimes, of the women who died, and of the society and times in which they lived that matters and holds the enduring fascination."[12] Granted, the identity of the Ripper is not at the center of any of Begg's published texts, but the vast majority of Ripper narratives are indeed focused on giving the killer a name. Even Begg's treatment of the murdered women might be considered out of the ordinary, since an even-handed approach is so striking as to seem almost too kind. In his concluding thoughts in *Jack the Ripper: The Definitive History* his argument shifts slightly, not attempting to dismiss the identity of the Ripper entirely but condemning the authors of both fact and fiction who have romanticized the series murders and placed them in the midst of a romantic Victorian fog. This is perhaps a more reasonable call for other authors, considering the usual research questions that have been brought to bear on the subject.

In *Jack the Ripper: The Definitive History* Begg also makes another move toward a more relatable representation of the murdered women when he brings up for the subject of pathos. For Begg, three of these women exhibit moments of pathos on the last night of their lives: Mary Ann Nichols takes pride in her new bonnet, the act of a poor woman reveling in the simplest of things; Elizabeth Stride borrowed a clothes brush before going out for the evening, as though her outfit were fine enough to look all the better for using one; and Catherine Eddowes laments the response she will receive for arriving home hours later than she had promised. This is the only rhetorical term Begg uses, calling these instances "moments of pathos"[13] without clarifying either the term or what it is about each scenario that makes it pathetic. They are simply snapshots in which these women tug the heartstrings, everyday tasks that can be seen as relatable or pitiful even more than a century later.

Even when conscientiously aligning his representation of these women with information gleaned from contemporary sources, Begg manages to avoid either extreme and give a more balanced presentation. They are not horrific, irredeemable wrecks of women who threw themselves into prostitution without a care, and neither are they saints. Begg tempers reports that skew to either end with more information, either placing these women and their actions in the historical context or reminding readers of previously stated evidence to combat the tendency to clean up a person's reputation after death. These biographies do not necessarily eclipse the mystery of the killer's identity or his methods, but they offer more than scant repeated facts.

Questions of Redemption

Paul Roland's 2006 book *The Crimes of Jack the Ripper* once again directs focus back to the Ripper himself, concluding that the accusations against a mad Jewish butcher were in fact correct, and that his name was Jacob Levy. Roland also returns to the typical method of presenting each of the women's biographies in a paragraph or two, painting their lives in broad strokes. He may be choosing to reflect the opinion of the day, the same way in which he observes that the only way lower-class women could "redeem themselves"[14] would be to find themselves a respectable paid position, either as a maid or in one of the factories. If a women were ever forced to resort to prostitution, then she was indeed in need of redemption, and Roland declares that any woman who could not—or would not—apply herself to an occupation other than prostitution deserved whatever end she might meet, even if that end came on the Ripper's knife. This is an opinion that was not left in the Victorian era.

Polly Nichols indeed seems to have bought and paid for her violent end—or rather, to have chosen to spend her money on alcohol instead of on the bed that would have kept her off the street. "Had she saved just a few coppers," Roland laments, "she would not have been soliciting"[15] and therefore on the street and in the path of the Ripper. The focus is not on the fact that there was a killer on the loose, attacking women with his knife, but that Polly was so much of an alcoholic that she was unable to keep herself out of his way.

Her alcoholism was what put her in the East End in the first place, separating her from both her husband and her children and forcing her to depend on the kindness of strangers through various workhouses. This is a woman who seemed unable to redeem herself no matter what options were presented to her because her priorities centered around the bottle instead of some higher form of salvation. Roland does credit her with a higher level of education than is commonly assumed of East End prostitutes, referencing a letter Polly wrote to her husband, but even the ability to read and write did not mean that she possessed the motivation or the character to stick with the domestic position that had been obtained for her. It would seem that no amount of help that came to Polly was enough to change her situation, since she herself would have needed to change, as well.

Annie Chapman, on the other hand, was not able to reject all attempts at help since it seems none were offered her. The fact that "she looked as if life had knocked her around a bit"[16] was likely because it had: out of her three children, there was one dead, one institutionalized, and one placed in a home for cripples. Her husband had reportedly drunk himself to death, and Roland reports that it seems Annie had set out to do the same. In stark contrast to Polly, Annie's marriage is not shown to end because of her drinking. Instead it seems that she was only separated from her husband through his death, and that the heavy drinking of the parents is understandable considering the fates of the children. Annie's situation is sympathetic and relatable instead of pathetic and distant.

It is Elizabeth Stride who might come off as pathetic, not only being a foreigner who left her home country in order to escape the blows of her parents' death and a stillborn baby but also emerging from a short-lived marriage and ending up on the street. Still Elizabeth manages to remain "slim and pretty, a more attractive prospect than the dowdy bawds with whom she shared a pitch,"[17] prostituting herself only when she could not earn enough money as a cleaner. Her looks put her in clear contrast with Polly and Annie, as well as the fact that she is not an alcoholic and thus her drinking could not have caused her marriage to fail. This is an Elizabeth who is trying to make the best of a bad situation to the point where she even borrowed a clothes brush before going out to solicit for the night, as though the men who sought out East End prostitutes might be more inclined to favor the slim and pretty Swede if her clothes were also as clean as she could get them. This is the plight of a woman who, apparently through no fault of her own, has suffered multiple losses in life and yet pays attention to the small details that likely go unnoticed by those around her.

Catherine Eddowes is not pathetic and not even relatable. She is simply released from her cell, not entirely sober, and sets off into the night to her death. Clearly drinking put her in the wrong spot at the wrong time and meant she crossed paths with the Ripper, but if the bottle had cost her anything else in life—or if there was even anyone to miss her—Roland does not mention it.

Being younger than the other women, Mary Jane Kelly is also the prettiest—even more so than Elizabeth, perhaps because she had not been occupying the East End for quite as long. She had been sharing various lodgings with her boyfriend, Joe Barnett, although the couple preferred to spend their rent money on alcohol and be forced to move, multiple times over. It seems that, when they drank, they also fought, and this "volatile"[18] relationship left Mary Jane alone in her rented room, with no man to protect her and the need to go out soliciting for customers in an attempt to pay off some of what was owed.

Whether or not Barnett can be blamed for leaving her, it would seem that he was not the sole cause of her drinking, since she was drunk on her last night. Granted, she may have turned to the bottle for solace in what might have felt like a hopeless situation, or for courage to go out and sell herself, but Roland suspects that the Ripper chose her as his victim precisely because she was not sober. He speculates that other women who were out and about that night, in full control of their facilities, avoided the Ripper because of their intuition, "whereas Mary Kelly was too drunk to have heeded hers."[19] It was once again not the responsibility of the Ripper to not have murdered, but the responsibility of his victims to have recognized him for what he was and gotten out of his way. It would seem that the punishment for drink, as well as for prostitution, was death.

The question of redemption is thus posed in relationship to the murdered women and not to the murderer himself. It seems that the women—prostitutes and alcoholics—would have been able to have been redeemed, had they simply tried harder or wanted it more. Giving up alcohol would have meant more money in their pockets for food and shelter, and having shelter would have meant that they would not have been on the street at the same time as the Ripper. Having an income that did not require occasional or continual prostitution would also have worked in their favor, both from a moral standing and to have kept them off the street. These women thus put themselves perfectly in the path of the Ripper's knife, so their deaths were bought and paid for through the choices they made in life. Whether or not the Ripper is capable of—or in need of—redemption is not discussed.

Vulnerable Victims

In his 2009 book *Jack the Ripper: Quest for a Killer*, M. J. Trow makes the interesting move of connecting his Ripper suspect with the murdered women outside of the murders themselves. When Trow provides readers with the women's backgrounds, he mentions where Robert Mann was and how old he was at the time of their births. Even though the Ripper and his victims are separated by miles and will not cross paths for decades, Trow cannot introduce the women without reminding readers of his true focus. Even though he condemns prior authors from either turning the Ripper narrative into entertainment or for presenting situations and people involved falsely, part of his means of grounding his own narrative in fact comes from this continual turning back to remind readers of where the young Ripper was and what he was up to when his victims were born.

Trow connects the Ripper not only to his victims, but also to twentieth century serial killer Ted Bundy, making multiple references to the man who was executed for his crimes over a century after Mary Kelly's death. Bundy was, after all, a suave killer, much as the Ripper was assumed to have been. This assumption seems to have been based mostly on the fact that the Ripper was not caught, and Trow's description of Robert Mann does not impress readers with the idea of the same charisma. His observation that Bundy would not have been identified as a stereotypical serial killer by those who passed him on the street, however, does hold for Mann, although perhaps not for the same reason. As a law student, with his clean-cut good looks, Bundy seemed above reproach; workhouse inmate Mann would have been overlooked as being too dull and ordinary.

The observation that "the Ripper's victims were considerably more vulnerable than any killed by Gacy or Bundy"[20] is certainly a means by which to separate Mann from the more recent serial killer. In part due to his looks and his education, Bundy was not perceived as a threat and was thus able to approach college co-eds who were meant to have been given the proper background and tools to prevent themselves from becoming victims. Mann is not a threat because of charisma and appearance, but rather because he is deemed as too low to be much of one. He is an inmate at a workhouse and thus has no money and no education, placing him in opposition to Bundy. Bundy's victims were mainly young women who had been living comfortable middle-class lives and could afford to go to college, thus making them women whose absence would be noted and lamented much more quickly than missing Victorian prostitutes.

When Trow brings John Wayne Gacy into discussion, he includes another segment of the victim population. Instead of college co-eds or prostitutes, Gacy murdered boys and young men. They were usually hitchhiking or in search of a job, which allowed Gacy to convince them to get into his car or come to his house. Trow states that the women murdered in Whitechapel were even more vulnerable than the young men and boys Gacy killed in the 1970s, although this claim seems to be more complicated than it first appears. True, the number of victims of the Ripper changes depending on the narrative, but Gacy was convicted of thirty-three murders, which is more than have been attached to the Ripper. The East End—and indeed the world—was made aware of the Ripper murders at speed, thanks to newspaper reports, meaning that readers could both learn the identity of the murdered women and be aware that there was a threat. Women who had no other source of income were still forced to walk the streets, but their plight came under discussion and it was reported that many began to carry knives. Even if they did not know what the Ripper looked like, they knew enough to be on the lookout.

Gacy's victims, on the other hand, responded to a seemingly jolly man offering them a ride or a job. This was a man who, by the time he was caught, had buried twenty-nine bodies on his property and tossed four more into the river because he was running out of space. Because he chose to murder runaways and hitchhikers, many of them were not reported as missing and their deaths were unknown until the property was excavated and the remains began to be identified. Even though Gacy murdered more people, the fact that he hid their bodies instead of leaving them to be found means that the horror of his actions was only uncovered after the disappearance of his final victim, whose family missed him immediately.

This is not to say that the East End prostitutes were not a vulnerable population, since they clearly were, but that they are not the only vulnerable category of victims. The five murdered women in Whitechapel were identified with varying degrees of difficulty in the days after their murders, but they were still given names, and their loved ones were made aware of their fates. Although some printed responses suggested that murdered prostitutes deserved their deaths, others came forward to protest the current conditions of the East End and suggest various ways and means—not all of them practical—to protect the women. The Ripper murders have been pointed to as a locus for social change, as though the murderer himself might have been a reformer, whereas a discussion almost a century later of murdered boys and homosexuality did not produce the same effect. The media flocked to the Gacy murders, yes, and certainly turned them into a spectacle, but the question of whether the Ripper victims or Gacy's victims were more vulnerable does not have a clear-cut answer.

The vulnerability of the Ripper's victims comes from their occupation, which stems from their common history of failed relationships and alcoholism. Polly is once again unable to seize "[h]er one chance—as it turned out her last"[21] to set her life straight, but she fails at being a maid just as she failed at being a wife and mother, due largely to alcohol. Eliza Ann Smith—also called Annie Chapman, or simply Annie—may have only begun drinking because one of her children was born crippled and another died, but alcohol still cost Annie her marriage and likely fed her temper. Although Liz Stride may not have been an alcoholic herself, the man she took up with after the failure of her marriage certainly was and Michael Kidney, like Annie, had a fierce temper. Kate Eddowes faired better in that her long-term relationship with John Kelly seemed steady in spite of the bottle, although Trow's description of a "relatively loyal and happy"[22] couple is at odds with his initial description of Kelly merely as Kate's "sometimes lover."[23] Finally Mary Kelly, despite her presumably superior position, seemed to share Annie's temper as well as her love of alcohol, since "drink turned her from a quiet woman into a terrifying harpy."[24] Both prostitution and alcoholism made these women vulnerable, frequently placing them in the company of strange men and thus overlooked by the supposedly better classes.

What set Bundy's victims apart was that so many of them came from those supposedly better classes. They were young, good-looking, and the sort of women said to have their whole lives ahead of them. They were also, unlike Gacy's choice of victim, generally white and heterosexual. This placed Bundy's victims on a level above Jack the Ripper's, increasing Bundy's risk when he murdered them and thus elevating Bundy in the pantheon of serial killers. The Ripper's victims, like many of Gacy's, were ignored and dismissed as having no future or no means of improving themselves. The fact that society has already begun to ignore them is a large part of what makes the East End women such likely victims, especially when two aspects of their lives seem to have been their own personal choices: prostitution and alcohol. Whether these are tantamount to hitchhiking and homosexuality is still up for debate.

"By no means unique"

Trow is by no means the only author to make the point that aspects of the murdered women's lives did indeed mean that they were more likely to fall prey to the Ripper's knife. It is a concept that serial killer expert Steven Egger defines as the "less-dead," an idea he has been refining since first proposing it in 1994. For Egger, the less-dead category encompasses "the marginalized members of society"[25] who are overlooked in life and most often described as having put themselves in harm's way. He includes such populations as hitchhikers, the homeless, and prostitutes, although race and sexual preference are also likely categories. These groups are ignored, if not exiled, and therefore less-alive when living, making them less-dead when murdered. What M. J. Trow describes when he labels the Whitechapel women as "vulnerable" fits into this category of the less-dead, and he is not alone in this assessment.

After more than a century of discussion about the Ripper narratives, it is perhaps difficult for authors to continue to present the murder victims in new and individual ways. Although it is common enough to take a few provable facts about a suspect and build up a life story around him in order to prove that he could have been the Ripper, the interest in the victims lies in their bodies and what clues can be gathered from them in order to point to that killer. Thus, while the basic facts of their lives might be dutifully repeated, there is not necessarily enough information to provide readers with distinct personalities or identities of the murdered women. A number of books from the twenty-first century, therefore, are notable for this study only in that they echo Egger's assessment of the less-dead similarly to Trow, putting the idea in their own words.

In his 2011 book *Jack the Ripper and the Case for Scotland Yard's Prime Suspect*, Robert House ferrets out the life of the mysterious Aaron Kosminski, one of the three possible suspects named by Sir Melville Mcnaghten. Since the Mcnaghten notes were made public in the middle of the twentieth century, researchers have been attempting to track down the three he named and make their argument for or against them. House has uncovered more information about the Polish Jew and apparent hairdresser who spent the last decades of his life in an insane asylum.

While House does indeed provide each murdered woman with a chapter in her name, the majority of each chapter concerns itself with the discovery of her body and the resulting investigation. House is, after all, concerned with making the case that Kosminski could have encountered each woman on the night of her death and enacted both the murders and the mutilations involved, and this argument needs only the women's bodies and descriptions of their wounds. Indeed, when he reaches the murder of Kate Eddowes, House simply declares that she "was another fairly typical East End prostitute."[26] It would seem that all five of these women were typical, since none of them stand out in the usual ways as being most pathetic, or the biggest liar, or the prettiest. They are simply five women whose names are known and connected because of Jack the Ripper.

In their 2013 book *The Complete and Essential Jack the Ripper*, Paul Begg and John Bennett take this a step further when they point out that "these women were by no means unique in the mighty city that was London."[27] This is the realization that occurs to the public, both in London itself and the wider world, after Annie Chapman was murdered. Not only were the murdered women not unique in and among themselves, but they belonged to a wider pool of women whose situations were very much like their own. This was the realization that led to responses ranging from praise for the Ripper for cleaning up the streets—which in itself was an overstatement, considering the number of prostitutes in the East End alone—on the one hand and social reform on the other.

Begg and Bennett also take the time to reflect on the state of Ripper narratives and express their concern with the state of recent critique. They acknowledge that many of these narratives have fallen prey to decades of myth making and that, by the anniversary of the murders, Ripper narratives were "essentially commemorating the century of a fictional creation"[28] and not of a real man who murdered and mutilated real women. These myths surround the figure of the Ripper and allow for the dismissal of his victims, and the authors further argue that these, like other serial killer tales, direct their focus in ways that do not touch on the actual reactions to the murders. At this distance, both emotionally and chronologically, readers have been directed to focus more fully on the mystery of the Ripper's identity instead of on the true fates of his victims.

This is a tendency that Begg and Bennett do not lay solely on authors writing during or after the anniversary of the murders. Rather, they suggest that "there simply *had* to be a reason for the Whitechapel murders in order for people to attempt to come to terms"[29] with them. This search for an explanation that would lead to closure is made easier if the murdered women are considered as a homogenous group instead of distinct individuals. First, it allows for distance even in those living through the murders, holding the women at arm's length instead of personifying them and presenting readers with the complete horror of their deaths. And secondly, placing the murdered women into a single group allows for the explanation that the killer held something against that group. If the Ripper's victims were all prostitutes and by no means unique, then he clearly held something against that specific class of people. He was not even alone in his negative feelings—the Ripper simply took common public reaction a step too far.

Although it may have begun in 1888, this grouping and dismissal of the victims remains in recent texts. Robert Keller's 2016 *The Devil in Whitechapel: The Untold Story of Jack the Ripper* declares it bluntly: "Prostitutes make easy victims. They were simply unfortunate enough to cross the Ripper's path while he was hunting."[30] If it hadn't been Polly, Annie, Long Liz, Catherine, and Mary, it would have been other women. These five were not the only sad, broken-down, alcoholic prostitutes in the East

End, after all, and if they had not been murdered they would have simply been part of the larger statistic of numbers of prostitutes and the homeless in the East End. Once again there is the suggestion that these women might have been lucky to have been murdered, since it means their names and a few facts about their lives are indeed known. Yes, they might have been fairly typical prostitutes, not unique in any way, but it is still their lives that have captured public attention—or, at least, their deaths. Just how little their lives honestly seem to matter in the Ripper narrative is taken up in 2015 by Bruce Robinson.

Thirty-Five Minutes

They All Love Jack (2015) by Bruce Robinson is an education not only in all that he feels has gone wrong with Ripper investigations of the past, but in casual British swearing. Robinson works to set himself apart from those that have gone before, not only in the fact that he holds the truth to the Ripper's identity—Michael Maybrick—but also in his language choice. In his preface Robinson firmly takes up his stance about the figure of the Ripper himself when he states that many Ripper authors present the murderer "as though he were someone special, rather than the epitome of all that is cruel, and a God-damned repugnance."[31] Further reading reveals that Robinson's frustrations appear to be directed more at past researchers, who have made mistakes and repeated false information than at the Ripper and his cronies.

Robinson's blunt style results in his saying outright what many authors have enacted but few have stated. "As far as this narrative is concerned," he confesses glibly, "Catherine Eddowes' life lasted about thirty-five minutes: from the time she left the police lock-up to the time the Ripper killed her."[32] There is no apology offered. As far as Robinson is concerned, Catherine was forty-six years old and a drunk, and that is all that is relevant outside of her autopsy reports.

All the same, despite this dismissal of the living Catherine Eddowes, Robinson mocks the treatment she has been given when he reflects on the contemporary assessment that "Catherine Eddowes was complicit in the loss of her ear, kidney and womb. She shouldn't have been walking around flaunting such stuff at a murderer."[33] He takes the idea of vulnerability presented by the above authors and dismisses the declaration that either her occupation or her fondness for alcohol was at fault for her death. Ears, kidneys, and wombs are not usually among the list of what murder victims are meant to have flaunted at their killers, and any killer whose murderous streak is aroused by any of these three would have been confronted with them everywhere. It was not how Catherine was dressed or her level of sobriety that resulted in her death, but, rather amazingly, something beyond her control. Could it be, perhaps, that Jack the Ripper was the one solely responsible for the murders and it wasn't the women he killed who brought it on themselves?

It would seem that Robinson's remark about the interesting length of Catherine Eddowes' life has more to do with making a blunt statement about the way in which the murdered women are generally treated in a text and not so much that he, personally, feels the need to dismiss the women's lives that easily. More often he dismisses the usual dismissals, such as when he mocks Coroner Wynn Baxter's claim that Annie Chapman was murdered because of a request for wombs. Each specimen would be well paid for, of course, and Robinson rejects the idea that a woman would have been murdered for the price of a single body part—even such a ridiculous price. "Mrs. Chapman was the victim of a commercial enterprise,"[34] he marvels, as though Baxter might honestly have thought murder might have been performed for a few coins. True, Robinson's main point is that Baxter was a Mason, and the Masons were heavily involved with the Ripper murders, but when he picks at common elements of the Ripper narrative, some of these do involve the traditional representations of the murdered women.

Although Robinson does not concern himself greatly with the biographies of these women, when he groups them into a single category, it is once again to critique. Just as these women should have known better than to flaunt common body parts at a prospective murderer, that same murderer need no longer actually go on the hunt for his next target. Instead, "it is the victims who 'prowl,' making themselves targets for the perfectly reasonable attentions of a psychopath with his knife."[35] This sentiment has, after all, been stated before, although the fact that the Ripper's desire to murder is "reasonable" is usually left unsaid. By taking the assumed and making it obvious, Robinson's attacks on previous authors have to do not only with the lamentable state of their research, but their continued parroting of cultural values without considering their full implications. After all, telling a woman to make herself less of a target is asking her to ensure that the predator kills someone else instead.

Although Robinson's style—and his word choice—might put readers off because they are so different from previous authors, and his dismissal of so many respected names in the field might make his actual audience even smaller, readers who do wade through his more than 700 pages will stumble across these gems. The direction of his critique does not point him to a close study the victims, and, as we have seen, he freely admits this. Once again stating baldly what many have done but not admitted, Robinson owns up to this lack instead of ignoring it, and takes the time at other places in his book to indicate how nonsensical past representation of these women has been. His casual and slang-filled approach might count against him among more "serious" works, but Robinson certainly attempts to uproot more than the Ripper's identity.

Pushing the Boundaries

Although these books tended to continue along the same narrative lines as those that preceded them, it can still be seen that they adopted their own individual approaches to the Ripper narrative. The same handful of facts about each woman was available for selection, and authors picked and chose in the way that best suited their own arguments. When the women have very little to do with the story outside of their own deaths, the discussion of each woman shows it. At other times the approach to the murdered women betrays personal or public opinion about them, be it an opinion that was held in the Victorian era, in the twenty-first century, or perhaps one that has seen little change. With so many books now written about Jack the Ripper it is unsurprising that many have adopted the same approaches to their subject, since they are expected and perhaps even anticipated by readers and fellow authors.

Alongside the more commonly expected authors and narratives there emerged others with more varied backgrounds that allowed them access to modern uses of police work and technology. This particular knowledge allowed them to approach the Ripper mystery with their own specialties in mind. Much in the same way that authors made use of the FBI's behavioral profiling in the 1980s and 1990s, these individuals relied on their own experiences with modern police techniques of their knowledge of—or access to—DNA technology. The Ripper mystery could once again be scrutinized in a new light and with new methods, this time related to twenty-first century technologies not accessible to the general public.

EIGHT

Enter DNA

Victim Descriptions
in Light of 21st Century Uses
of Technology in Ripper Theories

A common lament about the Ripper crimes is that, even with full access to the coroner's reports and the rest of what was kept in the sealed files, very little new information was actually discovered. This is not simply because the files have been picked over or lost through the years, or because much of the information surrounding the crimes had already been printed in various newspapers. The details surrounding the Ripper case seem minimal today because the police and doctors had little access to forensic knowledge that seems so prevalent even to the average citizen in the twenty-first century.

Between the true crime boom of the 1980s and forensics-heavy television shows of the twenty-first century like, *CSI:*, including its variants and knockoffs, the average viewing and reading public has been exposed to ideas involving fingerprints, DNA, and young, hip scientists in a dramatically lit lab able to tease clues almost out of thin air. Profilers, professional and amateur, attempt to suss out the killer's identity before the characters manage it, relying on popular representations of crime and criminals in order to do so. The prevalence of this knowledge is shown through "the CSI effect" in which jurors have an overinflated expectation of both the abilities of forensic science and the proceedings within a courtroom based on the fast-paced, easy to follow through-lines of these types of shows. In the rare cases when the criminal is not caught, with full proof, by the end of the episode, it is likely to be part of an arc about a serial killer who return next sweeps week to once again boost the ratings.

"The CSI effect" not only leads amateur detectives to believe that science borders on the magical, but also that every killer will be caught. It is rare even for texts that fall under true crime instead of crime fiction to be about unsolved cases, although Jack the Ripper is, of course, the most famous exception. By the twenty-first century the Ripper himself is clearly no longer a threat—even if he was not one of the identified suspects, with a death date, enough time has passed that he cannot possibly still alive. The safety readers feel of not being a prostitute, especially not one in the East End, is therefore further compounded by the passage of time.

The same passage of time that leads to feelings of safety also saw developments in technologies and techniques that were not present in 1888. Even if twenty-first century detectives, armchair or professional, wish to cast an eye over the crimes, they find themselves limited. Although morgue photographs were taken of the victims, only Mary Kelly's corpse was photographed where it was found. Catherine Eddowes' location and position in Mitre Square was sketched, but none of the previous crime scenes were given such attention. The only clues toward the positioning of the women's bodies came through the written descriptions.

Fingerprinting would not come into practice for another few years, and DNA matching was a century away. Although doctors were called to the scenes of the crimes, it was generally to pronounce death and then return to bed until it was time for the autopsy. The bodies were removed in carts to the nearest mortuary before being undressed and washed, at times without supervision from the doctors or police and even without permission. Those doing the work were often inmates of the workhouse attached to the mortuary and thus not specifically trained. Even the physicians who consulted on the case were working with minimal training and often disagreed with each other. There were no sterile theaters or labs for testing.

In the face of these deficiencies, from a twenty-first century perspective, the Victorian police force and armchair detectives, perhaps imagining themselves to be Sherlock Holmes, engaged in pseudo-scientific practices. One was handwriting analysis, feeding off the many letters sent to both the newspapers and the police claiming responsibility for the crimes. Due to the amount of letters, this analysis was generally used to determine which, of any, were likely to be from the "real" Ripper, or at least which had probably been written by the same person. The handwriting and spelling were inspected to inform opinions about the letter writer's level of education. Another pseudo scientific practice came from piecing together the evidence uncovered at coroners' reports. Much of this came from witness testimony, and these armchair detectives were able to engage in the process of constructing an image of the Ripper himself. Some newspapers took this literally at the time, printing sketches born of the verbal portraits of men supposedly seen with the murdered women shortly before their deaths.

If the police in 1888 had had access to modern techniques and technology, it is frequently argued that they would have solved the case and named Jack the Ripper once and for all. The common lament seems to be one of "if only." If only they had known about fingerprinting. If only the doctors had recorded more exact information during the autopsy. If only suspicious characters had been subjected to much more vigorous inquiry. In an attempt to combat the lingering feeling of "if only," modern Ripper authors have taken multiple approaches to apply updated procedures and technologies to the Ripper murder mystery.

The Ripper for a Modern Era

In 1998, John Plimmer published his book *The Whitechapel Murders Solved?* and his question mark is indeed apt. Plimmer's focus was not so much on the Ripper case itself but how modern procedures would have approached the murders. He intermingles fact and fiction, allowing investigators to find clues that were not actually presented, appointing a media liaison, and giving Chief Inspector Fredrick Abberline a press conference complete with video cameras. Although the microphones might strike the casual reader as anachronistic and be a clue that Plimmer's scenarios are indeed only imagined, discussions of blood spatter and footprints might not be so obvious. Plimmer's narrative is a clear mix of fact and supposition, ending with a transcription of a fictionalized interview with the killer.

Plimmer includes little information about the murdered women, prefacing his narrative with the argument that "[t]he circumstances of the murders have been well documented."[1] Although Plimmer does not introduce the idea of DNA evidence into his fiction, he apparently also does not need to further investigate the biographies of these women in order to profile the murderer. Despite his short descriptions, Plimmer still introduces tidbits about the lives of these women, even if some of it is in contrast with information presented by other authors.

His Mary Nichols, for example, parted from her husband due to drunken brawls in which her husband was the beaten party. He does not indicate which half of the marital pair was drunk, but it is clearly Mary who became violent. Further, this Mary is not ejected from her lodging house for being penniless, but is instead accosted on her way to her lodging house. Apparently she was in possession of the money necessary for her bed, having had two clients and not spent that money elsewhere. Likely this Mary did not need to spend it elsewhere, since "poor wretched Mary was extremely drunk"[2] already and apparently not in need of food. However miserable her life may have been—or may not have been—she was still able to secure multiple clients in a day and keep herself in drink and shelter.

Plimmer does take a moment in his description of the police response to the murder to point out that modern police activity would include a much closer look at Mary's history than was undertaken at the time. This comes in relation to the criminal profiling introduced and made popular in the 1980s in which the victims' biographies would be examined in order to determine what sort of person would undertake the risk of murdering them. The fact that Mary is clearly identified as a prostitute both widens her circle of acquaintances and places her at greater risk for stranger violence. Plimmer gives no indication that any of Mary's family members would have come under suspicion over her death.

Like many other authors, Plimmer presents his Annie May Chapman as a largely sympathetic figure. Instead of the negative physical descriptions, she is "an attractive, well-proportioned woman"[3] who, unlike Mary, does not seem to have a drinking problem. The end to Annie's marriage has blame placed equally on husband and wife with the suggestion that they each fell on hard times, perhaps through no fault of their own, and this— along with the fact that their son needed care in a home for cripples— seems to be a rational reason why two people would agree to go their separate ways.

This Annie clearly has access to money, since she pays extra at her usual lodging in order to have a double bed that she does not have to share. Doss houses that had double beds were the only ones in which men and women were allowed to sleep together, and the more usual scenario involved a man paying for the bed and allowing a woman to join him in exchange for favors. Considering how many women were forced to walk the streets all night, even at the height of the Ripper murders, the fact that Annie could afford twice what the other women lacked indicates that her income was steady and perhaps almost extravagant for the area.

It is therefore much more of a shock for this Annie when she is forced to leave her usual lodging for not having any money, although the rules had not changed and lodgers were fully expected to pay in advance. This Annie becomes "disillusioned"[4] when she is turned out. Despite the fact that she had parted from her husband and her children and had been living in the East End for years, it is only now that Annie suffered disillusionment. Somehow her double bed and the income that allowed her to pay for that bed meant that her life was not nearly as terrible may have been suspected. Perhaps this Annie was used to being on the receiving end of human kindness, and being ejected from the place where she was known and usually accepted proved to be the defining moment of her predicament.

Once Annie is murdered, however, she loses all vestiges of humanity and empathy. In his description of her injuries, Plimmer reduces her to a genderless body. She transitions from "Annie May Chapman" to the body, the corpse, the dead woman, and the victim. All of these indicate not Annie herself but the effects of Jack the Ripper's intervention in her life. The term "victim" especially indicates her relationship to another person, presupposing an enactor of the crime. She is also a victim who was unable to react in the expected manner of self-defense, since later it is revealed that she was already quite ill and therefore could not have been able to defend herself. This attractive woman, somehow untouched by the ravages of the East End, was finally disillusioned and this, on top of her physical ailments, led directly to her death.

Less information is available about Elizabeth Stride. Although Plimmer dismisses the story of the sinking of the *Princess Alice* and its effects on her family, he does indicate that, during her marriage to John Stride, "she helped raise three children."[5] It was not the seven or nine of her usual stories, and apparently none of the three offspring mentioned were involved in any sort of disaster, ship-related or otherwise, but the wording itself is curious. The fact that she "helped raise" instead of simply "raised" indicates that there was another person involved in the upbringing of these children, and that these children were possibly not her own. If they had been, she would have done more than *help* raise them—Elizabeth would have birthed them and been expected to be the main caregiver. There is no indication as to whose children they might have been: John's from a previous marriage? A friend's? Does Plimmer suppose that Elizabeth had family in London? Whoever these children are, they disappear from the narrative as soon as they surface. Her death, for whatever reason, does not seem to effect them in any way.

Unlike Mary Nichols, when Elizabeth engages in violent arguments with her on-again, off-again boyfriend Michael Kidney there is no indication as to whether this violence was directed at him, her, or went in both directions. There is also no suggestion that these outbursts were drunken instead of sober or what the subject of these arguments may have entailed.

Elizabeth is a known prostitute and thus might be assumed to be able to support herself without Kidney's help, but she still presumably kept returning to him despite these violent arguments. Plimmer gives little enough information about the couple, so readers are left with a lack of information from which to make such judgments.

Unlike the other women, Catharine Eddowes is first introduced as a corpse. While the figures of Mary, Annie, and Elizabeth were introduced with descriptions and brief biographies, Catharine is first described as "an alarming and terrifying sight"[6] encountered by a police officer walking his usual beat. She is a body before she is a woman, although her narrative rivals Annie's as far as Plimmer is concerned.

Orphaned at a young age, passed between relatives, and running off with a much older man, "Eddowes experienced most of the hardships of life in Victorian England during her early years."[7] Perhaps Plimmer does not have to limit her hardships to merely her early years, since Catharine never seemed to be able to reach any level of comfort. Although she found a second common-law husband after leaving the father of her children and the couple remained together for years, neither seems to have had steady work. She would often pawn items in an attempt to make money for survival, and Plimmer also says that she worked to sell trinkets and things on the street during the day. Apparently the prostitution at night was either supplemental to this income when the couple needed more money, or prostitution alone was not enough to support them. In contrast to Annie's solitary double bed, Catharine and John Kelly's failure to maintain a steady income seems puzzling. Perhaps she is simply not as young and beautiful as those who were better off, either Annie in her lodging house or Mary Jane Kelly and her rented room.

Mary Jane is, of course, "a different kind of prostitute"[8] than the others, not just in age and looks but apparently also bearing and education. While Plimmer does not discuss whether Michael Kidney and John Kelly were aware that Elizabeth and Catharine were prostitutes, he declares that it seems obvious that Mary Jane kept her prostitution from Joe Barnett. Although the pair had been living together, perhaps Barnett had been engaged in more continual labor that would have allowed Mary Jane to know when to expect him home and therefore limit her hours of operation. This situation might also raise questions about the character of Kidney and Kelly, or perhaps their practicality. If they knew about their lovers' means of making money, they might have accepted it as a fact of their situation or perhaps encouraged it as a means of income. If Barnett did not know how Mary Jane earned her money, it might have been a statement of his personality and morals, or perhaps of her own cunning. If Barnett did not know how she earned money, then perhaps he did not know that she earned any at all, and she was free to spend it as she wished.

If she did earn money, however, there is the question of what she did with it. When Barnett moved out of their small room Mary Jane was already behind in rent and was, on the last night of her life, "fairly desperate"[9] to earn some. She knew that her landlord would send someone to collect as least a portion of what was owed, and indeed her body was found because of this very situation. If Mary Jane Kelly, young and attractive, could not earn money when Mary Nichols found two customers in one day and Annie Chapman routinely paid for a double bed, what reason is there for this discrepancy? If she were indeed a prostitute and accustomed to walking the streets, perhaps during the day when Barnett would have been at work, why would she have encountered such difficulties during the last months of her life? These are questions that Plimmer does not think to address.

Plimmer does acknowledge that, in a modern murder investigation, the police would offer victim support to the friends and family of the dead woman. He does not indicate whether this support would be offered to her lover immediately or only after he had been determined not guilty—Plimmer suspects that Elizabeth may have been murdered by boyfriend Michael Kidney—but he does acknowledge that loved ones, even estranged loved ones, may be in need of such a service. Most Ripper narratives end their concern for the relatives after the inquest and the funeral, where all loved ones' reactions are scrutinized for signs of guilt and then generally dismissed. In the quest for discovering the identity of the Ripper, interest in the women and their families ends there as the investigation moves on.

Before his final contribution of the fictionalized interview with the killer, Plimmer reviews the facts of the case with victim profiles. These are apparently geared more toward the Behavioral Science Unit's approach to murder, with the focus being on what these profiles can tell us about the identity of the man who murdered the women and not on the subjects of the profiles themselves. As much as the Victorian era may be chastised for being cold in the face of death, accounts such as these victim profiles strip these women to the bare facts of their bodies' existence.

Chasing the Ripper with Forensics and Fame

In 2002, Patricia Cornwell presented the first Jack the Ripper book to make use of modern DNA extraction technology in order to support her argument that artist Walter Sickert was Jack the Ripper. Her book *Portrait of a Killer: Jack the Ripper Case Closed* came at great personal expense, since Cornwell not only paid for analysis of DNA evidence on a small sample of Ripper letters but also purchased a number of paintings by the artist to analyze. What the book does not emphasize is how many Ripper theorists do not believe that the killer himself wrote any of the letters— and thus did not lick the envelopes or the stamps—or how the analysis actually involved mitochondrial DNA. While mDNA is much more likely to have survived the passing decades, what Cornwell was able to conclude is that Sickert was not excluded from the population that might have licked the areas she tested. This is a topic that Cornwell does feel the need to address in the 2017 updated and expanded text, *Ripper: The Secret Life of Walter Sickert*.

Before becoming a best-selling novelist, especially known for her series centered on medical examiner Kay Scarpetta, Cornwell worked in the Office of the Chief Medical Examiner in West Virginia. Although not a medical examiner herself, through both her fiction and nonfiction works Cornwell became known for her representations of the lives of medical examiners and their use of forensic science. The combination of her reputation for forensic writing, the fact that Cornwell spent so much of her own money, and her identity as one of the few female authors to tackle the subject helped with the popularity of *Portrait of a Killer*, even in the face of controversy from those who had already been studying the crimes. In short, no matter how much money Cornwell pours into her research or how passionately she argues her case, there is still no proof that any of the evidence she tested would have been touched—much less licked—by the real murderer.

Cornwell, like previous authors, focuses her narrative on proving the identity of the killer and not on the women themselves, a direction that has been magnified through book reviews and counter-arguments that followed publication. Although she does indeed devote the majority of her text to Sickert's biography and proof of his alternate identity, Cornwell does take the time to set the scene, giving details about life in the East End for women who lacked the support of family or husbands. Like others before her, Cornwell describes the condition of the local doss houses, but she also explains the process by which the mortuary photographs were taken. These photographs—the most well-known and widely circulated of the murdered women—were the result of a heavy camera, fixed in position, that meant the women's bodies had to be propped up against or hung from a wall.[10] Although Cornwell's description of the process is matter-of-fact, she is clearly presenting readers with a facet of the proceedings that is not commonly published and thus may serve to present readers with a moment of reflection. Not all of the indignities done to their bodies were performed by the Ripper.

At other times, however, her manner of blunt presentation detracts from the humanity of her subjects. When discussing the differences between nineteenth century and modern approaches to murder scenes, Cornwell is more likely to use language expected from the fields of medicine and forensics. She declares that "[t]he most important piece of evidence in any homicide is the body,"[11] reducing the women to mere evidence after the Ripper has turned them from living women to inanimate bodies in the eyes of those called upon to handle the case. These women's bodies are not only objects but also evidence, with the purpose of directing others to the identity of the killer. Not only did they need men in life to protect them from walking the streets, but their deaths are also entangled with—and directed toward—a man.

So much of these women's lives is oriented toward others. Mary Ann Nichols is described as having "nothing left, not even her children,"[12] positioning her as a mother and former wife. Annie Chapman's husband left her "nothing but two children who wanted nothing to do with her."[13] Catherine Eddowes is "a drunken, immoral woman who belonged in the dustbin … and a disgrace to her children"[14] as well. Only Elizabeth Stride and Mary Kelly escape the fate of having failed children as well as spouses and other family members. Then, after death, each is confronted with a new failure: a failure not only to protect herself and stay alive, but also to allow the expects who had full access to their bodies to identify their killer.

It is interesting that, when Cornwell observes that "a woman [at the time] had no legal grounds to leave her husband unless he was unfaithful and cruel or deserted her,"[15] she is referring to Sickert's wife at the time of the murders. Her concern is for Ellen Sickert, who may or may not have known that her husband was not only murdering multiple women but also writing myriad letters to newspapers and the police about his deeds. Certainly a woman who discovered this sort of secret about the man she married would deserve sympathy and should have been able to extract herself from that marriage without social condemnation. But what about those murdered women, four of whom had seen a marriage dissolve? Only Mary Kelly, in the biography she related to "her man, Joseph Barnett,"[16] was widowed and then forced to fend for herself. Mary Ann, Annie, Liz, and Catherine had all seen the end of a marriage—likely common-law in Catherine's case—and the loss of the security and support provided by that husband, but presumably none of these women was married to a serial killer.

These women drank and lied about their pasts and may themselves have been the troublesome spouse in previous relationships. It is possible that Catherine was not a prostitute, since Cornwell presents her and Kelly as cobbling together a living from other temporary positions, but her discussion of alcoholism and the late-nineteenth century approach to it comes after the narrative of Catherine's death. Even if Catherine had not put herself at risk by walking the street as a prostitute, available for any man who had the money, she still made the unwise decision of drinking too much and putting herself in danger by not being in full control of her faculties. Although Cornwell does not say this outright, she does mention in passing that the Ripper "murdered them because it was easy."[17] Murdering women of the East End was easy because they were likely to be prostitutes, likely to be drunk, and unlikely to cause much of a stir if they were missed. Clearly these women had already been rejected by their husband and children, and whatever men they had taken up with since would have been East Enders themselves and hardly respectable.

There is, however, one moment of stark contrast in which Cornwell once again presents readers with a scenario that is unusual for the Ripper narrative. It is common to assert that any and all mutilations to their bodies took places after their throats were slit, and that in itself was likely after they had been choked to unconsciousness. Readers are free to engage in this scrutiny of the women's corpses and other evidence because they have been reassured that the women did not suffer. Cornwell, however, takes a moment to discuss the murder of Mary Jane Kelly and argues that "[s]he may have felt the cuts as the loss of blood quickly caused her to shiver. Her teeth might have begun to chatter, but not for long as she grew faint, went into shock, and died. She may have drowned as blood gushing out of her carotid artery was inhaled through the cut in her windpipe and filled her lungs."[18] Cornwell does not give her readers a Mary Kelly whose death was instantaneous and painless. This Mary Kelly suffered, and her suffering will not be ignored.

Readers are presented with the usual photograph of Mary Kelly's body as it was found the next day, as well as the litany of her injuries. There has always been a question of how quickly the Ripper worked, debated using timelines of when policemen walked their beats and when the women's bodies were discovered, and now readers are confronted with some uncomfortable questions: how long was Mary Kelly conscious of what was happening to her? And how many of those injuries could have been inflicted in that amount of time?

The usual means of presenting the murdered body as evidence involves a time skip between the last known sighting of the woman in question and the discovery of her body. Somehow, between these two points in the time-line and perhaps around the estimated time of death given by the doctor called to the scene, the woman transitioned from a living, breathing person—rejected by her family, a disgrace to her children, an alcoholic and a prostitute—to a corpse and hopeful source of evidence. The transition from life to death is glossed over and, when the coroner's report is dutifully provided, the injuries described are presumed to have been inflicted on a dead body and not one still clinging to life.

Cornwell's description of Mary Kelly's death is visceral and uncomfortable. It confronts readers with the idea of shivering not because of the temperature in the room, but because of massive blood loss, as well as the thought of drowning in blood. This blood, of course, would not have been inhaled through Mary Kelly's mouth, but from the slash in her throat since her windpipe was no longer connected—a graphic image indeed. Cornwell is simply presenting her readers with medical commentary not much different from the litany provided in the coroners' reports, except for the fact that the coroners are clearly describing a body where the life is already absent. The coroners came upon these women already as bodies and already dead, while Cornwell takes this moment to confront the very end of Mary Kelly's life and fill in that time skip between last known living sighting and discovery of the body. In this moment Mary Kelly is confronted as a living, breathing human being—although not for long.

With her background in a medical examiner's office and her history of writing a best-selling series about a medical examiner, it is perhaps not surprising that Cornwell remains largely within the usual expectations of a Ripper narrative. Much of this language and the approach gained popularity in the 1980s, not only with the century mark of the murders but also with the emergence of the FBI's Behavioral Science Unit and the new specific language for discussing serial murder, the killers, and the victims. It is even possible that Cornwell, as one of the few women to write on the subject, consciously made the effort to avoid too many deviations from the standard approach to the subject of the Ripper and his identity. The traditional Ripper narrative has always been more matter-of-fact and distanced, referencing the murdered women exactly as Cornwell describes: as evidence and nothing more. Their importance to the mystery is solely in what clues they can provide.

Despite this, Cornwell does manage to insert some comments that veer away from the usual and by now expected representation, the most obvious being her observation about Mary Kelly's death. Even then the language itself is medical and distanced, presenting a visceral subject almost dispassionately while at the same time grabbing readers in a way few Ripper authors even attempt. Even if the bodies Cornwell examines are currently lifeless, they are not simply objects that were never alive and thus cannot be dead. They are women's bodies, of women whose lives were taken from them.

In a section added for the 2017 revision and expansion, Cornwell remarks that it is "appalling"[19] that so many of these people put themselves in a position where their powers of observation were limited, either by the fact that they were drunk, they were in areas that were not well lit, or they were not wearing any corrective lenses that they needed but were unable to afford. This is a regular sentiment concerning murder victims and a common way of not only indicating how the victims could have prevented their own deaths, but also how readers might be able to protect themselves. The difference in this case, however, is that Cornwell is not discussing the murdered women. She is listing all of the reasons she does not put her faith in the testimony of eyewitnesses.

Perhaps the accusations are similar in more than just their wording. When a victim is mentioned as having failed in some way, it means that she has become a victim in the first place. The least she could do in this situation would be to offer evidence as to the identity of her killer, and, in the case of Jack the Ripper, the women fail do have done that. Now Cornwell is moving beyond blaming the murdered women to blaming the eyewitnesses who have spread their tales—and, perhaps, to the many authors who have also believed them.

It is now no longer a question of decreased ability, either through alcohol or multiple factors concerning eyesight, allowing the crime to happen in the first place, but these issues interfering with the identification and arrest of the person responsible. Those who are too drunk or otherwise incapacitated are no longer women who have thus bought and paid for their fate, allowing the Ripper an easier time at his task, but the innocent bystanders of both genders who were unable to help bring the murderer to justice. Responsibility for the deaths and the escape of the Ripper is thus shared out not only among the dead, but among the living, and given to men as well as women—although still kept from the figure of the Ripper himself. The comment in and of itself might be easy to overlook, perhaps as readers assume that such familiar critiques must once again be heaped against the victims and no others, but this shift in blame is interesting. Cornwell may not go so far as to present Sickert as possessing full responsibility for his crimes, but that blame is at least shared by people who were not his victims.

Just the Facts?

Trevor Marriott's 2007 book, *Jack the Ripper: The 21st Century Investigation*, does not make use of the same sort of DNA evidence as Cornwell's, but Marriott's background is similarly based in the real-life field that proves support for his investigation. As he explains in his introduction, Marriott was hired to the Bedfordshire Police and quickly put in the Criminal Investigation Division,[20] giving him real world experience with murder investigations. Although he does not have the same forensic evidence as Cornwell—he presumably also lacks a spare million or two with which to have conducted such an investigation, since Marriott is not the author of a best-selling crime fiction series—Marriott, like John Plimmer, seeks to bring modern approaches to bear on the Jack the Ripper case.

Despite the fact that his book comes to more than 300 pages, Marriott himself has very little to say about the Ripper's victims. Instead of providing his own descriptions and insights, Marriott introduces each woman with her name and age before reproducing pages of the coroners' inquests. Although he argues that "[n]one of this testimony furnished wholly accurate description of anyone who appears more than one throughout the enquiry into the series of murders,"[21] Marriott himself does not attempt to clarify any individual's identity or sort through these discrepancies. He simply offers up the information collected at the time with only a single instance of analysis.

This comes in his discussion of Catherine Eddowes or, rather, during his discussion of the Goulston Street graffiti. On the night when Catherine's body was discovered, a piece of her apron, shown to fit the one she was wearing, was found in a doorway on Goulston Street beneath some chalked graffiti. Never photographed and thus much contested, this message—generally reproduced as "the Juwes are the men that will not be blamed for nothing"—was only one such slogan chalked on the walls, but the piece of apron meant it was closely scrutinized. Did the Ripper take a piece of Catherine's apron, use it to wipe his hands, and discard it—either beneath an existing message or without noticing the message—or did he take the time to chalk it himself?

Marriott, in an argument expanded in his 2013 eBook *Jack the Ripper: The Secret Police Files*, suggests that Catherine had made use of the cloth as toilet paper. As the graffiti was found near a stairwell and public toilets charged their customers, it is his contention that Catherine made use of this semi-private space before her death and then disposed of her soiled apron. Since graffiti itself was common, this action then unintentionally led to the mystery of the message chalked nearest to the apron. Discussions of feminine hygiene related to the Ripper narrative are rare indeed and somehow gritty in a way that coroners' reports are not, and thus this deviation from contemporary reports stands out in Marriott's discussion.

This approach to the representation of the victim in which Marriott relies heavily on contemporary reports and withholds his own interpretations could have been done for a number of reasons. First, it might be that Marriott wished to play it safe, presenting readers with contemporary accounts rather than attempting to form his own opinions of women who had lived and died over a century earlier. It might be an acknowledgment that a man born and raised in a world vastly different from the one these women inhabited could not properly assess their situations. Or it could be the decision of a policeman who wants to present readers with the facts and just the facts, remaining distant in order to allow them—and himself—to form an unbiased opinion. Marriott, following the inquest reports, jumps between the women as alive and the women as dead, once again glossing over the transition as has long been expected. Although murdered, these women have not suffered.

Back to the DNA

Over a decade after Patricia Cornwell faced criticism for issues of mitochondrial DNA and imperfect sample sources, Russell Edwards found himself facing those same critiques. His 2014 book *Naming Jack the Ripper* recounts his attempts to match the DNA sample on a shawl with both Catherine Eddowes and his chosen suspect, Aaron Kosminski. Like Cornwell, Edwards finds himself only able to test for mitochondrial DNA and thus make sweeping conclusions that the results do not rule out Catherine or Kosminski, instead of pinpointing them. Further, in the same way that research has not proven that the Ripper wrote, stamped, or sealed his own letters, Edwards admits that the provenience of the shawl is itself in question. He has "no proof it had belonged to the victim Catherine Eddowes, just a long family history,"[22] making his claim that it relates to the Ripper murders even more difficult to substantiate.

Unlike Trevor Marriott, Edwards presents his readers with the women's biographies in his own words, reflecting his own opinions. His Mary Ann Nichols abandons her family for reasons he does not fully discern, leaving all of her children in the care of multiple others and therefore presumably not together. It is during this time, when she has to fend for herself, that Mary Ann undertakes prostitution as her means of income, and it is this prostitution that leads to her dubious fame as being the first Ripper victim. Edwards makes a valiant attempt to remind his readers that these victims were first and foremost women, with their own histories and personalities, before they were lumped together and numbered according to the time of their deaths, but even he seems unable to fully pursue those histories and personalities. Very little information is offered about Mary Ann the person, since it is as a victim she has achieved what Edwards terms "a strange immortality."[23] No matter what their lives or personalities as individuals, these five women are forever lumped together through their deaths, which were not of their own choosing. Their individuality is subsumed under the Ripper's activities and his identity.

Annie fairs little better. Edwards presents his readers with an alcoholic prostitute who, despite having family nearby—and presumably being on better terms with them than Mary Ann was with hers—struggled to make a living. He declares that Annie, like most of the women in the East End, attempted to piece together enough money through selling goods instead of herself. Here Edwards suggests that, despite the large number of prostitutes in the East End, it was not the first choice in vocation for the majority of them. While many Victorians and still more recent authors seem to think that many of these women made a beeline for prostitution at the least provocation, Edwards acknowledges the difficulties women faced in this period when they lacked support, either from a husband or extended family. It is a broader acknowledgment that most of these women, and not just Annie herself, did what they could in the hopes that they might be able to keep themselves off the streets.

Edwards also brings his readers closer to Annie's experience than many other authors. While discussions of the weather and temperature are usually put forward in order to facilitate estimates of time of death of these women, he brings up the conditions during Annie's last night alive and presents her in them *as* alive instead of as a cooling corpse. "It was cold for that time of year," Edwards informs his readers, as many authors have, adding that the chill and rain made it "an unpleasant night to be out, especially for someone who was so clearly unwell."[24] Annie's inability to produce money for a bed that night is now framed not merely as a moment that would facilitate her death, but as an occurrence that would not have turned out well for Annie even if she had not met the Ripper. She would likely have lived—for another few months, at least—but the experience of merely being out on the street in those conditions would have been miserable even for a healthy woman. Annie's recent stay in the infirmary and her various post-mortem diagnoses mean she was hardly in the best of shape to have been kicked out of her lodging house in the first place, and suggest that her last night was miserable indeed.

Although Annie's alcoholism is not in question, and although Edwards gives it as the reason she ended up alone in the East End, he does not blame her final night's misery on alcohol. In the end his Annie is a woman fighting to maintain herself through means other than prostitution, unknowingly suffering from a number of illnesses and with the bad luck to have crossed paths with the Ripper on her last night. Even though she spends her money at the pub first, thinking of food and shelter second, her recent stay in the infirmary means that she likely had no money for a bed simply because she was unable to earn it. This Annie is not drunk when she meets her fate and is able to be seen as more of a sympathetic figure.

Liz, though, is a different story. Even if her marriage, like Annie's, ended because of her drinking habit, Edwards makes it clear that Liz's drinking led to many arrests. Whatever Liz's personality, she became violent and out of control when she drank, an assessment that was not made of Annie. Although Liz does indeed try to find work outside of prostitution, "there simply wasn't enough work to keep her going, especially with her drink habit."[25] Oddly enough, even though Liz was not on the street because she had been thrown out due to a lack of doss money—she was seen preparing for a night out and leaving freely—her alcoholism can still be positioned as the cause of her murder. If she did not want more money, presumably for drinking, then she would not have needed to seek a secluded location with a strange man.

In a fit of generosity Edwards at least declares his forgiveness of the lies she told about herself, since empathy moves him to comprehend why a woman in her position might make up romanticized versions of her past. He even suggests that Liz might have come to believe her own stories, considering the frequency with which she told them, likely showing an understanding of how difficult and depressing life in the East End must have been. The fact that he admits seeing he might have done the same had he been in her position makes it unlikely that he would be condemning a pathological liar unable to separate truth from her own fiction.

Catherine Eddowes is, like the others, an alcoholic, and once again a past relationship has dissolved because of this. Edwards allows that, at the time, "she was using the surname Conway, a common enough thing to do when a couple were living as a man and wife,"[26] although his wording makes it very clear that the couple had not in fact married. Clearly the relationship ended by Catherine's alcoholism, although long-lasting, was merely common-law and had not seen the benefit of a wedding. Unlike other authors Edwards does not begrudge her the use of the name, nor mock her adoption of it. It almost comes off as a mild rebuke against anyone who would choose to focus on the fact that the relationship was not legalized, indicating that this was "common enough" in the time and place. Whatever morals twenty-first century readers may have involving marriage—and, of course, prostitution—Catherine's lack of a proper signed paper is dismissed without fanfare.

While Catherine's alcoholism would seem to have been enough of a reason for the relationship to end, considering how the previous women's stories were told, Edwards gives her a reason for not wanting to stay with Conway. Perhaps in relation to her alcoholism, Conway himself had occasional bouts of violence that were directed toward Catherine. Her later long-term relationship with John Kelly was presumably free from such violence, even if she continued to drink to excess. Although an alcoholic, Catherine seems to have preferred serial monogamy to a string of men in her life, and her assumed role as prostitute is questioned. If most of the women in the East End did what they could to avoid prostitution, and if Catherine had her long-term steady man in John Kelly, then perhaps prostitution was not her main means of earning money.

Catherine is at the center of Edwards' argument since the source of DNA is a shawl that he claims was on her body when she died. Since there is no written history of the shawl he must spend some time making a case for its importance and indeed its existence. Edwards ends up concluding the expensive silk shawl had never actually belonged to Catherine for two main reasons: first, since the dye ran when the shawl got wet, it "could never have been used as an outer garment."[27] Catherine, having no fixed address, would not have always had a place to go when it rained or a layer to put over the shawl, so the dye would likely have already run had she owned and worn the shawl. Perhaps more compelling is the argument that, during their last days together, Catherine and Kelly pawned items in order to make money for food, including his boots. Surely if they were so desperate to make money that they would pawn the very boots off his feet, they would have pawned her silk shawl instead—and surely said boots would not have been pawned if the couple had been accustomed to making money through Catherine's prostitution. Through these arguments Edwards once again shows an understanding of the position these women found themselves in and thus attempts to connect the shawl to his Ripper suspect as a more believable provenience of such a fine garment.

These moments of connection and apparent deeper understanding are still interspersed among the more common, distancing language. In reference to Mary Kelly, for example, Edwards writes, "Again, thank God, the victim was dead swiftly."[28] Comparing this to Patricia Cornwell's description of Mary Kelly's death shows that Edwards has fallen into the trope of quick deaths, although at least he does not attempt to make hers painless, as well. Although the coroners' reports indicate that Mary Kelly did not have any defensive wounds, those reports from 1888 cannot always be taken as though they were the full, comprehensive, and strictly regimented documents of the twenty-first century. It is simply easier for Edwards to dismiss Mary quickly, especially when her background is only obtained third-hand and he suspects that even her name might not have been the truth. Unlike many authors, Edwards does not ascribe some deeper meaning so special attributes to Mary, since his main focus is on a garment he does not believe she ever touched.

Jack the Ripper and the CSI Treatment

Instead of using modern technology to illustrate proper procedure for a murder investigation or to identify the Ripper himself at this late date, Paul Begg and John Bennett's 2012 book *Jack the Ripper CSI: Whitechapel* seeks not to investigate, but rather to illustrate the Whitechapel crime scenes. Although other books have relied on photographs of the scenes themselves, not from 1888 but from before any time any of the locations was destroyed or remodeled, Begg and Bennett present readers with an illustration-heavy volume of computer generated images of the crime scenes. They are meant to help readers imagine the place and not the crime itself, since the spaces themselves are empty. They are not occupied by people, living or dead, or any other possible clues.

Because the identity of the Ripper himself is not under discussion, each of the women's biographies for once outshines discussion of the killer. Begg and Bennett do not even bother listing possible suspects or refuting the less likely. Indeed, their entire focus is on recreating the spaces of 1888 to help readers place themselves in that distant time and place.

Mary Ann Nichols is at times called Mary Ann and at other times addressed simply as Nichols. The authors hit the high points of her biography, including the dissolution of her marriage and the existence of her five children, adding once again that "the couple's eldest son would have nothing to do with his father at his mother's funeral."[29] Both father and son attended that funeral, despite the fact that Mary Ann had apparently abandoned them, and the fact that this son still avoided his father indicates that, whatever may have been said, not all of the blame fell on Mary Ann herself. It is a pointed observation, given without extra comment but presented to readers so that they might reflect on the fact that, even if she had been given to drink, Mary Ann might not have been the more offensive of the married couple.

Begg and Bennett also point out that the blacksmith Mary Ann had a long relationship with after leaving Nichols was not a complete stranger. Thomas Stuart Drew had apparently courted Mary Ann before her marriage and was a widower at the time when Mary Ann left her husband. Although that relationship also faltered, this information puts it in a different light. Instead of the possibility of Mary Ann grasping for any man who would support her, it could be in fact Mary Ann returning to a man who cared for her and might have made a better husband in the first place. Or, considering the reasons for the breakdown of her marriage, Drew might have been the cause for Nichols to accuse his wife of cheating on him. Whichever way Mary Ann's relationships went, Drew separates from her just as Nichols did, leaving Mary Ann to make her own way in the world and thus putting her on the street to die at the scene Begg and Bennett illustrate.

Annie is not accused outright of cheating on her husband, but she was given to drink and, in the course of her alcoholism, became an embarrassment. This is not entirely clarified, but considering the fact that the Chapmans tended to live in in wealthier homes in the course of his work, it seems there would be a wide variety of ways a servant's wife might embarrass him and threaten his position. Like Mary Ann, Annie left children behind when she walked out of her marriage, but John Chapman apparently gave all of them a good education and thus no reason to avoid him.

He also seems to have been a kinder man than William Nichols, although Begg and Barnett's description of the allowance he gave his wife seems baffling. According to the authors, Annie received "a hefty chunk of John's earnings, probably half of what a good labourer would hope to make."[30] If he had the children and was paying for their schooling, why would Annie then receive a whole half of what he brought in? Other authors have pointed out that this sum was large and likely more than a woman in the East End would need to live comfortably, but this comparison shows just how shocking the payments were. Begg and Bennett even give Annie credit for struggling against her alcoholism and getting it more or less under control, meaning she would not necessarily have needed to spend all of her allowance to keep herself in relative comfort. As much of an embarrassment Annie may have been during her marriage, it would seem that her time in the East End had the effect of helping her straighten up and gain control over her drinking.

Elizabeth Stride receives no such positive concessions. Even her mortuary photograph and a contemporary drawing are deemed unflattering by the authors, leaving her no redeeming features. After being registered as a professional prostitute in her home country of Sweden, they declare that "[h]er life was going horribly wrong."[31] Even her reaction to her mother's death is given a negative cast, since it becomes the impetus for her arrival in London not because she was fleeing the terrible thing that had happened, but because she was able to pay her way with her small inheritance. Instead of a flighty dreamer, Liz seems to be a shrewd opportunist.

Begg and Bennett give her more nicknames than the usual "Long Liz," although they cannot quite imagine why she might have been called some of them. Others stem from her habit of faking epileptic fits or perhaps her smile, which they likewise deem must have been unattractive. The sham elliptic fits were presumably Liz's way of getting out of drunk and disorderly charges, once more displaying a woman willing to take advantage of a situation so she could turn it to her favor. The sinking of the *Princess Alice* is not part of the main narrative but rather occupies a box labeled "Background Intelligence," mimicking a police file, just another illustration of the situations Liz would use in order to show herself in a better light.

Even Catherine Eddowes has "a dark side to her character,"[32] although with the authors' description it would seem that the dark side is nearly her only side. Although she was orphaned at a young age and ran away from the aunt and uncle who had been charged with caring for her, Catherine's drinking and her temper override any sympathy. This is a Catherine who is not only forced to break with her family but is thrown out of the casual ward during her final stay. Her marriage to Thomas Conway and her relationship with their children fall apart due to her drinking, and perhaps her relationship with John Kelly was not as rosy as others have seen it. Kelly told police that Catherine was going to her daughter's on her last day in order to borrow some money, but that daughter had moved without leaving a forwarding address so that she could avoid her mother, the scrounger. Begg and Bennett suggest Kelly told this story to cover for the fact that he knew Catherine would be out seeking clients and earning money through prostitution.

Mary Jane Kelly, also simply called Kelly by the authors, is perhaps treated more kindly solely because there were fewer people to speak about her after her death and there is no way of proving or disproving what little was said. Perhaps the biggest argument in her favor was that "her lover" or "former lover"[33]—he is referred to as both on the same page—Joseph Barnett continued to give her money even though they were no longer living together, and appeared to hope that their separation was only temporary. Kelly seemed to inspire tenderness in him, and although the authors speculate that she might have also had trouble with her parents, there was no record of what that trouble may have been, and no family stepped forward to support a negative reputation. Even though Kelly has been surrounded with all kinds of speculation, Begg and Bennett stick to the most factual evidence they can find, and it seems to tend toward the positive.

Despite, or perhaps because of, their focus on the locations of the crimes and not the enactor thereof, Begg and Bennett are able to paint brief pictures of the victims shot through with moments of intense clarity. They return to the seafaring theme when they point out that these women were "the flotsam of society, the unwanted and uncared about victims of their own vice and misfortune,"[34] and illustrate this through the women's biographies. Few of those who even knew them seem to have cared about their lives or the deaths, and Begg and Bennett point out that their deaths would likewise have gone unnoticed if not for the fact that they were murdered. Because they are not concerned with the identity of the Ripper but instead with the locations of the murders, Begg and Bennett are able to focus on these women not as clues to solve a mystery but in order to ask the question of how these women had ended up there in the first place.

Under a Microscope

The introduction of new technologies and police procedures is meant to increase the speed and ease at which law enforcement officials can solve crimes. At the time of the Ripper murders even fingerprint identification was still in the future, much less tests to determine blood type or DNA. Twenty-first century readers exist in an age permeated with narratives of stalking and catching serial killers that began in the 1980s when the FBI assumed the title of serial killer expert. Since then the figure of the almost psychic law enforcement official has found roles in books, movies, and popular television shows, proclaiming the near omniscient powers of these specially trained individuals. These narratives also include the required forensic evidence to prove this official correct.

Although the behavioral science experts and their work has been used to analyze the Ripper since the 1980s, the use of modern technology has been more recent. Patricia Cornwell and Russell Edwards took it upon themselves to, at their own expense, procure and test artifacts that were associated with the Ripper in 1888. Unfortunately these tests could not rely on DNA to specifically point to their chosen suspects and instead had to use mDNA, due to the age of those artifacts. mDNA can be used to exclude suspects but not to identify them, and both Cornwell and Edwards were able to show that the tests their experts administered did not put their personal suspects out of the running. Unlike a good crime novel or CSI episode, however, technology did not point the finger at an individual and, since their suspects are long dead, there was no hope of confronting them in an interrogation room and attempting to elicit a confession.

John Plimmer was able to interrogate his suspect, although that interview transcript—and indeed much of the evidence used to point to him in the first place—was only a fiction. In his attempt to present readers with a modern investigation into the Ripper murders, Plimmer had to create evidence for his case simply because policemen in 1888 would not have thought to have looked for it. Even if they had discovered the specific evidence Plimmer points to, it would have been of little use to them. Plimmer thus manufactures a case based on true events, although he manipulates details in a way that would not stand up to cross examination.

Plimmer, Cornwell, and Edwards all make use of modern technology in order to light the way toward the final, conclusive identification of the mysterious Jack the Ripper. Their focus is still on the Ripper himself, which comes at a cost to the representation of the women he killed. True, there are moments in which authors bring these women to the fore and present them as living people worthy of empathy, instead of bodies meant to only be searched for clues, but those moments are rare. The identity of the Ripper is the grail and the women's bodies are merely signposts indicating the way.

Paul Begg and John Bennet, on the other hand, use improvements in technology in order to focus their research on another aspect of the Ripper murders entirely. They utilize computer imaging to construct the scenes themselves, devoid of all human presence or evidence. Perhaps because their focus is not on the Ripper, they are able to more fully explore the lives of the women who met their deaths at these locations. They do not need to use the women's bodies as clues because they are not asking any questions that those clues would answer. Begg and Bennett therefore also belong to the category of authors who have chosen to direct their research about the Ripper murders to something other than the identity of the Ripper himself. They have selected a new angle with which to approach the case and in that new approach may have illuminated aspects that other researchers had not uncovered.

The authors in the next chapter have likewise incorporated something "different" into their books. Some of them, like Begg and Bennet, have chosen to focus on an aspect of the case that has not yet come to the fore. Others approach the same question of the Ripper's identity but from a new position, accusing family members of having been the Ripper or even crafting the narrative in order to propose that the Ripper was actually a woman. With each approach meant to clarify a new aspect of the Ripper mystery—or perhaps solely to sell a book when so many have already been written—the representation of, and time spent discussing, the murdered women continues to evolve.

NINE

Crimes for a New Age
Variations and Changes
in Victim Representation
of the 21st Century

Considering the vast outpouring of books about Jack the Ripper that occurred in the final decades of the twentieth century, it might be reasonable for researchers and authors to ask: what more could be said? Even if a new name is submitted as a suspect for the Ripper's true identity, what could be done to make that person stand out or be more of a possibility than the names already mentioned? How could authors take a narrative more than a century old and make it new and exciting again without simply being a repeat or a rehash of what has gone before?

The twenty-first century answered this call in the form of variety. New categories of suspects—including women, the author's own ancestor, and Americans—allowed for a different angle on the investigation into the Ripper's identity, as did two more supposed autobiographies. Other authors took their research further, ignoring the idea of the Ripper's true identity completely to focus on a gap or previously unexplored facet of the Ripper narrative, shining more light on the mystery without specifically focusing on the Ripper himself. Although some of these approaches minimized the discussion of the murdered women, others allowed new angles of insight to be brought forward.

Women Against Women

Although he does not make an entirely new accusation in his 2012 book *Jack the Ripper: The Hand of a Woman—The Compelling New Account,*

John Morris' claim that Jack the Ripper was in fact a woman was not one that had received serious consideration since William Stewart's book in 1939. While Stewart set his accusations on a profession instead of a specific person—choosing "midwife" instead of the figure of Olga Tchkersoff suggested by Edwin Woodhall two years earlier—John Morris names Lizzie Williams, wife to Sir John Williams. This does give him the distinction of naming a suspect who was, in fact, married to another suspect, although changing the narrative of the Ripper murders from a male to a female murderer comes with its own challenges.

According to Morris, Lizzie Williams set off on a very Dr. Stanley–type quest, with the ultimate goal being the murder of Mary Jane Kelly. This murderous spree began because she and Dr. Williams were unable to have children and, presumably because he suspected the issue lay with her, Dr. Williams sought out younger, prettier Mary Jane Kelly so that she might provide him with a child. Out of jealousy Lizzie decided she should kill Mary Jane, embarking on the initial murders purely to prove to herself that she could. Morris further suggests that John Williams, a respected gynecologist, not only failed to help his wife's infertility, but also taught Lizzie enough about anatomy and the surgeries he practiced that there were questions of whether or not the Ripper possessed medical training.

Perhaps because of Lizzie's obsession with her own barrenness, a litany of the victims lists their names, ages, number of children, and their occupations as common prostitute. Motherhood trumps even marriage or any current relationships in this list for all but Mary Jane Kelly. The other women's boyfriends matter little, since they were not John Williams. For Morris—and for Lizzie—it matters only that they were currently prostitutes, on the street looking for money, and mostly drunk. Indeed, "[i]f Nichols had been even half-sober, she might have fought off her murderer"[1] and brought Lizzie's murderous spree to a halt that night. Being a woman herself means that Lizzie would have been expected to have been weaker than a man and thus her approach to the murders would necessarily be different from the usual assumptions.

Although Morris makes it clear that East End prostitutes must have been used to women approaching them to buy sexual favors as well as men, he jumps to say that he is not "suggesting for one moment that Lizzie Williams was anything other than a heterosexual."[2] It is unclear whether the suggestions that Lizzie was either bisexual or a lesbian would be an insult to her, or whether Morris finds the prospect of a female serial killer difficult enough to present without questioning her sexual orientation as well. Indeed, Morris put himself in the position of being a man declaring such things as how only a woman would have placed Annie's belongings so carefully after her death,[3] even in the aftermath of a murder giving in to some innate feminine desire for order. Lizzie would have done this after finding a cloth or rag in Annie's pocket meant for personal hygiene, so that the killer could clean her hands—Morris points out that no such cloth was found, so Lizzie must have taken it away with her—and the scatter of belongings was simply too out of order to Lizzie to leave. Her compulsive urge to straighten the items was a clear indication of her femininity, although this judgment of her actions comes from a member of the opposite sex.

As other authors have suggested, Morris claims that Catherine Eddowes' death was a mistake born of her use of the name "Mary Kelly." Rather than being old and haggard like the previous women, Catherine looked younger and had apparently kept herself better. Naturally if Lizzie thought Catherine was Mary Kelly she would have suspected she was looking at her husband's mistress, and Morris suggests that an "attractive young woman who was always happy"[4] would have seemed different enough from Lizzie herself. This says some negative things about Lizzie and makes Catherine's death all the more tragic, since she wasn't simply an old hag waiting for the end of her joyless life, as the other women presumably were. Although little is stated about Catherine beyond the fact that she had three children and that she was drunk when Lizzie encountered her, only Mary Kelly has more information presented about her past. Morris depicts Lizzie as attacking Catherine in a jealous rage, with the facial mutilations enacted to destroy the other woman's femininity and the missing kidney Lizzie's attempt to remove Catherine's heart.

Lizzie's desire to remove the heart of her husband's mistress was indeed fulfilled once she had tracked down the real Mary Kelly, "a captivating, fertile Irish girl"[5] whose short-lived marriage had produced a son. This son was not present in Mary Kelly's room on the night of her death—and indeed, Morris admits to being unable to track him at all—but was clear proof that Mary Kelly, unlike Lizzie, was capable of bearing children. Again the idea of fertility and the focus on the womb is tracked through the storyline, along with Lizzie's desire to utterly and completely destroy the woman her husband had chosen to father his child. Unlike the other women, Mary Kelly is allowed a past of broken relationships, making John Williams just another man for her. Even though her marriage ended because of her husband's death, she is then shown to foist her son off on friends when she wanted privacy in her room, either to pursue her latest doomed relationship or to support them through prostitution. The other women may have been prostitutes, but Mary Kelly was carrying on with a married man, which made her worse.

Morris makes two other notable moves when discussing the murdered women. First, when describing their injuries, he does not refer to them by name. They become simply "the victim" or "the woman," impersonal and distant. Second, when Morris describes the position in which these women were found, he seems incapable of mentioning the position of their legs without immediately connecting it to the sexual act. Granted, the women were indeed known to be prostitutes, and this might be an aspect of arguing that the killer was female instead of male, but the repetition is almost overwhelming. Even dead, the women are nothing more than vessels for their wombs.

Two years later, in 2014, Tom Wescott makes a similar shift in his book *The Bank Holiday Murders: The True Story of the Whitechapel Murders.* Unlike Morris, Wescott is not certain of the identity of the Ripper himself, but rather focuses on a woman who is usually relegated to a bit part in the Ripper narrative, arguing that she seems to be an accomplice. Wescott does not discuss all five canonical murders, instead focusing mainly on Polly Nichols and some earlier murders he connects with his suspected accomplice, Pearly Poll.

Wescott identifies Pearly Poll as "a minor and rather whimsical character in the modern re-telling of the Ripper story,"[6] known for being the prostitute said to have been out with Martha Tabram on the night she was murdered. If Tabram is added to the list, Polly becomes the second Ripper victim, and Wescott draws connections within the small geographical area to show how Pearly Poll might have influenced the investigation into Polly's death the same way she interfered with the investigation into Martha's. He further suggests that the woman Annie Chapman fought with before her death was a friend of Pearly Poll's, connecting Pearly Poll to yet another murder.

There is not much personal information given about the women Wescott does discuss, mostly because he marvels that "it's as though someone were killing the same women over and over,"[7] considering how similar their stories were. This is not a new observation and has been used by authors both to dismiss the individuality of the murdered women and to make a case for the Ripper's victim type. At the same time Wescott does give the women he discusses moments of individuality, such as when he notes that Polly "did all she could in those final days to keep from having to 'go out' for money,"[8] marking her as something other than a professional prostitute.

With his focus on the bank holiday murder victims and on Pearly Poll, Wescott does not present readers with the normal, expected Ripper narrative. He is not explicitly searching for the Ripper's identity—although he does suggest that further investigation into Pearly Poll might reveal him—and he does not expand his timeline to include all five canonical victims. The decision to focus on bringing Pearly Poll to the forefront limits his scope and shifts his attention from the murdered women to one who was still alive—and possibly manipulating the police to prevent the murdered women from seeing justice.

The Ripper Murders as Ancestral Tales

As seen above, John Morris accused Lizzie Williams of being the Ripper in his 2012 book, but seven years earlier Tony Williams and Humphrey Price wrote *Uncle Jack*, accusing Lizzie's husband—and William's great-uncle—of that same title. Williams explains that he was intrigued when he came across a letter written by his famous ancestor and looked more deeply into his papers, discovering that the collection of John Williams' journals included one for 1888 that had a number of pages missing. It seems that Williams may have set out to disprove his suspicions that Sir John Williams, respected obstetrician and gynecologist and contributor to the National Library of Wales, was Jack the Ripper, but ends up actually finding information that supports his relative's secret identity.

Since his choice for Ripper suspect is not only a physician but on his own family tree, Williams emphasizes that the "[h]e killed the women quickly and cleanly"[9] and "in each case death was almost instantaneous."[10] It is perhaps the only defense that can be made for the Ripper, who was after all a murderer and mutilator of women. Williams assures readers that those mutilations were only affected after the quick death—the blood in his veins might be tainted with a murderer, but not a monster.

The murdered women themselves are likewise quickly dismissed, first in a list that contains only their names, locations and dates of death, and ages at the time of death, sandwiched by the above reassurances. He then turns to further investigating the life of his uncle, only coming back to the women ninety pages further on. They are still easily disregarded and clearly downplayed, since Williams' focus is indeed on Sir John and he seems to have reached the conclusion that the physician was responsible for the violent acts. After all, if Sir John were innocent, then it would not matter if the dead women had been the most highly respected in the land since he had no hand in their deaths. It is only his guilt that makes the identity of the women of any importance to Williams as he tracks his ancestor's history.

Mary Ann Nichols is an alcoholic who lost every good thing that ever came her way to drink, including her marriage, her children, and the possibility of steady employment. Presumably drink would likely have stolen any possible good thing yet to come. Annie Chapman has "little to live for,"[11] what with her husband's death and her children dead or living abroad. She even spent time in the infirmary before her death, so Annie could not be said to even have her health. These women, like those who came after them, were prostitutes, and Williams makes the case that most, if not all of them, likely encountered his uncle through the course of his occupation before their deaths. It is a reference to Mary Ann Nichols in his uncle's notes that started him on this quest.

Liz Stride, like those before her, suffered from a failed marriage, a dead husband, and drink, but despite these shortcomings and her propensity to tell lies, she seems to have been well-liked. This is, of course, by the standards of the East End, which perhaps makes it easier for Williams to think of his uncle as having murdered her, since she would not have been so warmly received outside the poorest area of London. Catherine Eddowes is likely a bit dimwitted, since it took her twenty years to leave Conway despite the fact that he was beating her, and she willingly went with the Ripper into Mitre Square on the night of her death at the height of the murders. If Williams' Uncle John were indeed the murderer, then perhaps Catherine could be forgiven for having accompanied a well-dressed man of his standing, especially if she had known him as a physician, but even then meeting Sir John in Whitechapel after midnight should have been enough to make her wonder. If Catherine were stupid enough to stay in an abusive relationship, she can't entirely have been expected to have the wits to avoid her own murder.

The description of Mary Kelly includes the fact that, after arriving in London, "she went off the rails, and then fetched up dead in a Whitechapel hovel"[12]—as though Mary herself were solely responsible for all that had happened in her own life. Williams has her end up "dead" instead of "murdered," supposedly as a result of her own trajectory in life, and she is as disposable as the rest. Although Morris argued that Mary Kelly was key to the murders and a significant player in the life of Sir John, she is just another expendable prostitute for Williams.

He likewise dismisses the plight of East End women in general, explaining that many of them—and likely even the Ripper's victims—were only casual prostitutes who resorted to selling themselves when desperately in need of money. He minimizes the act of casual prostitution by saying that "in the end they all fell back on what came easiest."[13] Not only does everyone resort to it, but for a woman, the act of selling herself for sexual favors is easy. Perhaps this is only true for the class of women who have already seemed to have lost everything, so respectability has already fled, but Williams also completely dismisses the idea that accompanying strange men to secluded places in the hopes of receiving a few pennies could be difficult or dangerous. Williams is, of course, not alone in his minimization of the victims or his grouping of women together in order to dismiss them—he simply has the added pressure of discussing a man whose name falls on his own family tree, and thus has the extra incentive of downplaying the horrifying nature of these murders, especially when he cannot prove that his uncle did not commit them.

Antonia Alexander takes up the idea of Sir John as Jack the Ripper in her 2013 book *The Fifth Victim*, likewise placing a famous name in her ancestry. In Alexander's case, however, the name is that of Mary Kelly, who is her own great-great-grandmother. The confusing aspect, at least for those familiar with the Ripper narrative, is the fact that Alexander's Mary Kelly, while targeted by the Ripper, is not in fact the victim Mary Kelly. Instead she is a woman who left her family—including her living husband and children—in order to flee to London to be with Sir John. Despite being apparently more appealing than her husband, Sir John tires of this Mary Kelly, although she lives and returns to her family. The Mary Kelly who was the final Ripper murder victim had borrowed Alexander's great-great-grandmother's name, since the pair had come to London at the same time.

Despite the fact that the book's title is *The Fifth Victim*, the focus of Alexander's text is first Sir John—she extensively repeats Williams' research—and then her own ancestor, who was not a murder victim at all. There are few notes about the other murdered women, who apparently did not know Alexander's great-great-grandmother and thus do not impact the storyline. Mary Ann Nichols lived in workhouses and Annie had sought treatment at an infirmary after a fistfight, but otherwise no information is offered about the other women. Alexander even admits that she has no idea who the murdered Marie Kelly—who may have affected the French spelling in order to differentiate herself from her namesake—actually was. Otherwise they are simply "poor vulnerable women"[14] who, unlike her own ancestor, were not able to dodge the Ripper's knife.

Despite the focus of her narrative indicated by her title, Alexander spends much of the text recounting the argument for Sir John and Jack the Ripper. The focus on her own great-great-grandmother is limited to the final ten pages of the text, and even this is not entirely sympathetic. Alexander points out that "[s]ome women ... were bored with a husband who was loyal and dependable and family oriented, a man who'd want nothing more than to make them happy,"[15] clearly criticizing Mary Kelly for giving up such a relationship in order to pursue one with a married man in the big city. Despite her claim that she is not here to judge, Alexander makes her own feelings clear, both about her ancestor and the man she abandoned her family for.

The intriguing aspect that Alexander does not explicitly mention is that, in forming her narrative this way, she is struggling with the same familial guilt that seems to plague Williams. While he could only find information that seemed to corroborate his ancestor's identity as a murderer, Alexander's narrative has Mary Kelly being the reason that Sir John began to murder in the first place. This once again situates Mary Kelly—albeit not the murder victim Mary Kelly—as the cause of the murders due to the reactions and emotions she brings out in the killer. The five women Alexander glosses over are only dead because of her great-great-grandmother, and Alexander may be attempting to avoid any sense of familial guilt when she condemns the fact that her ancestor left a presumably good marriage without explicitly placing any blame on her shoulders for the murders that followed.

Although both Williams and Alexander are far enough removed from their ancestors so as to never have met them and thus never formed a personal attachment or impression of them, they each chose to align those ancestors with the Jack the Ripper narrative. Williams gives his great-uncle the defining role and places him at center stage as the Ripper himself, while Alexander presents readers with the addition of her great-great-grandmother as Sir John's lover and the reason he murdered so many strangers in the first place. While engaging in a narrative that was already more than a century old, each sought to personalize it by literarily relating to a figure within the story while at the same time enacting a number of rhetorical moves in order to minimize the lives of the murdered women and the violence—and guilt—of their deaths.

Foreigner Jack

Although it was popular at the time to accuse Jack the Ripper of having been a foreigner, "foreigner" was most often interpreted to have meant that the Ripper was a Jew and likely fleeing pogroms in Eastern Europe. Over a century after the crimes, Stewart Evans and Paul Gainey wrote *The Lodger: The Arrest & Escape of Jack the Ripper* (1995)—or, as the title was printed for the later editions, *Jack the Ripper: First American Serial Killer.* Working off a name taken from a letter written by Inspector John Littlechild, Evans and Gainey make the case for American Francis Tumblety as having been the Ripper. Since the Littlechild letter—and thus Tumblety as a suspect—had been ignored for so long, the authors devote their text to exploring his biography and viability as a suspect.

Evans and Gainey seem sympathetic to the idea that women in the East End would need to resort to prostitution, since "[t]he few jobs available to women ... hardly provided appealing alternatives"[16] considering the long hours and dismal conditions women would face in factories or as maids. Their assessment of each of the murdered women, however, veers toward the negative. When discussing Polly's alcoholism, for example, they say she "would sell her body and soul for a drink"[17]—her body quite literally—and that her drinking was what kept her from succeeding in both her marriage and any attempts to reform her life. In fact they frame the dissolution of Polly's marriage as having set her free, since she no longer held responsibilities as a wife or mother and had no one to look after except herself. Granted, her alcoholism prevented her from doing well at that, and it is likely her alcoholism that was to blame for her being on the street the night of her murder. Whatever chances Polly had in life, she could not overcome her drinking to take full advantage of them.

Less is said about Annie, although the authors refer to her as "unfortunate"[18] twice in four pages. Despite the fact that she was unattractive, Annie seemed to make her way well enough with two men in the East End. They presumably both paid for her bed and did not mind that she was working as a prostitute. Evans and Gainey name two men specifically who were known to associate with Annie, but add that she was not above sharing her bed "casually"[19] with other men. Clearly selling her body was a casual act for Annie, not worth worrying over or thinking about as long as it resulted in money.

Intriguingly Evans and Gainey find Long Liz to be the most sympathetic of the women, noting that her arrival in London came after the death of her parents and the birth of a stillborn child, both understandable reasons for a woman to want to leave her home country and that life behind. Yes, Liz is an alcoholic, but certainly not on par with Polly. Liz was also "in better health and better looking"[20] than the other two women—not difficult, especially considering Annie's health and appearance—and may not have been prone to the others' less appealing habits. They note that Liz, unlike Polly or Annie, was not kicked out of her lodging house that night for lack of funds. If Liz did drink, she apparently was not such a slave to the bottle that she would spend her last coins on alcohol and forgo a place to sleep.

Little is said about Kate aside from the fact that she tended to call herself Kate Kelly despite not being married into the last name. This is almost emphasized, although there is no such discussion of whether or not she had adopted the name of Conway previously. Her relationship with John Kelly is thus established as being both steady and of a long enough duration to be common-law, although Evans and Gainey do not believe Kelly when he reported ignorance of Kate's working as a prostitute. The authors suspect that Kelly knew about, and possibly even supported, this vocation, especially when the couple found themselves low on funds. They also say that it is "interesting to note"[21] the fact that, having no fixed address at a lodging house as the other women seemed to, Kate was in possession of a much lengthier list of belongings the night she died. It is perhaps less interesting than simply indicative of the fact that she was likely worse off than the other women despite the fact that she was in possession of so many items. Without a usual bed, Kate had no place to leave even the smallest belongings without them getting stolen.

Mary Jane Kelly had a regular bed in her rented room, of course, although there seems to be doubt over whether she was even in full possession of her name. Evans and Gainey insist on calling her Mary Jane despite the fact that "her man friend"[22]—not her lover or her common-law husband, perhaps because they were no longer living together at the time of her death—insisted that she called herself Marie Jeanette. Because Mary Jane's history is only passed down verbally through that same man friend and not substantiated through other reports or even other people from her past, Evans and Gainey have little to say about her outside of her youth and beauty. These, at least, were reported by others who had known her, even if she had not opened up to tell them more about her past.

Almost two decades later Dane Ladwig also decided to put forth an American as his chosen suspect for Jack the Ripper, writing *Dr. H. H. Holmes & the Whitechapel Ripper* (2014). Unlike Tumblety, who was a fraudulent doctor often in trouble with the law but died of natural causes, Holmes—real name Herman Webster Mudgett—went to medical school and ended up being executed for murder. Granted, he was hanged based on a single case of murder, that of business partner Benjamin Pitezel, but it was clear that he had also murdered the Pitezel children that had supposedly been in his care. Before his execution, Holmes also confessed to have murdered multiple women in his so-called "Murder Castle" in Chicago around the time of the World's Columbian Exposition. There is suspicion that his victim count is well into three digits, and that is before the Whitechapel women are factored in.

Thus instead of a narrative that must encompass one murderer and five victims, Ladwig is faced with an unknown number of victims—the women in Whitechapel, the women in Chicago, and various members of the Pitezel family—although at least he is focusing on a confessed murderer. Instead of making the five canonical Ripper victims the focus of the suspect's criminal activity, they become more of a prelude to Holmes' more spectacular murders. The Chicago murders were committed in a building he constructed specifically to aid him in that task and thus even the Murder Castle rivals the setting of Victorian England. On the other hand, the true number and identity of the women murdered in Chicago is unknown, while at least Ladwig is able to name the women of the East End.

He begins with a dedication to the victims who, in part, "left behind unsolved and unfinished business."[23] While the unfinished business might refer to their lives, cut short by murder, anything "unsolved" would be related to the crime itself. For the Whitechapel women, the "unsolved business" would be the identity of their killer and, to an extent, their own identities. Many of the Chicago victims are unknown, since there were so few remains to be identified. Many young women used the opportunity of the World's Fair to disappear of their own accord, and thus it is difficult to determine which may have taken off under their own free will and which may have discovered the darker secrets of Holmes' Murder Castle. Ladwig gives his dedication to victims in general, and not specifically to those of Holmes, but once again the idea of "unsolved business" seems to relate more to the one who made them victims and not to the victims themselves.

In his preface Ladwig foregrounds his focus on the idea of victims, this time specifically directing attention toward those mentioned in his book, declaring that "[t]he public, and certainly the families of the victims, deserve the answers that will give them closure."[24] In this sentence the interests of the public come before the interests of the family members, although—considering Holmes was executed in 1896—any family members alive to read Ladwig's words would only know their ancestors the same way Williams and Alexander do: as names on the family tree and not as a personal loss. Over a century after the murders perhaps the public and the family are indeed comparable, being so far removed from the individuals whose lives were ended, although the curiosity of the general public seems to supersede any desire the family might have for a resolution. It would seem, however, that the family members most in need of closure would be the ones who had personally known the murdered women and had lived through not only their lives, but also their deaths.

Unlike many authors, Ladwig does fully acknowledge that his fascination lies in a direction other than the victims. He insists that he has no empathy for the murder, but confesses that "there has piqued in me a certain amount of interest and curiosity"[25] about Holmes and the sort of person he must have been in order to commit all of these crimes. That curiosity outweighs any repulsion or disgust Ladwig might feel, since he does indeed explore the personality and biography of Holmes, both to prove that Holmes could have been Jack the Ripper and in an attempt to discover how Holmes could have turned into a murderer in the first place. For Ladwig the murdered women are just part of the narrative, and not even the most torturous aspect. Holmes' life holds its own horrors.

The Whitechapel murders are confined to only a handful of pages. Elizabeth Stride, Catherine Eddowes, and Mary Kelly are presented as names and dates only, all on the same page. They are simply part of Ladwig's timeline for Holmes. The only woman who has any indication of a biography is Mary Nichols—whom he later refers to as "Ann Nichols"[26]—who "sacrificed her marriage and five children for her addiction to alcohol."[27] If readers were only familiar with Ladwig, it would seem that Mary Nichols was the only woman who drank. Otherwise Ladwig reproduces the original Scotland Yard reports of the murders, as difficult as the handwriting might be for twenty-first century eyes to read. These copies take up seventy pages, offering readers the chance to acquaint themselves with the opinions and observations that were made at the time.

It is only later, after the original reports, that Ladwig offers some more information about the Whitechapel women, treating them as a homogeneous group and listing their similarities instead of any individual characteristics: they were prostitutes who had drinking problems and scrounged pennies for a bed. They kept to themselves—perhaps an explanation for why there are no individual characteristics—and they "were all estranged from their families."[28] There is no indication of whether this means from parents and siblings or from husbands and children, or if there might be a difference depending on the woman in question. Apparently none of this information seems relevant to Ladwig's piqued interest in Holmes, since the Whitechapel women were victims of opportunity who found themselves crossing the killer's path at the wrong moment. The closure he seeks for the public and the families lies in identifying their killer and not in a deeper exploration of their lives.

Ladwig does bring things back around full circle, returning to the victims at the end of his narrative and echoing the sentiments from his dedication and preface. As a partial admission that it cannot be proven that Holmes was also the Whitechapel murderer, Ladwig's writes that "the victims of Jack the Ripper may remain un-vindicated for all of eternity,"[29] a prospect that threatens Ladwig's goal of closure. The question, however, is which definition of "vindicate" he intended: to be cleared of blame, or to be proven to be right? His presentation of the murdered women places blame upon them only as much as any author blames a prostitute for risking her life daily in her profession, since Ladwig does not present any conspiracy or relationships that would direct the blame otherwise. If Ladwig wishes them to be proven right, there is the question of what has been presented that makes them wrong in the first place. True, many authors have approached the idea that these women engaged in prostitution as being wrong, as tough they could have made other, more moral, life choices, but Ladwig does not argue either way about their occupations. It would seem that Ladwig is perhaps more concerned about the victims being unavenged, considering his earlier concerns for unsolved mysteries and closure.

The shifting of the Ripper's origins to make him American therefore also assists in the shift away from attention on the murdered women. Evans and Gainey set themselves the task of suggesting a suspect who had not previously been explored at such depth, while Ladwig chose one whose already explored biography offered up many more victims and many more points of interest. Because neither case involved a personal motive for the crimes, the murdered women only matter inasmuch as whether the timing and method of their deaths could be used to disprove the identity of the chosen suspect. As long as Tumblety or Holmes could have been in Whitechapel on the given dates, and could be imagined to be the sort of man to inflict such brutality, then no more information about the victims is necessary.

Confessor Jack

Although the controversy of the Maybrick diary was largely left behind after the 1990s, the twenty-first century still has room for volumes supposedly written by the Ripper himself. David Monaghan and Nigel

Cawthorne present one of them in their 2010 book *Jack the Ripper's Secret Confession: The Hidden Testimony of Britain's First Serial Killer.* They resurrect the autobiography of a man known only as "Walter," making the claim that, in the middle of his explicit confessions of sexual perversion, "it is quite possible to identify some of the victims of Jack the Ripper."[30] Despite this claim—and the extensively quoted, originally banned and often pornographic text—"Walter's" description of the murders is nowhere to be found. Instead the authors reproduce his reminiscences of spying on women as a child and his sexual exploits with women and many children once he had moved past the voyeur stage. Indeed, the fact that Jack the Ripper is mentioned in the title seems to be largely so that this reproduced narrative of raping minors and paying for virgins will sell.

Interspersed with the reproduced text that seems to have nothing to do with the Ripper murders are the authors' descriptions of the crimes. The price of an East End prostitute is equated with a glass of gin but less than a bed at a doss house, so this Mary Nichols needs to find two clients in order to pay for the night. Her new bonnet is questioned, since she has no money, and the fact that she was found in possession of a clean handkerchief is likewise brought up as being odd. Why would a prostitute who was fond of drink have spent her hard-earned money on either or a bonnet or a handkerchief, which would not have been clean for long? The authors suggest that "Walter" was fond of giving women both bonnets and handkerchiefs, explaining their provenance. The fact that Mary's hands were bruised, "showing that she had been involved in a ferocious struggle for her life,"[31] is mentioned and then just as quickly dismissed. Her killer had no sympathy for her and did not care about the details of the life he was ending, and neither the struggle nor her death is discussed. Mary is simply a puzzle because of the items not expected to have been found on a prostitute from Whitechapel.

Annie Chapman is also likely to have spent her money on drink before she would have purchased anything else, although Monaghan and Cawthorne draw another comparison between Annie and Mary: the fact that each had daughters "who might follow them into their trade."[32] This is important to their argument because "Walter" confesses to paying for access to young girls and gives full descriptions of the acts he performed on them. The suggestion seems to be that Mary and Annie may have caught "Walter's" attention because of their daughters, as though each woman could routinely be seen wandering the streets with a child in tow. The fact that neither woman took her children with her when she left her marriage makes this statement all the more confusing, since it seems difficult to see how their daughters might be similarly tempted if the rest of the family meant to keep them away from their mothers. Outside of being an alcoholic and a mother, there is nothing of interest about Annie.

Liz Stride, on the other hand, is no one's mother—despite the once again repeated *Princess Alice* story—and had been attempting to improve her situation at the time of her death. Although her life had gone downhill since the days in which she had helped out at her husband's coffee shop, Liz is shown making steps toward respectability once more. There had been no steady improvement in her situation, and her encounter with "Walter" removed any possibility of success.

There is little enough to be added about Kate or Mary, although Monaghan and Cawthorne confirm that each was in a relationship. Kate had her common-law husband,[33] John Kelly, while Mary had a boyfriend, Joe Barnett, even though he "had been out of her life—or at least her room— for over a month."[34] The presence of a steady man does nothing to influence their fate, however, since each was looking for money on the last day of her life. Although a common-law husband might be more respectable than a boyfriend, Kate was still an alcoholic and thus not raised to the hopeful level of Liz Stride. Even Mary, so often separated from the others, is mentioned and quickly dismissed.

In a near reversal of *Jack the Ripper's Secret Confession*, 2013's *The Autobiography of Jack the Ripper* discusses the murdered women solely in the text of James Carnac's supposed confession, with no outside information about them. Paul Begg wrote an introduction to the reproduction of the text, but his discussion is merely of its provenance and, in a later chapter, whether or not this confession might be believed. The representation of the murdered women within this narrative, then, is supposedly from the point of view of the Ripper himself and limited only to their final moments. The fact that he describes meeting "the woman whose name I afterward learned was Mrs. Stride"[35] drives home the lack of information the Ripper himself possessed. It is only because Carnac was writing this text after the murders were committed—and thus after he had read about them in the paper—that he is able to provide this much information, and Stride is the only woman given a name.

Otherwise Carnac writes of his encounters with the women, describing their appearances—Polly is "slightly less degraded"[36] than the other women in the area, for example, while Kate is both "elderly" and "pathetic"[37]—and presenting Annie as an incredibly chatty woman. He writes her monologue with a heavy cockney accent, apparently recalling each and every word she said to him despite the passage of time. Carnac even belittles Kate for being so bold as to accompany him to Mitre Square despite the murders, and Mary Kelly for taking him to her room and undressing as she, too, chatted away, apparently without any concern. Throughout he does not use their names, instead referring to the women as subjects or, when he is on the lookout for his next victim, a possible subject. They are clearly not individuals in Carnac's mind and, outside of the chatter, there is little to distinguish one from another.

Once again, with the shift in focus from the murder narrative itself—this time to first person confessions—these books have little to say about the murdered women. Monaghan and Cawthorne must present this information on their own, since they do not reproduce any of their chosen confession that would show why, exactly, they have decided that "Walter" makes a viable suspect. It is therefore unclear what "Walter" himself thought of them, or even why he resorted to murder when the rest of his confession deals with other sexually deviant exploits that center on children bought and paid for, often at extravagant rates. *The Autobiography of Jack the Ripper*, on the other hand, is clearly meant for readers who already have knowledge of the Ripper case, since its purpose is to present the original confession written by a man who knew less about the women he killed than was printed in the newspapers. These books are clearly moving away from recounting the murder narrative as a whole in order to focus on an aspect that the authors believe has been ignored or simply undiscovered and, in these cases particularly, this means that the murdered women are once again relegated to the position of placeholders in the face of other, more important, information.

Minding the Gaps

Perhaps because of the emphasis on the retelling of the original Ripper crime narrative, with adjustments and additions based on newly discovered information or newly proposed suspects, the twenty-first century has seen a number of books devoted to a specific facet of the Ripper crimes and not to the entire narrative. In many of these cases, that facet shifts focus away from the murders themselves and thus the victims almost completely.

Stewart P. Evans and Keith Skinner chose to focus on the various missives received by the press and the police in their 2001 book *Jack the Ripper: Letters from Hell*. The book offers reproductions of many of these letters and transcribes the text, as well, to aid in reading the various handwritings. The book opens with a description of the murder discoveries but otherwise refers to the murders only to compare that information with details found in a letter. The discussion centers on whether the letters could be proven to only have been able to be written by the killer or whether anyone with access to a newspaper might have been able to compose them. Throughout the book, the murders themselves are often identified based on the location of the murder, and not the name of the woman killed.

In 2003 R. Michael Gordon presented readers with *The American Murders of Jack the Ripper*, focusing on a series of murders that happened in that country after the Whitechapel murders had ceased. Gordon suggests that his suspect, George Chapman, did not simply stop murdering but instead moved and thus changed the location of the murders. The Whitechapel murders are listed together in the preface, but the main focus of the book follows the women listed in Gordon's dedication: Carrie, Hannah, Elizabeth, and Mary.[38] Of the four, Carrie Brown, also known as "Old Shakespeare," receives the most attention and most detailed biographical treatment. They, and not the Whitechapel women, are the focus of this text.

In 2006 Robin Odell set out to summarize the body of works written about Jack the Ripper in his book *Ripperology*. In his preface he provides readers with a summary of the murders, "intended to remind readers of the essential features of each murder without going into excessive detail."[39] Presumably anyone interested in a review of the literature composed about these murders would already be familiar with the details of the murder narrative itself. Odell traces the discovery and introduction of new information—as well as pointing out the dissemination of facts now known to be untrue—with a focus on Ripper suspects. Odell does not set forth to make the case for any specific suspect of his own, but evaluates the arguments put forward and allows the books he discusses to be in conversation with each other.

The Victims of Jack the Ripper (2007) by Neal Stubbings Sheldon focuses solely on the facts known about the canonical five victims, although nearly half of the short volume is devoted to photographs, mainly of the murdered women's descendants. Each chapter is devoted to a single woman, although those chapters also contain the continuation of her family tree, if known. Sheldon's focus is indeed on the murdered women, although he limits himself to reporting confirmable facts. Although it has become tradition, or perhaps expected, to take scarce facts and turn them into a narrative for a Ripper suspect, the same has not been done with the facts surrounding his victims. In Sheldon's short book, the women are presented as a gathering of facts, more extensive than many authors offer, but there is no attempt to take these pieces and reanimate them into people with personalities. Since no attempt had been previously made, the simple fact that Sheldon produced a text devoted solely to the murdered women and not to discovering the identity of their murderer is, in and of itself, a notable goal. Sheldon chooses to focus on the canonical five, much in the same way that all Ripper authors must mention them, if no one else.

Jack the Ripper: The Forgotten Victims (2013) by Paul Begg and John Bennett instead broadens the definition of "victims" to include not only the women the Ripper may have personally murdered, but all of those living at the time whose lives were impacted. Begg and Bennett go beyond the canonical five or even the expanded number of women murdered in Whitechapel alone to include women who died of fright or because of copycat killers who might not have been inspired to murder had they not read about the Ripper. Their main argument is that the canonical five victims "live on"[40] through the already published works about the Ripper, with their lives and families trees having already been subjected to extensive research, while this wider net of victims has remained nameless, unrecognized, and forgotten.

For Begg and Bennett, the canonical five are bound together through their murders, since they are "women of whom we never would have heard"[41] and women "who would otherwise be unknown to history"[42] if they had not met such violent ends. We have only heard of them, and their names have only been recorded in history and our collective consciousness, because of the man who murdered them. It is through no action of their own—and indeed, no reason other than an attempt to discover their murderer's identity—that all of this recognition has come about. Begg and Bennett wish to argue that the attention these five women have received has allowed them "to be remembered, and not just as victims,"[43] but even they themselves cannot mention them without that victim status. The horrific extent of the Ripper's crimes means that their identities will always be as his victims first, and anything else—if anything else is deemed worthy of mention—second. The fact that their graves are marked and their names, according to the authors, known and recognized around the world is meant to elevate them somehow above any woman who falls outside the canonical five. Although the names of the canonical five have indeed been mentioned over and over in nearly every retelling of the Ripper narrative—which is, of course, the reason this very book has chosen to focus on them—there is certainly not the trend of viewing them as women instead of victims or bodies.

Begg and Bennett do acknowledge that the amount of attention these women receive does not necessarily equate to good attention when they ask if the effect their story has on readers is "a genuine sympathy, or is a by-product from a sense of guilt."[44] Is the attention given to the canonical five victims an honest attempt to present them as women in their own right, or has it been an outgrowth of the desire to finally identify Jack the Ripper? Does tracing the biography of a murder victim allow an author to breathe the life back into her, or does it mean the author can support the argument for a new suspect? It is a fine line for an author to walk, one that might be predetermined by decades of previously written narratives and the expectations inherent within the genre of crime narrative, where the slightest increase in attention to detail in one text might make it stand out as vastly more attentive than the others.

Have these women been discussed most thoroughly and satisfactorily? Was the information available about them "enough" at the time or their murders, or did that completeness emerge in the intervening years? Can we trace any sort of improvement of the written treatment of the Ripper's victims through the years? After this survey of books published about the case, we can begin to piece together the answers to these questions.

Conclusion
What Possible Use?

From the very beginning, starting with Leonard Matters' book in 1929, authors have been arguing that the women murdered by Jack the Ripper were all but indistinguishable from each other. This insistence has carried across the decades, from Tom Cullen in 1965 to Jean Overton Fuller in 1990, Robert House in 2011, and Paul Begg and John Bennett in 2013. Each of these authors stresses that the women were anything but unique, marking them as simply select individuals that represented the teeming masses of the East End poor.

Even in the midst of this protestation that these women are the same, distinctions emerge. At times those differences are negative, such as when Elizabeth Stride is dismissed completely, either because she was not a Ripper victim or because there was nothing new to learn from her death. More often authors who declare that the murdered women are similar contradict themselves by adding more information about one or two of them in order to make them stand apart. Annie Chapman is a likely candidate for more information, especially more sympathetic information, and Mary Jane Kelly is by far most frequently separated from the others and held up for scrutiny.

What purpose could be served in lumping the murdered women together as a cohesive cohort? The more similar their stories, the more likely it would be that they shared a reason for being murdered. Likewise, the more similar they are, the less likely it would be that readers would be able to identify with the women. By grouping the victims as uninteresting prostitutes, any reader who finds herself—or her female family members or friends—to be interesting, and not a prostitute, would not need to worry that a similar fate could befall them. It is easy to point to the women's occupation as the reason they crossed paths with the Ripper in the first place, and thus women who are more cautious about meeting or going with strangers need not have the same fears.

Daughter, Wife, Mother, Woman

Even as they are lumped together, the women are still individualized through their various relationships—with men, of course. The main relationship they all share is that of being a victim of Jack the Ripper. Calling them "victims" defines them in relationship to a criminal, even if he is not named. The term in this case functions the same as "husband," presupposing that there is someone to occupy the other position and create a relationship in which the women in question can orient herself. However, these women are not only victims but also wives and mothers.

Although few details are known about their lives, the women are generally accepted to have had some say in the men they married. This is in stark contrast to their relationship to the mysterious figure of Jack the Ripper—no murder victim can be said to have wanted that fate. The choice of that husband, as well as the subsequent failure of that relationship, is used to position the given woman in many cases as a failure. It is generally her addiction to the bottle that is given as the reason for her husband abandoning her, and she rarely receives a sympathetic reason to have turned to the bottle in the first place. Due to the circumstances of her children, Annie Chapman is most likely to be presented empathetically when it comes to both her drinking habit and her separation from her husband. With one child born a cripple and a second dying young, Annie-as-mother seems to have every reason to turn to alcohol for comfort, and she and her husband are generally presented as separating through a mutual decision. This is in stark contrast to Elizabeth Stride since, even in the narratives in which she turned to the bottle after the drowning deaths of her husband and children, authors still resist treating her as kindly as they do Annie. Perhaps this is because so many others have completely rejected this tragic story from Liz's past.

This background of relationships made and broken serves to explain why each of these women was on the street, for the most part fending for herself. It is all a consequence of having been born as a woman in Victorian England—the need for a man to support a woman is paramount. Although women of the lower classes may have been able to find work to support themselves, such as Polly's failed attempt as a maid or the various items the women were meant to have hawked in the street, they were still meant to find themselves a good husband, and thereafter be a good wife and mother. A man was expected to bring in a steady income and provide her with security. The women in long-term relationships at the time of their deaths were not married to those men, although this was not the only aspect of those partnerships that has been derided. Michael Kidney, John Kelly, and Joe Barnett have all come under suspicion of having prostituted their women and lived off their earnings, while Kidney and Barnett have each been accused of murder—and Barnett of being the Ripper himself.

Although the women's first husbands, both legal and common-law, play only small roles in this narrative, since they were out of the women's lives before the murders took place, they, too, are grouped together to explain the women's current lifestyles. In 1987 Martin Fido described the situation in a single catch-all statement that labeled the men respectable and their wives alcoholic, and thus intolerable. Whether the women were simply drinking or drinking for a reason, it was enough of a cause for their men to leave them. It is commonly asserted that the husbands were indeed the ones to draw the line, since what Victorian woman would cut herself loose from a provider if she were not forced to do so?

This idea of the men tolerating and rejecting the behavior of the murdered women is also a throughline in the Ripper narratives, stated outright by Jean Overton Fuller in 1990 when she asserts that any man who was in a relationship with the women near the ends of their lives could only do so because he had "forgiven" her for prostitution. None of the men in these narratives, least of all Jack the Ripper, is in need of such defense or forgiveness, but the women face the question continually. Their husbands could not forgive them, although this is hardly a flaw on their parts, since they were themselves respectable and thus had expectations of their wives. The men who did forgive them were likewise only East Enders themselves. Perhaps their forgiveness is more freely given, although it might not mean as much as it would coming from a man of good standing.

Some authors refer to these women with the title of Mrs., or solely by their last names. Polly, Annie, and Liz took the last names of Nichols, Chapman, and Stride through marriage, and authors have routinely granted them the use of this name. Kate Eddowes, on the other hand, is routinely mentioned with her maiden name, since there is no record of her marriage to Thomas Conway as having been anything but common-law, and her seven-year relationship with John Kelly likewise did not see their signatures on a marriage certificate. The fact that she seemed to have called herself Kate Kelly is generally deemed inconsequential, especially in the face of the numerous other aliases she may have used. Mary Jane Kelly, on the other hand, is routinely referred to by her maiden name of Kelly—even if her given names vary—despite the fact that she reported she had once been married to a man with the last name of Davies or Davis.

It could be as simple as the fact that authors have chosen to use the names the women were buried under, except for the fact that many shorten their names or use the nicknames reported in the daily papers. Mary Ann Nichols is thus most often Polly, and other nicknames seem based on the appearance of the women: Dark Annie, for example, or perhaps "Long Liz." At times authors such as David Abrahamsen only use the women's last names, while others, like Richard Whittington-Eagan or A. P. Wolf, need to clarify which woman they are writing about since it seems unlikely that readers would have been given enough context for that information for remain in their short-term memories. Still others, of course, do not mention the murdered women at all, either because they choose not to discuss the crimes, or because they opt to focus on the clues and evidence left on the corpses who are, after their encounter with the Ripper, no longer people at all.

Since four of the murdered women were in their forties, it may make sense to identify them based on their choice of husband, since his personality and profession may reveal something about their pasts. However, certain authors, such as Paul Harrison in 1993, find it important to list their father's professions, as well. Since even the youngest woman—Mary Jane, in her twenties—had been living on her own and outside of her parents' home, this information seems at best introductory and at worst a token attempt at identity. If their fathers' occupations are part of a longer biography of the women, then this information serves to paint a fuller picture of their childhoods and thus perhaps their expectations. When Harrison mentions it, however, he also fails to discuss the women's husbands at all. Thus the presentation of this information, of victim-as-daughter, is only useful when it is part of a larger context of the women's backgrounds. Their fathers' occupations, like many tidbits that have emerged about these women, are nearly useless in reconstructing their identities unless they are accompanied by many more facts. After all, these women did not choose their families, although their expectations for their husbands and the path their lives should take would have been founded in their childhoods.

Is It Sympathy, Empathy or Respect?

Not every author has approached the murdered women purely in the negative, although that has largely been the trend. As seen above, it is easier to accept the horrific deaths of women if they somehow deserved it. If they were alcoholics who managed to make their respectable husbands drive them out of house and home, to the point where even their children wanted nothing to do with them, then they become less sympathetic female figures. Women especially are expected to fulfill distinct roles within society, and those who cannot are then somehow deserving of their fates, whether this meant life in the East End or death in the same place.

This extension of sympathy does not come often, and is not necessarily extended to all of the women each time it is present. Sometimes it seems more of a gesture of propriety, such as Edwin T. Woodhall's reluctance to actually use the term "prostitute" to refer to any of the women. At times even the empathy is dehumanizing, such as when Melvin Harris uses the phrase "tragic, lost creature."[1] The first two words are promising and meant to elicit an emotional response from readers, but he is discussing a creature instead of a woman or a human being. It seems that, for many of these authors, the path that the women took to the East End removed their humanity and, in a sense, their worth.

At times sympathy is extended to Liz or Mary Jane in outright defiance of the usual dismissal they receive for their fanciful tales of their own histories. Liz's supposed loss of husband and children on the *Princess Alice* and Mary Jane's unlikely tale of having been taken to France and then returned to London because she did not like it there are often reported and then scoffed at, dismissed as utter fairy tales used by women to prey on sympathetic others. These stories are in fact almost conniving, since the women telling them do so only to elicit a known reaction—hopefully in the form of coins—from their audiences. The less popular view is to acknowledge the desperation inherent in these women's situations. Women of a certain age living alone in the East End needed a tale to tell about how they ended up there, and if they wished to create their own biographies in order to give themselves distance from their own pasts, this seems to be only rarely understandable.

Prostitution is another issue that is generally derided by authors who seem to believe that there were many open positions simply waiting to be filled by women of this class. The empathy here, as seen for the first time in William Stewart, extends towards the "one-man women"[2] who have managed to hold on to an apparently steady relationship. These women—Stewart names Annie and Mary Kelly specifically, although other authors have also championed Liz and Kate—presumably have no need to walk the street at night, since they have managed to find a man who will care for them. They might do some work during the day to help supplement his income, but these women are not prostitutes. They might not be married, but they have managed to situate themselves in a long-term relationship of mutual benefit. It might still involve sex outside of marriage, but at least it is sex for money in a more roundabout, apparently acceptable way than outright prostitution. Prostitution is, after all, an act that must be forgiven, even by the men who apparently love and care for these women.

Authors who set out to provide a more rounded representation of these women must declare it specifically, as William Beadle, Philip Sugden, and John Tully do in the 1990s. They stand out for declaring that they are discussing people, not just victims, and that these women had already fallen victim to society before Jack the Ripper ever met them. These approaches attempt to situate the women and their murderer in a society far removed from what readers know, providing background information that helps clarify the situation more than other authors have done. Instead of condemning the women's apparent choice of prostitution, for example, these authors explore the conditions of women in Victorian England, especially women whose husbands have left them. This approach does not mean that the women are presented as having been perfect, but it does allow for a more critical look at their lives and the era and place in which they lived. It also complicates the question of why these women were selected to die, and perhaps threatens the reader's own feelings of safety since the answer is no longer cut and dry. These authors are not dealing with women who threw off the shackles of marriage and willingly walked the streets of Whitechapel looking for customers, but women whose lives were not always in their own control and thus women who may not have done anything specifically in order to deserve death.

Dehumanization and Separation

In many of these accounts, the murdered women are stripped of their humanity even before their deaths. Once they have encountered the Ripper—or rather, once their bodies have been discovered—their main importance is as clues or evidence that could point to the Ripper's identity. This is, after all, the reason why so many authors do not need to delve into the women's lives, since it is only the final encounter with their killer that is of interest. Even those that do present the women as living beings and not lifeless corpses do not always allow them their personhood.

Some of the earliest metaphors for describing the murdered women bear a seafaring theme when the women of the East End are often referred to as derelicts or flotsam, either drifting or washed ashore. Such items have no control over their paths or their usefulness and must depend on outside intervention in order to be directed or rescued. Although the items may have at one time been both functional and valuable, something happened to them so that, perhaps through neglect or disrepair, they have lost their worth.

Reducing human beings to derelicts or flotsam removes any possibility of agency. Perhaps the women had no hand in their own descent, but they also are now not given any opportunity for bettering their situations. They have been given up as a lost cause and, as such, their murders represent no great loss. If Jack the Ripper merely destroyed a derelict or some flotsam, well then, they were of no use to anyone anyway, and perhaps it is better to have them removed rather than eternally drifting.

The same change is affected when authors refer to the women as creatures. Annie is most often the target for such language, being a poor, sick creature on the last night of her life. While the adjectives are generally skewed toward the sympathetic and an unfortunate creature might indeed be the subject of pity, it is still a creature and not a person. The emotional response generated is more along the lines of an injured animal, since the use of the word "creature" indicates an other and does not encourage identification with the self. A creature is a thing and not a human being, and most often creatures take on the form of monsters or other figures that encourage emotionally distanced fascination.

That distance continues with phrases that mark these women as the "easiest prey" or "Jack's targets." Outside of a short story by Richard Connell, human beings are not thought of as the hunted and most dangerous game. It is animals who are hunted, and the prowess of the human hunter is tested by the skill and ferocity of his intended prey. Skilled hunters do not focus on the easier prey but rather seek to challenge themselves. Identifying these women as "easy prey" is not only an insult to them, but also to the Ripper, who somehow managed to avoid capture but limited his homicidal actions to a set of women who would not be missed very much.

As his targets, the women once again become objects. A target has even less agency than the easiest prey, which can at least be expected to move of its own free will. A target might be stationary, or it might be launched into someone's path, but it does not choose to be there. While the easiest prey might not offer much resistance, a target will not fight back. Its entire purpose is to allow the hunter to practice with a deadly weapon, and it acts as a stand-in for more challenging objects.

Some authors argue that the apparent lack of resistance on the women's part is a testament to the Ripper's skill, arguing that he must have caught them off guard completely. While Annie—the poor creature—is ill and not expected to have fought back, Liz is most often put forward as the candidate most likely to have been physically able to defend herself. More often the "easiest prey" makes itself even easier by spending coins on alcohol instead of a bed, and these women place themselves on the street, inebriated and clearly unable to fight back. The question of whether their lives would have been worth fighting for is rarely raised in the face of women expected to be unable to fight, much less to make the decision over whether their lives would be preferable to death.

Some authors go so far as to not even name the women, relying on location or date to distinguish which body is being discussed. Instead of Annie or Kate, these authors refer to the second victim or to the Mitre Square victim, as though order—or location—of death supersedes any individual identifying factors. Indeed, the identity of the Ripper can be investigated without the names of his victims, causing Bob Hinton to ask what use it is to research the biographies of these women, or Bruce Robinson to admit bluntly that, for him and for so many others, Catherine Eddowes' life was no longer than thirty-five minutes. The women—derelicts, creatures, or prey—are only notable because of their deaths, and thus their deaths are continually the focus while their lives are largely ignored.

Representations of the murdered women have caused some contention between authors who respond to previous books with arguments over whether earlier narratives depicted the women too kindly. Annie is most often at the center of these discussions, with authors arguing for or against the "romantic" view of a woman down on her luck, merely trying to make a living as best as she can. Arthur Douglas seems to praise the Ripper for "call[ing] a whore a whore and not a fallen angel,"[3] a jibe which is also directed as those who have written about the murders before he did. The representation of these women seems to swing between those two extremes—whore and angel—without the acknowledgment that people are rarely either just one, and that identity is in fact a spectrum. Authors tend to cling to what facts they can find and not extrapolate between them, very nearly the opposite of what tends to happen with their Ripper suspects.

A span of months or years with no documentation in the life of a suspect seems to be a blank canvas for authors to suppose and suspect. Patricia Cornwell has especially been accused of wildly filling in the blank spaces, but she is hardly the only author to do so. There are expectations of the sort of person the Ripper must have been, based largely on the FBI and popular culture representations of serial killers since the 1980s, and those gaps seem to be an invitation to authors to fit those pieces together for a compelling argument.

Thus we are confronted with Bob Hinton's entreaty to put ourselves in the Ripper's shoes and imagine ourselves as Hutchinson, scorned by the beautiful woman we have attempted to woo away from her dreary life and, finally, driven to murder her. We have David Abrahamsen, who argues that his Ripper suspects were themselves victims and thus made their families victims, as well. The murders they enact have become Martin Howells and Keith Skinner's "antiseptic and painless experience,"[4] creating a distance from which readers need not mourn the murdered women but from which they can also gaze upon the Ripper with fascination—and, if authors like Hinton and Abrahamsen have their way, with empathy.

The move, then, continually seems to be away from the murdered women. There is a small resistance in the 1990s when authors such as William Beadle, Philip Sugden, and John Tully attempted to give the women as much time and space on the page as they gave the Ripper, arguing for their humanity and dignity while deriding the Ripper. "Spare no thoughts for him,"[5] Beadle argues, although his narrative spares plenty. It is simply impossible to write a book about Jack the Ripper without dwelling on him, especially when that book means to argue a case for his identity. Some later books of the 2000s manage to devote more time and energy to the murdered women than to the Ripper, if only because they are specifically setting out not to champion a suspect. Even these are standouts among texts that fall back on, as Tony Williams put it, "what comes easiest"[6]—in the case of the authors not prostitution, but the ignoring and deriding of prostitutes. The Ripper narrative encourages authors to draw closer to the Ripper while shifting his victims out of the spotlight and at times even offstage entirely.

Sacrifice, Redemption, Immortality

The practice of referring to the murdered women as "sacrificial victims" began as early as 1937 with Edwin T. Woodhall, but it was not a passing fad. In 1975 Richard Whittington-Eagan suggested that the women were "redeemed by the enormity of their deaths."[7] In 1988 Paul Begg wrote that their deaths gave them "a sort of immortality"[8] that could not even be shared by the richer or more well-known figures of the day. Russell Edwards calls it a "strange immortality,"[9] but it is one that nevertheless exists.

R. Michael Gordon proclaims that the women "walked into history"[10] on the nights when they were murdered. It is not a constant refrain—not as constant as the denigration of these women, certainly—but it is one that has popped up occasionally, even within the past few years.

If the women's deaths were indeed a sacrifice, they were certainly not bloodless. Instead of being categorized in the same way as a shipwreck, the women now share space with ritually slaughtered animals in way that moves beyond Robin Odell's 1965 proposal that the Ripper was in fact a Jewish slaughterman. A sacrifice is performed in order to appeal to a higher power, whether in thanks or in pleading, and blood sacrifices are often highly ritualized and respected occasions. Human sacrifice is frequently relegated to pre–Columbian civilizations in the New World or ancient civilizations in Europe and is dismissed in recent times as divergent, underground behavior. If the victims of Jack the Ripper are meant as human sacrifices, then they are far removed from the religious practices of the day; if they are meant as animal sacrifices, then they are once again no longer human.

The use of the word "sacrifice" suggests that the act was made *to* someone or something, or *for* someone or something. A sacrifice involves the giving up of something, generally something that the enactor will miss. Sacrificing a good animal means that that person's family will not be able to eat it, but the ritual itself is made for a perceived greater good, such as the favor of a god. Such favor is only earned through this decision to take a personal loss and, as such, the size of the sacrifice should be large enough that the person is affected by it. A man who sacrifices a single goat when he has twenty is making a different offering than the man who kills his only animal.

What, then, was sacrificed in the deaths of Polly, Annie, Liz, Kate, and Marie Jeanette? Their killer certainly took a risk in breaking laws and taboos in order to commit both murder and multination, but he—or she, or they—was never caught. Perhaps, if the religious aspect of sacrifice is considered, he sacrificed his soul, but to what purpose? If the women's deaths were a sacrifice and not merely the actions of a person seeking a forbidden thrill, what was the intended outcome? What was meant to be the payoff of the sacrifice?

Various authors, Paul Begg included, have observed that the spate of murders drew attention to the appalling conditions of the East End and led to social change that was meant to help the people living there. Gas lighting was only one project implemented because of this attention. However, few are willing to credit the Ripper with such a social conscience, considering his method. If someone wished to literally and figuratively shed light on the East End, a "sacrifice" of numerous strangers would seem like a risky, if not entirely foolish, means of doing so.

The actual loss of this "sacrifice" is, first and foremost, the lives of the women murdered. Paul Begg and John Bennett argue that there were other losses, as well, in the form of simple fear—the loss of a feeling of safety—or copycat murders. It would seem, however, that the killer himself has lost nothing, not even his anonymity nearly 130 years on.

The women certainly did not choose to die. The very fact that these are called "murders" and Jack the Ripper labeled a "serial killer" shows there is no argument. They did not commit suicide because they had nothing to live for, and as of yet no author has suggested that the murdered women planned their own deaths for the sole purpose of social change and enlisted the killer of their own free will. Those who suffered the greatest loss did so unwillingly and with no promise of better things to come. Once again they are relegated to the position of the sacrificial animal. The lives they lost have even been argued to have been worthless in the first place and thus no great loss for anyone involved.

Their deaths, after all, are often argued to have been swift, with the mutilations being enacted after the slit throat. The lack of noise coming from any murder scene does suggest that the women were either dead or incapacitated before the mutilations took place, but the general narrative technique of jumping between the last sighting of the living women and the discovery of her body means that the deaths themselves go unseen and unexplored. Tony Williams, arguing that the Ripper both comes from his own family tree and was a doctor, has a specific vested interest in making the gruesome murders as sanitary as possible—a doctor, after all, is meant to preserve life, not to take it, and he is discussing a man rather closely related to him by blood. The continual insistence that death was swift, if not entirely painless, permeates the Ripper narratives, allowing authors and readers alike to skip the moment of transition from life to death and instead to be able to concentrate on the murdered women's bodies solely as objects.

This time skip supports both the practice of drawing the women away from the spotlight and the centering of the killer in its exact middle. By ignoring the acts themselves and instead concentrating on the amount of skill it would take to perform them in the dark, as well as the minimum amount of time required, the murder becomes distanced and antiseptic, presented in terms of a coroner and doctors and not blood on the cobbles. Any suffering the women went through in their deaths is minimized or outright dismissed, removing the need for empathy. The killer himself is rarely, if ever, depicted actually completing the act, allowing authors to craft their supposed Rippers as attractive, or troubled, or sympathetic. If they are not shown inserting the knife or rooting around in a still-warm body cavity for the desired organs, then perhaps those moments are the deviation and the killer's public face is the truth. The question becomes "What sort of man could commit these murders?" and not "What sort of man could hide behind his public mask of sanity?"

As sacrifices, if that was what they were, it would seem that the murdered women were flawed. Most religious sacrifices are meant to be of high quality—granted, at times so the temple might over-charge penitents with the argument that the sacrifice they personally brought was not pure enough—but, in terms of the moral standards of the day, prostitutes were not pure. Paul Roland is a rare author who suggests that the women have a chance to "redeem themselves"[11] on their own and in life, through honest labor and by getting themselves off the streets and away from the bottle. The mere statement that they *could* redeem themselves—ignoring the practicalities of how—indicates that the women are definitely in need of redemption.

This redemption is generally granted them through their murders. It would not have been enough for them to have died of other causes, or even to have been murdered by someone other than the Ripper. It is this public outcry and the newsworthiness of their corpses that provides redemption for their lives. More specifically, their murders provide redemption for their prostitution.

As early as 1965, Robin Odell puts forth the argument that prostitution was not a choice for these women but the only option that stood between them and starvation. Not every author chooses to stress this point. Many tales involve headstrong women willingly prostituting themselves, and Mary Jane Kelly is the most likely to take up prostitution as her own choice, wielding her youth and beauty as power over higher classes of men. Some variations have these women purposefully leaving their marriages in order to pursue prostitution, instead of being forced to engage in prostitution solely because their marriages fell apart. All failings of these women can be traced not to the bottle—although it is often part and parcel of the tale—but to sexual promiscuity. Those who still had living husbands often also possess a resentment of being tied down to the role of wife and mother. Somehow "prostitution" becomes equated with "freedom" in these narratives, and a woman seeking either is clearly in the wrong.

Although Paul Roland suggests that any woman in this possession might indeed be capable of orchestrating her own redemption, it would seem that only Polly is given the chance, and she is unable to maintain her position as a maid, especially in a tee totaling household. It would not have been enough for her to earn wages through honest means—means other than prostitution—but she would also have had to spend them on necessities and not drink. The Ripper's intervention stopped her from engaging in further prostitution or alcoholism, true, but also ended any chance the women might have had at improving their own lives.

And yet, in spite of the conditions they lived through and the manner in which their lives ended, there is still a sense of envy or perhaps a righteous justification of the Ripper's actions. Paul Begg and John Bennet write that the women "would otherwise be unknown to history"[12] if they had not been murdered, and compare the relative wealth of information available about them to the lack of information about more prominent figures of the day. It is an opinion Begg had already presented in 1988, like Richard Whittington-Eagan before him when he suggests that their position might be one to envy. It is their "fame" that is the subject of such envy, since the women's names—with various spellings and in various forms—are still written today, more than a century after their deaths, when even the name of their murderer might forever be unknown. It seems doubtful that this envy would stretch to being remembered as a common whore, a pitiful creature, or looking like a bad drawing of a human being, much less having had to go through the life experiences that landed these women in Whitechapel in the first place.

The indication seems to be that, given the choice, many people—from prostitutes to politicians—would have gladly met the Ripper's knife. It is a baffling proposition, since their deaths are the only event in their lives for which these women are known. In many cases, it is only their deaths and their mutilated bodies that deserve mention in the narratives, with even their names being left aside. Any woman murdered by Jack the Ripper is forever known as a Ripper victim above and beyond all else, although "all else" is hardly any more flattering: women abandoned by their husbands and children; alcoholics; and prostitutes to boot. Any kindness shown to their memory is attributed to their friends' desire not to speak ill of the dead, or to other authors over-romanticizing the situation. The women are also frequently depicted as having put themselves in harm's way and all but offered themselves up to the Ripper by not having the money for a bed that night, and thus they are not only ugly, dirty prostitutes but stupid, as well. It would seem that authors suggesting that theirs is a position to envy have not fully contemplated what, exactly, they are envying.

Granted, a politician or person of higher birth might have had a better chance at an extended biography simply because someone on that position would be given a more complete of existence to start with. There is, however, no point of comparison between the murdered women and those imagined to be jealous of their enduring legacy, and thus no clear indication whether such a politician would be remembered for his own acts, or solely for the acts of the Ripper. It would seem, on the surface, that being murdered would be the easiest way to make it into the history books, although no one seems to want to consider whether the murdered women would have chosen that opportunity themselves. They were simply not given the option.

Any acknowledgment of the tragic nature of the women's murders tends to come by way of authors suggesting that, with the mystery solved, their souls might now rest peacefully. As enviable as their positions might be, the fact that their murderer has so long escaped justice is unacceptable. So many authors make a token acknowledgment to the victims in their dedications, introductions, or final paragraphs, a variation on R. Michael Gordon's entreaty that the women should now "rest well"[13] because the identity of their killer is known. Their violent deaths, unable to be prevented, are avenged by the naming of a suspect who is dead by the time his—or her, or their—name is published. Indeed, by the time of many of these accusations, anyone who personally knew the women would also be dead. Closure, such as it is, is meant for the interested public and the descendants of those involved, should they know who they are. The raging curiosity behind the Ripper's true identity is presented as a quest for justice for those who did not see much of it during their lives, or even in the narrative proclaiming vindication. The immortal women who are envied, redeemed, and avenged are still little more than East End whores who might not actually be deserving of envy, redemption, or vengeance, but who still somehow bought and paid for their deaths.

Blame Lives On

It would seem that the focus of so many Ripper narratives would be the person guilty of committing these crimes, when in fact responsibility for this string of murders is most often placed elsewhere. The Ripper was frequently driven to kill, and then by something other than his own demons—something outside of himself. Perhaps it was an overbearing mother or the absence of a father figure that shaped him, the way many serial killers have been presented since the 1980s. Perhaps there were warning signs that someone close to him should have caught, thus preventing the Ripper from ever murdering anyone. Instead of any of these explanations, however, so many authors prefer to assign guilt to the women the Ripper murdered instead of to the Ripper himself.

From the very first book about Jack the Ripper, the killer has been given explanations for his actions. Leonard Matters began by arguing that the Ripper was in fact Doctor Stanley, bent on seeking revenge for the death of his son. That son had, of course, died because of a disease passed on to him by the harlot Mary Kelly. All murders preceding hers were committed in order to help the doctor cover his tracks; the severity of her mutilations are explained because her death was personal; and the theory neatly explains why the string of murders suddenly stopped. Matters introduced the idea of revenge as the Ripper's motivation.

This revenge is presented as a response to an act of free will. Mary Kelly is meant to have known exactly what she was doing when she seduced the younger Doctor Stanley and passed on the infection that killed him rather quickly. The younger Doctor Stanley names her on his deathbed, and his father is so consumed with grief that he will let nothing stand in his way of killing the woman who killed his son. This is the first time that Mary Kelly will be blamed for not only her own death, but for the entirety of the Ripper's spree. It will not be the last.

Because all of the Ripper's victims were prostitutes, it is also possible to present the theme of revenge as against a certain class of person, and not as against specific people. Edwin T. Woodhall and William Stewart take this route, proposing two alternate scenarios: first, that a woman was seeking to avenge her sister against the class of women who turned her into a prostitute and led her to the disease that caused her death; and second, that a midwife had been imprisoned for performing abortions and wished to get back at the sort of women who had betrayed her. This idea of a killer's anger and violence directed at a class of women or a specific occupation carries over to the male suspects, as well. Some are meant to be killing the sort of women who have infected him, while others see a beloved female family member wasting away and cannot stand the sight of other presumably healthy women degrading themselves on the street. The theme of the Ripper wanting to hurt the people who have hurt him comes in both the generic and specific varieties.

When the focus is specific, Mary Kelly once again comes off the worst of all. She is not only the most viciously mutilated—she is the most often cited instigator of the murders. While it is common to blame each woman for her own murder, arguing that she should have saved her pennies for a bed instead of spending them on drink, Mary Kelly, it seems, must pay for all. Whether it is Stephen Knight's conspiracy theory of 1976 or Antonia Alexander's family history written in 2013, Mary Kelly did something to cause the Ripper to act.

The proponents of Stephen Knight's theory and its variations indicate the cause of the Ripper murders to be Mary Kelly's blackmail threat against the crown. When she finds herself in possession of royal secrets, Mary cannot help but tell three of her friends. This is her first false step. Those friends are the ones who convince her to seek blackmail. In most cases Mary Kelly would not have thought of blackmail on her own, so the greedy trio of Polly, Annie, and Liz might still take some of the blame, but Kate is often cited as a mistake based on the fact that she gave her name as Mary Ann Kelly. Even if Mary Kelly might be absolved of the guilt of the deaths of her friends—who would never have suggested such a thing had she not spoken up in the first place—she is still responsible for the death of an innocent.

Her role is taken to the extreme by John Wilding in 1993. Perhaps the simple blackmail of Knight's theory could be construed as a bout of peer pressure that got out of control before Mary Kelly had any idea what was going on, but Wilding's Kelly is as shrewd and calculating as the Mary Kelly who seduced the likes of the young Doctor Stanley. She still seeks to blackmail the royal family, yes, but this time because she is pregnant with the crown prince's child. This Mary accidentally causes the murder of her friend Polly, perhaps only hoping to throw the strangers off her trail when she gave Polly her bonnet. She slips up when she tells the killers that she has given proof of her tale to her friend Annie—again, possibly a mistake made by a woman who found herself in over her head. She may have only been thinking of a way to save herself.

But then things change. Wilding gives Mary Kelly the role of personally selecting Catherine Eddowes and priming her with alcohol so that the killers might have their next victim. The alcohol itself is shown to be a measure of guilt, since Mary Kelly did not want her friend to be fully aware of what was happening to her. The plan went awry, but Mary Kelly was there to meet Catherine when she was released from her cell and led her, no longer drunk, to meet the killers. Finally, Mary Kelly is shown to handpick one of her friends to stay the night at her small room in Miller's Court and be discovered dead and horribly mutilated on the morning of November 9. Wilding does allow her an attack of conscience and lets her flee to a pub to attempt to drink it away, but this is still a Mary Kelly who has a clear hand in the murders. She may not have held the knife and she may not have purposefully caused the deaths of Polly and Annie, but she was clearly involved in the deaths of Kate and the mystery woman buried under the name of Marie Jeanette. No longer simply a young and beautiful prostitute intent on using men for she could get, this Mary Kelly sells out her own friends in hopes of a better future for herself.

Wilding's Mary Kelly and the Mary Kelly of the various royal conspiracy theories had some sort of active role in causing the series of Ripper murders. Even if all Mary Kelly was meant to have done was demand blackmail, this was still an act of her own instigation. She may not have been intelligent enough to realize that there would be consequences and that the royal family would not simply comply, but it was still one specific act that cause the death of five women. Authors have blamed Mary Kelly for less than that.

For Paul Harrison, Bob Hinton, and Antonia Alexander, the Ripper was a man intent on driving Mary Kelly off the street—and, in the case of Alexander's tale, out of London entirely. Harrison proposes that Mary Kelly's boyfriend, Joe Barnett, instigated the murders in order to keep his girlfriend from continuing her life as a prostitute. Mary Kelly, however, is not above manipulating multiple men at once in order to get what she wants. Poor Barnett, who had struggled mightily against the sort of life in which he had grown up, finally realizes that this woman has no interest in respectability. Had Mary Kelly not played Barnett and strung him along, Barnett would not have read of the murder of Martha Tabram and decided on his specific plan of action. This was a man who was only trying to make a better life for himself and the woman he loved, but the woman he loved was far from true to him.

Hinton's choice of George Hutchinson meant that Mary Kelly was never in an established relationship with the killer, although she does not escape culpability. Much like Harrison's Mary Kelly, this woman is a user, willing to string along any number of men in order to get what she wants. One of those men is Hutchinson—a poor choice, Hinton notes, because Hutchinson fixates on her. He murders the other women out of frustration with being continually snubbed by Mary Kelly, and finally murders her when he is confronted with the fact that she is not actually an angel in rags, but a common, filthy whore. At least Hinton's version does not turn his killer into an altruistic dreamer, but again, if Mary Kelly had not used Hutchinson in the first place, he would not have fixated on her.

Antonia Alexander, although writing about a different Mary Kelly, blames her great-great-grandmother for the murders. This Mary Kelly abandoned her husband and children in order to move to London to be with Dr. Williams, who was also married. This Mary Kelly, like the others, proved difficult to get rid of, although she did eventually return to her family while another Mary Kelly was murdered and made the headlines. Once again a woman did not comply with the expectations of her lover, and so he was driven to murder in order to right the situation.

A woman does not have to be a Mary Kelly stringing along multiple lovers in order to be blamed for her death. In 2006 Paul Roland observed the expectation that women are meant to avoid crossing paths with killers, and in 2015 Bruce Robinson mocked the common depictions of victims being on the prowl for their killer, flaunting such things as ears and uteruses, since those seem to have had a special appeal for the Ripper. Being so careless with money as to be forced onto the street at night means that the women quite literally placed themselves in his way, and the fact that many, if not all, were reported to have been drinking means that their senses were dulled and they were in no condition to fight for their lives. It would seem that every East End prostitute needed to at all times be on full alert, in complete control of her senses and every situation, so that she might avoid being murdered.

Life After Death?

The big question this book set out to answer was one of change: how have the representations of the canonical five Jack the Ripper victims changed? It was my hope to track these changes and show an improvement in narrative descriptions of victims across decades, dozens of books, and millions of words. From previous research I already knew that many true crime texts present murder victims as objects and sources of evidence that can be used to point to the killer, but given the vast array of writings about Jack the Ripper and so many different voices and areas of focus, I had hoped to see a constant, steady movement toward the humanization of the murdered women.

This was not what I found.

In 1939 William Stewart described Mary Jane Kelly as being an "accessory to her own death"[14] due to the fact that she was drunk and a prostitute who walked the streets, presumably flaunting her wares, and took strange men back to her small room. In 2015 Bruce Robinson mocked the very idea of victim guilt, but not because he had recently read Stewart. Robinson was responding to so many authors across so many years. The Ripper's victims are still whores, likely better off dead, and their lives are of no use to anyone since their biographies can tell us nothing about their killer.

Yes, there have been standouts and moments when it seemed change was likely. The 1990s brought multiple books in which the authors strove to give the women as much attention as their murderer, but it also brought Bob Hinton asking what use their biographies were, after all. In 2007 Neal Stubbings Sheldon published a short book focusing on the murdered women, sticking with the facts he could verify through documentation and adding in photographs of their descendants to make up almost half the book. Arguments that these women live on and have become immortal are also used to dismiss them so that authors can pursue other avenues of investigation. The apparent focus on five otherwise unremarkable women has raised responses of envy and the thought that, really, they should be happy that their names are still spoken, considering how many of their contemporaries have been forgotten.

It is true that humanizing murder victims would force other changes to the traditional murder narrative structure. Especially when a serial killer is concerned, bringing his victims in to share the spotlight would quickly crowd him out, and Jack the Ripper is practically unproductive by today's standards. The balance of five—or more—against one has continually been shifted in favor of the Ripper and fascination with this mysterious figure, but in order to feel that fascination and not repulsion, his victims must be pushed aside. They can be nobodies, or they can be blamed for their own deaths, but they must always be clues: objects, and not people.

What does it matter if women who were killed more than a century ago are continually denied humanity, empathy, and attention? What does it mean when attempts to change this representation are continually the exception instead of the rule? Does it minimize or even normalize instances of violence in a world where news reports are continually full of new accounts? If representation matters—and it does—then victim representation matters, too.

The depictions of Jack the Ripper's victims across the decades says far less about them than it does about the culture which chooses to describe them. Although the amount of information available about them likely reached a plateau long ago, the approach to telling their story—or to not telling it—is the choice of the author situated in a distinct time and place. The lack of changes in these stories has far less to do with the number of facts available about the women in question, but how the author's culture reacts and responds to the idea of victimhood. The frequency at which Polly, Annie, Liz, Kate, and Mary Jane appear in writing does not mean that those appearances are satisfactory. They are so often simply a name, a location, or an ordinal number with a coroner's report attached. For so long Jack the Ripper has inspired "interest and curiosity"[15] among researchers who seek to discover the person behind the monster and the myth. Researchers are more than willing to play connect the dots with confirmable information about their chosen suspect, crafting varying degrees of three dimensional humans who are neither saints nor the devil incarnate. After nearly ninety years of books, it might be too late to argue for that same consideration to be given to the victims, since the narrative structure is already long established, but the first step is certainly to recognize it— in the case of Polly, Annie, Liz, Kate, Mary Jane, and so many others.

Chapter Notes

Introduction

1. casebook.org.

Chapter One

1. Stuart P. Evans and Keith Skinner, *The Ultimate Jack the Ripper Companion: An Illustrated Encyclopedia* (New York: Skyhorse, 2009), 26.
2. *Ibid.*, 50.
3. *Ibid.*, 71.
4. *Ibid.*, 82.
5. *Ibid.*, 172.
6. *Ibid.*, 22.
7. *Ibid.*, 224.
8. *Ibid.*, 404.
9. *Ibid.*, 381.

Chapter Two

1. Leonard Matters, *The Mystery of Jack the Ripper* (London: W. H. Allen, 1929, reprinted 1948), 16.
2. *Ibid.*, 26.
3. *Ibid.*, 27.
4. *Ibid.*, 30.
5. *Ibid.*, 46.
6. *Ibid.*, 50.
7. *Ibid.*, 67.
8. *Ibid.*, 70.
9. *Ibid.*, 113.
10. Edwin T. Woodhall, *Jack the Ripper or When London Walked in Terror* (Runcorn, Cheshire: P & D Riley, 1997 facsimile edition, first published by Mellifont Press, 1937), 7.
11. *Ibid.*, 11.
12. *Ibid.*, 9.

13. *Ibid.*, 11.
14. *Ibid.*, 15.
15. *Ibid.*
16. *Ibid.*, 30.
17. *Ibid.*, 37.
18. *Ibid.*, 89.
19. *Ibid.*, 93.
20. *Ibid.*, 96.
21. William Stewart, *Jack the Ripper: A New Theory* (London: Quality Press, 1939), 27.
22. *Ibid.*, 19.
23. *Ibid.*, 37.
24. *Ibid.*, 58.
25. *Ibid.*, 63.
26. *Ibid.*, 69.
27. *Ibid.*, 76.
28. *Ibid.*, 83.
29. *Ibid.*, 172.
30. *Ibid.*, 199.

Chapter Three

1. Donald McCormick, *The Identity of Jack the Ripper* (London: Jerrold's, 1959), 23.
2. *Ibid.*, 38.
3. *Ibid.*, 71.
4. *Ibid.*, 106.
5. *Ibid.*, 109.
6. *Ibid.*, 120.
7. *Ibid.*, 109–110.
8. *Ibid.*, 111.
9. *Ibid.*, 149.
10. Tom Cullen. *Autumn of Terror* (London: The Bodley Head, 1965), 14.
11. *Ibid.*, 30.
12. *Ibid.*, 49.
13. *Ibid.*, 50.

14. *Ibid.*, 116.
15. *Ibid.*, 131.
16. *Ibid.*, 132.
17. *Ibid.*, 164.
18. *Ibid.*, 166.
19. *Ibid.*, 179.
20. *Ibid.*, 211.
21. Robin Odell, *Jack the Ripper in Fact and Fiction* (London: George G. Harp, 1965), 24.
22. *Ibid.*, 57.
23. *Ibid.*, 109.
24. *Ibid.*, 178.
25. *Ibid.*, 31.
26. *Ibid.*, 37.
27. *Ibid.*, 66.
28. *Ibid.*, 70.
29. *Ibid.*, 109.
30. *Ibid.*, 113.
31. *Ibid.*, 226.
32. *Ibid.*, 258.

Chapter Four

1. Michael Harrison, *A Biography of the Duke of Clarence: Was He Jack the Ripper?* (New York: Drake, 1972), 139.
2. Stephen Knight, *Jack the Ripper: The Final Solution* (London: Book Club Associates, 1976), 14.
3. *Ibid.*, 25.
4. *Ibid.*, 236.
5. *Ibid.*, 56.
6. *Ibid.*
7. *Ibid.*
8. *Ibid.*, 235.
9. Jack Spiering, *Prince Jack: The True Story of Jack the Ripper* (Garden City, NY: Doubleday, 978), 15.
10. *Ibid.*, 30.
11. *Ibid.*, 66.
12. *Ibid.*, 72.
13. *Ibid.*, 129.
14. Daniel Farson, *Jack the Ripper* (London: Michael Joseph, 1972), 21.
15. *Ibid.*, 23.
16. *Ibid.*, 26.
17. *Ibid.*, 36.
18. *Ibid.*, 37.
19. *Ibid.*, 46.
20. *Ibid.*, 98.
21. Richard Whittington-Eagan, *A Casebook on Jack the Ripper* (London: Widly & Sons, 1975), xiv.

22. *Ibid.*, 155.
23. Donald Rumbelow, *The Complete Jack the Ripper* (Boston: New York Graphic Society, 1975), 113.
24. Arthur Douglas, *Will the Real Jack the Ripper* (Brinscall, Chorley, Lancashire: Countryside, 1979), 6.

Chapter Five

1. John Douglas, "Subject: Jack the Ripper," 1.
2. John Douglas and Mark Olshaker, *Journey Into Darkness* (New York: Scribner, 1997), 54.
3. Douglas, "Subject: Jack the Ripper," 2.
4. Martin Fido, *The Crimes, Death, and Detection of Jack the Ripper* (London: Weidenfeld & Nicolson, 1987), 18.
5. *Ibid.*, 20.
6. *Ibid.*, 57.
7. *Ibid.*, 43.
8. *Ibid.*, 87.
9. *Ibid.*, 98.
10. Melvin Harris, *Jack the Ripper: The Bloody Truth* (London: Columbus Books, 1987), 17.
11. *Ibid.*, 18.
12. *Ibid.*, 19.
13. *Ibid.*, 23.
14. *Ibid.*, 24.
15. *Ibid.*, 26.
16. Martin Howells and Keith Skinner, *The Ripper Legacy: The Life & Death of Jack the Ripper* (London: Sedgwick & Jackson, 1987), 3.
17. *Ibid.*, 67.
18. *Ibid.*, xiii.
19. *Ibid.*, 16.
20. *Ibid.*, 26.
21. *Ibid.*, 156.
22. *Ibid.*, 191.
23. Terence Sharkey, *Jack the Ripper: 100 Years of Investigation* (London: Ward Lock, 1987), 18.
24. *Ibid.*, 30.
25. *Ibid.*, 42.
26. *Ibid.*, 47.
27. *Ibid.*, 57.
28. Peter Underwood, *Jack the Ripper: One Hundred Years of Mystery* (London: Blandofrd Press, 1987), vii.
29. *Ibid.*, 1.

30. *Ibid.*, 4.
31. *Ibid.*, 10.
32. *Ibid.*, 11.
33. *Ibid.*, 18.
34. *Ibid.*, 21.
35. *Ibid.*, 23.
36. *Ibid.*, 73.
37. Colin Wilson and Robin Odell, *Jack the Ripper: Summing Up and Verdict* (London: Bantam, 1987), 24.
38. *Ibid.*, 24.
39. *Ibid.*, 42.
40. *Ibid.*, 235.
41. *Ibid.*, 60.
42. Paul Begg. *Jack the Ripper: The Uncensored Facts* (London: Robson Books, 1988), 28.
43. *Ibid.*, 39.
44. *Ibid.*, 53.
45. *Ibid.*, 94.
46. *Ibid.*, 111.
47. *Ibid.*, 115.
48. *Ibid.*, 142.
49. *Ibid.*, 148.

Chapter Six

1. Jean Overton Fuller, *Sickert & The Ripper Crimes* (Oxford: Mandrake, 1990), 89.
2. *Ibid.*, 223.
3. *Ibid.*, 155–156.
4. *Ibid.*, 22.
5. *Ibid.*, 197.
6. *Ibid.*, 142.
7. *Ibid.*, 61.
8. *Ibid.*, 206.
9. *Ibid.*, 12.
10. Shirley Harrison, *The Diary of Jack the Ripper: The Discovery, the Investigation, and the Debate* (New York: Hyperion, 1993), 3.
11. *Ibid.*, 61.
12. *Ibid.*, 76.
13. Paul Harrison, *Jack the Ripper: The Mystery Solved* (London: Robert Hale, 1991), 33.
14. *Ibid.*
15. *Ibid.*, 40.
16. *Ibid.*, 47.
17. *Ibid.*, 57.
18. *Ibid.*, 70.
19. *Ibid.*, 79.
20. *Ibid.*, 162.
21. *Ibid.*, 78.
22. *Ibid.*, 85.

23. *Ibid.*, 198.
24. *Ibid.*, 219.
25. *Ibid.*, 240.
26. *Ibid.*, 239.
27. *Ibid.*, 161.
28. John Wilding, *Jack the Ripper Revealed* (London: Constable, 1993), 11.
29. *Ibid.*, 150.
30. *Ibid.*, 22.
31. *Ibid.*, 46.
32. *Ibid.*, 180.
33. David Abrahamsen, M.D., *Murder & Madness: The Secret Life of Jack the Ripper* (New York: Donald I. Fine, 1992), 77.
34. *Ibid.*, 8.
35. *Ibid.*, 81.
36. *Ibid.*, 12.
37. *Ibid.*, 56.
38. *Ibid.*, 75.
39. *Ibid.*, 202.
40. William Beadle, *Jack the Ripper: Anatomy of a Myth* (Essex: Wat Taylor Books, 1995), 170.
41. *Ibid.*, vii.
42. *Ibid.*, 16.
43. *Ibid.*, 25.
44. *Ibid.*, 35.
45. *Ibid.*, 42.
46. *Ibid.*, 58.
47. *Ibid.*, 114.
48. *Ibid.*, 66.
49. *Ibid.*, 73.
50. Philip Sugden, *The Complete History of Jack the Ripper* (London: BCA, 1994), 34.
51. *Ibid.*, 45.
52. *Ibid.*, 96.
53. *Ibid.*, 196.
54. James Tully, *The Real Jack the Ripper: The Secret of Prisoner 1167* (London: Constable & Robinson, 1997), vxii.
55. *Ibid.*, 114.
56. *Ibid.*, 157.
57. *Ibid.*, 318.
58. *Ibid.*, 206–207.
59. *Ibid.*, 232.
60. Melvin Harris, *The True Face of Jack the Ripper* (London: Michael O'Mara Books, 1994), 3.
61. *Ibid.*, 111.
62. Paul Feldman, *Jack the Ripper: The Final Chapter* (London: Virgin, 2007), 2.
63. A. P. Wolf, *Jack the Myth: A New Look at the Ripper* (London: Robert Hale, 1993), 34.

64. M. J. Trow, *The Many Faces of Jack the Ripper* (West Sussex: Summersdale Publishers, 1997), 22.

65. *Ibid.*, 44.

66. *Ibid.*, 63.

67. Richard Wallace, *Jack the Ripper: "Lighthearted Friend"* (Melrose, MA: Gemini Press, 1996), viii.

68. *Ibid.*, 147.

69. *Ibid.*, 174.

70. *Ibid.*, 261.

Chapter Seven

1. R. Michael Gordon, *Alias Jack the Ripper: Beyond the Usual Whitechapel Suspects* (Jefferson, NC: McFarland, 2001), dedication.

2. *Ibid.*, 18.

3. *Ibid.*, 66.

4. *Ibid.*, 93.

5. *Ibid.*, 105.

6. *Ibid.*, 153.

7. Paul Begg, *Jack the Ripper: The Definitive History* (Harlow: Pearson Education, 2005), 106.

8. *Ibid.*, 188.

9. Paul Begg, *Jack the Ripper: The Facts* (New York: Barnes & Noble Books, 2004), 139.

10. *Ibid.*, 166.

11. *Ibid.*, 268.

12. *Ibid.*, 418.

13. Begg, *Jack the Ripper: The Definitive History*, 212.

14. Paul Roland, *The Crimes of Jack the Ripper* (Edison, NJ: Chartell Books, 2006), 11.

15. *Ibid.*, 30.

16. *Ibid.*, 38.

17. *Ibid.*, 52.

18. *Ibid.*, 76.

19. *Ibid.*, 80.

20. M. J. Trow, *Jack the Ripper: Quest for a Killer* (Barnsley, South Yorkshire: Wharncliffe True Crime, 2009), 98.

21. *Ibid.*, 100.

22. *Ibid.*, 135.

23. *Ibid.*, 47.

24. *Ibid.*, 155.

25. Steven A. Egger, *The Killers Among Us*, 2d ed. (Upper Saddle River, NJ: Prentice Hall, 2002), 88.

26. Robert House, *Jack the Ripper and the Case for Scotland Yard's Prime Suspect* (Hoboken: John Wiley & Sons, 2011), 110.

27. Paul Begg and John Bennett, *The Complete and Essential Jack the Ripper* (London: Penguin, 2013), 51.

28. *Ibid.*, 216.

29. *Ibid.*, 11.

30. Robert Keller, *The Devil in Whitechapel: The Untold Story of Jack the Ripper* (Create Space Independent Publishing Platform, 2016), 152.

31. Bruce Robinson, *They All Love Jack* (New York: HarperCollins, 2015), xii.

32. *Ibid.*, 162.

33. *Ibid.*, 225.

34. *Ibid.*, 113.

35. *Ibid.*, 550.

Chapter Eight

1. John Plimmer, *The Whitechapel Murders—Solved?* (Thirsk, North Yorkshire: House of Stratus, 2003), iii.

2. *Ibid.*, 6.

3. *Ibid.*, 29.

4. *Ibid.*, 30.

5. *Ibid.*, 70.

6. *Ibid.*, 72.

7. *Ibid.*, 73.

8. *Ibid.*, 128.

9. *Ibid.*, 135.

10. Patricia Cornwell, *Portrait of a Killer: Jack the Ripper—Case Closed* (New York: Berkley Books, 2008), 154.

11. *Ibid.*, 310.

12. *Ibid.*, 108.

13. *Ibid.*, 199.

14. *Ibid.*, 297.

15. *Ibid.*, 421.

16. *Ibid.*, 434.

17. *Ibid.*, 122.

18. *Ibid.*, 443.

19. Patricia Cornwell, *Ripper: The Secret Life of Walter Sickert* (Seattle: Thomas & Mercer, 2017), 472.

20. Trevor Marriott, *Jack the Ripper: The 21st Century Investigation* (London: Jonathon Blake, 2007), ix.

21. *Ibid.*, 29.

22. Russell Edwards, *Naming Jack the Ripper* (Guilford, CT: Lyons Press, 2014), 3.

23. *Ibid.*

24. *Ibid.*, 59.

25. *Ibid.*, 70.
26. *Ibid.*, 86.
27. *Ibid.*, 196.
28. *Ibid.*, 108.
29. Paul Begg and John Bennett, *Jack the Ripper: CSI: Whitechapel* (London: Andre Deutsch, 2012), 73.
30. *Ibid.*, 97.
31. *Ibid.*, 115.
32. *Ibid.*, 149.
33. *Ibid.*, 168.
34. *Ibid.*

Chapter Nine

1. John Morris, *Jack the Ripper: The Hand of a Woman* (Brigdend, Wales: Seren, 2012), 148.
2. *Ibid.*, 146.
3. *Ibid.*, 84.
4. *Ibid.*, 131.
5. *Ibid.*, 68.
6. Tom Wescott, *The Bank Holiday Murders: The True Story of the First Whitechapel Murders* (CrimeConfidentialPress, 2014), 152.
7. *Ibid.*, 1.
8. *Ibid.*, 145.
9. Tony Williams with Humphrey Price, *Uncle Jack: The True Identity of Jack the Ripper—Britain's Most Notorious Murderer—Revealed at Last* (London: Orion Books, 2005), 11.
10. *Ibid.*, 13.
11. *Ibid.*, 101.
12. *Ibid.*, 20.
13. *Ibid.*, 124.
14. Antonia Alexander, *The Fifth Victim: Mary Kelly Was Murdered by Jack the Ripper and Now Her Great Great Granddaughter Reveals the True Story of What Really Happened* (London: John Blake, 2013), 182.
15. *Ibid.*, 183.
16. Stewart Evans and Paul Gainey, *The Lodger: The Arrest & Escape of Jack the Ripper* (London: BCA, 1995), 17.
17. *Ibid.*, 26.
18. *Ibid.*, 45 and 48.
19. *Ibid.*, 52.
20. *Ibid.*, 68.
21. *Ibid.*, 82.
22. *Ibid.*, 130.
23. Dane Ladwig, *Dr. H. H. Holmes & the Whitechapel Ripper* (Chicago: Ink Slinger Enterprises, 2014), dedication.
24. *Ibid.*, preface.

25. *Ibid.*, 24.
26. *Ibid.*, 159.
27. *Ibid.*, 116.
28. *Ibid.*, 243.
29. *Ibid.*, 262.
30. David Monaghan and Nigel Cawthorne, *Jack the Ripper's Secret Confession: The Hidden Testimony of Britain's First Serial Killer* (New York: Skyhorse, 2010), vii.
31. *Ibid.*, 7.
32. *Ibid.*, 63.
33. *Ibid.*, 213.
34. *Ibid.*, 232.
35. James Carnac, *The Autobiography of Jack the Ripper* (Naperville, IL: Sourcebooks, 2013), 185.
36. *Ibid.*, 165.
37. *Ibid.*, 189.
38. R. Michael Gordon, *The American Murders of Jack the Ripper: Tantalizing Evidence of the Gruesome American Interlude of the Prime Ripper Suspect* (Guilford, CT: The Lyons Press, 2005), dedication.
39. Robin Odel, *Ripperology: A Study of the World's First Serial Killer and a Literary Phenomenon* (Kent, OH: Kent State University Press, 2006), xviii.
40. Paul Begg and John Bennett, *Jack the Ripper: The Forgotten Victims* (New Haven: Yale University Press, 2013), 66.
41. *Ibid.*, 19.
42. *Ibid.*, 65.
43. *Ibid.*, 262.
44. *Ibid.*, 263.

Conclusion

1. Harris, *The True Face of Jack the Ripper*, 3.
2. Stewart, *Jack the Ripper: A New Theory*, 19.
3. Douglas, *Will the Real Jack the Ripper*, 6.
4. Howells and Skinner, *The Ripper Legacy: The Life & Death of Jack the Ripper*, xiii.
5. Beadle, *Jack the Ripper: Anatomy of a Myth*, 170.
6. Williams, *Uncle Jack: The true identity of Jack the Ripper—Britain's Most Notorious Murderer—Revealed at Last*, 124.
7. Whittington-Eagan, *A Casebook on Jack the Ripper*, xiv.
8. Begg, *Jack the Ripper: The Uncensored Facts*, 28.

9. Edwards, *Naming Jack the Ripper*, 55.

10. Gordon, *Alias Jack the Ripper: Beyond the Usual Whitechapel Suspects*, dedication.

11. Roland, *The Crimes of Jack the Ripper*, 11.

12. Begg and Bennett, *Jack the Ripper: The Forgotten Victims*, 65.

13. Gordon, *Alias Jack the Ripper: Beyond the Usual Whitechapel Suspects*, dedication.

14. Stewart, *Jack the Ripper: A New Theory*, 199.

15. Ladwig, *Dr. H. H. Holmes & the Whitechapel Ripper*, 24.

Bibliography

Abrahamsen, David, M.D.. *Murder & Madness: The Secret Life of Jack the Ripper.* New York: Donald I. Fine, 1992.

Alexander, Antonia. *The Fifth Victim: Mary Kelly Was Murdered by Jack the Ripper Now Her Great Great Granddaughter Reveals the True Story of What Really Happened.* London: John Blake, 2013.

Beadle, William. *Jack the Ripper: Anatomy of a Myth.* Essex: Wat Tyler Books, 1995.

Begg, Paul. *Jack the Ripper: The Definitive History.* Harlow: Pearson Education, 2005.

_____. *Jack the Ripper: The Facts.* New York: Barnes & Noble Books, 2004.

_____. *Jack the Ripper: The Uncensored Facts.* London: Robson Books, 1988.

Begg, Paul, and John Bennett. *The Compete and Essential Jack the Ripper.* London: Penguin, 2013.

_____. *Jack the Ripper: CSI: Whitechapel.* London: Andre Deutsch, 2012.

_____. *Jack the Ripper: The Forgotten Victims.* New Haven: Yale University Press, 2013.

Carnac, James. *The Autobiography of Jack the Ripper.* Naperville, IL: Sourcebooks, 2013.

Cornwell, Patricia. *Portrait of a Killer: Jack the Ripper—Case Closed.* New York: Berkley Books, 2008. Originally published 2002.

_____. *Ripper: The Secret Life of Walter Sickert.* Seattle: Thomas & Mercer, 2017.

Cullen, Tom. *Autumn of Terror.* London: The Bodley Head, 1965.

Douglas, Arthur. *Will the Real Jack the Ripper.* Brinscall, Chorley, Lancashire: Countryside Publications, 1979.

Douglas, John. "Subject: Jack the Ripper." July 6, 1988. Retrieved from vault.fbi.gov.

Douglas, John, and Mark Olshaker. *Journey Into Darkness.* New York: Scribner, 1997.

Edwards, Russell. *Naming Jack the Ripper.* Guilford, CT: Lyons Press, 2014.

Egger, Steven A. *The Killers Among Us,* 2d ed. Upper Saddle River, NJ: Prentice Hall, 2002.

Evans, Stewart P., and Paul Gainey. *The Lodger: The Arrest & Escape of Jack the Ripper.* London: BCA, 1995.

Evans, Stewart P., and Keith Skinner. *Jack the Ripper: Letters from Hell.* Stroud: Sutton, 2001.

_____. *The Ultimate Jack the Ripper Companion: An Illustrated Encyclopedia.* New York: Skyhorse, 2009.

Fairclough, Melvyn. *The Ripper & the Royals.* London: Duckworth, 1991.

Farson, Daniel. *Jack the Ripper.* London: Michael Joseph, 1972.

Feldman, Paul H. *Jack the Ripper: The Final Chapter.* London: Virgin, 2007. First published 1998.

Fido, Martin. *The Crimes, Death, and Detection of Jack the Ripper.* London: Weidenfeld and Nicolson, 1987.

Fuller, Jean Overton. *Sickert & The Ripper Crimes.* Oxford: Mandrake, 1990. New revised edition 2003.

Gordon, R. Michael. *Alias Jack the Ripper: Beyond the Usual Whitechapel Suspects.* Jefferson, NC: McFarland, 2001.

_____. *The American Murders of Jack the Ripper: Tantalizing Evidence of the Gruesome American Interlude of the Prime Ripper Suspect.* Guilford, CT: The Lyons Press, 2005. First printed 2003.

Harris, Melvin. *Jack the Ripper: The Bloody Truth.* London: Columbus Books, 1987.

_____. *The Ripper File.* London: W. H. Allen, 1989.

_____. *The True Face of Jack the Ripper.* London: Michael O'Mara Books, 1994.

Harrison, Michael. *A Biography of the Duke of Clarence: Was he Jack the Ripper?* New York: Drake, 1972.

Harrison, Paul. *Jack the Ripper: The Mystery Solved.* London: Robert Hale, 1991.

Harrison, Shirley. *The Diary of Jack the Ripper: The Discovery, the Investigation, the Debate.* New York: Hyperion, 1993.

Hinton, Bob. *From Hell ... The Jack the Ripper Mystery.* Abertillery, Gwent: Old Bakehouse, 1998. Reprinted 2005.

House, Robert. *Jack the Ripper and the Case for Scotland Yard's Prime Suspect.* Hoboken: John Wiley & Sons, 2011.

Howells, Martin, and Keith Skinner. *The Ripper Legacy: The Life & Death of Jack the Ripper.* London: Sedgwick & Jackson, 1987.

Keller, Robert. *The Devil in Whitechapel: The untold story of Jack the Ripper.* CreateSpace Independent Publishing Platform, 2016.

Knight, Stephen. *Jack the Ripper: The Final Solution.* London: Book Club Associates, 1976.

Ladwig, Dane. *Dr. H. H. Holmes & the Whitechapel Ripper.* Chicago: Ink Slinger Enterprises, 2014.

Marriott, Trevor. *Jack the Ripper: The 21st Century Investigation.* London: Jonathon Blake, 2007.

_____. *Jack the Ripper: The Secret Police Files.* Amazon Digital Services, 2013. E-book.

Matters, Leonard. *The Mystery of Jack the Ripper.* London: W. H. Allen, 1929. Reprinted 1948.

McCormick, Donald. *The Identity of Jack the Ripper.* London: Jerrold's, 1959.

Monaghan, David, and Nigel Cawthorne. *Jack the Ripper's Secret Confession: The Hidden Testimony of Britain's First Serial Killer.* New York: Skyhorse, 2010.

Morris, John. *Jack the Ripper: The Hand of a Woman.* Brigdend, Wales: Seren, 2012.

Odell, Robin. *Jack the Ripper in Fact and Fiction.* London: George G. Harp, 1965.

_____. *Ripperology: A Study of the World's First Serial Killer and a Literary Phenomenon.* Kent, OH: Kent State University Press, 2006.

Plimmer, John. *The Whitechapel Murders—Solved?* Thirsk, North Yorkshire: House of Stratus, 2003. Originally published 1998.

Robinson, Bruce. *They All Love Jack.* New York: HarperCollins, 2015.

Roland, Paul. *The Crimes of Jack the Ripper.* Edison, New Jersey: Chartwell Books, 2006.

Rumbelow, Donald. *The Complete Jack the Ripper.* Boston: New York Graphic Society, 1975.

Sharkey, Terence. *Jack the Ripper: 100 Years of Investigation.* London: Ward Lock, 1987.

Sheldon, Neal Stubbings. *The Victims of Jack the Ripper.* Knoxville: Dan Norder, Inklings Press, 2007.

Spiering, Frank. *Prince Jack: The True Story of Jack the Ripper.* Garden City, NY: Doubleday, 1978.

Stewart, William. *Jack the Ripper: A New Theory.* London: Quality Press, 1939.

Sugden, Philip. *The Complete History of Jack the Ripper.* London: BCA, 1994.

Trow, M. J. *Jack the Ripper: Quest for a Killer.* Barnsley, South Yorkshire: Wharncliffe True Crime, 2009.

_____. *The Many Faces of Jack the Ripper.* West Sussex: Summersdale, 1997.

Tully, John. *The Real Jack the Ripper: The Secret of Prisoner 1167.* London: Constable & Robinson, 1997.

Underwood, Peter. *Jack the Ripper: One Hundred Years of Mystery.* London: Blandford Press, 1987.

Wallace, Richard. *Jack the Ripper: "Light-hearted Friend."* Melrose, MA: Gemini Press, 1996.

Wescott, Tom. *The Bank Holiday Murders: The True Story of the First Whitechapel Murders.* CrimeConfidentialPress, 2014.

Whittington-Egan, Richard. *A Casebook on Jack the Ripper.* London: Wildy & Sons, 1975.

Wilding, John. *Jack the Ripper Revealed.* London: Constable, 1993.

Williams, Tony with Humphrey Price. *Uncle Jack: The True Identity of Jack the Ripper—Britain's Most Notorious Murderer—Revealed at Last.* London: Orion Books, 2005.

Wilson, Colin, and Robin Odell. *Jack the Ripper: Summing up and verdict.* London: Bantam, 1987.

Wolf, A. P. *Jack the Myth: A New Look at the Ripper.* London: Robert Hale, 1993.

Woodhall, Edwin T. *Jack the Ripper or When London Walked in Terror.* Runcorn, Cheshire: P & D Riley, 1997 facsimile edition. First published by Mellifont Press 1937.

Index

237